The Politics
of Hope

Critical Social Thought

Series editor: Michael W. Apple
Professor of Curriculum and Instruction and of Educational
Policy Studies, University of Wisconsin-Madison

The Politics of Hope

Bernard P. Dauenhauer

Foreword by Paul Ricoeur

Routledge & Kegan Paul
New York and London

First published in 1986
by Routledge & Kegan Paul Inc
in association with Methuen Inc

29 West 35th Street, New York, NY 10001

and in the UK by
Routledge & Kegan Paul plc
11 New Fetter Lane, London EC4P 4EE

Set in 10 on 12 pt Times
by Inforum Ltd, Portsmouth
and printed in Great Britain
by TJ Press (Padstow) Ltd,
Padstow, Cornwall

Library of Congress Cataloging in Publication Data

Dauenhauer, Bernard P.
The politics of hope.

(Critical social thought)
Bibliography: p.
Includes index.
1. Political science — Philosophy.   I. Title.
II. Series.
JA74.D268   1986   320'.01   85–24328

British Library CIP data also available

ISBN 0—7102—0823—5

In memoriam
Thomas J. Brennan
1905–1982
philosopher, friend

Contents

Foreword by Paul Ricoeur

It is with a feeling of deep thankfulness that I start writing these few pages as a foreword to Bernard Dauenhauer's book *The Politics of Hope*. I must say that I find myself in so close an agreement with the main lines of this work that I can hardly do anything better than emphasize the themes that seem to me to be its major contribution to understanding political thought. I will do that by following a formal course of thought aiming at reconstructing the string of arguments that make up the strength of this unusually original work.

I will relate my remarks to two questions: in what sense is this a book about political philosophy? and to what extent does it deserve its title, which connects politics with hope? The first question concerns the descriptive purpose of the work, namely its assessment of the place of politics in the field of human activity. The second one concerns the normative purpose of the work, namely the kind of intervention thanks to which this book is itself a political act.

I

I see the contribution of this work to political philosophy as stemming from the convergence that it establishes between the specific features of *political action* and some general characteristics of the *human condition*. In this way, the content of this book may be approached from two opposite sides. You may start from the political field in order to delineate the privileged place where the basic constitution of the human being reveals itself. Or you may start from some major presuppositions concerning the human condition and draw from them some appropriate implications for political action. The book may be seen as located at the intersecting point of these two lines of thought and as drawing its strength from the mutual support that a properly political thought and what I would like to call a philosophical anthropology provide one another with.

Let us start from the *political pole*. With Hegel, Arendt, Merleau-Ponty and others, the author holds politics as the privileged *mediation* through which human action is made *efficient*. This concern for efficiency traverses the whole book as its major *ligne de force*. Thanks to this nonsubstitutable role, politics is both an activity among others and the activity which frames all the other activities; to use Arendt's terminology, politics delineates the 'space of appearance' for any kind of human achievements, including those of knowledge, of art, of religion, even of wisdom. By marking their place, politics preserves their relative autonomy and secures their public efficiency. This role is what makes politics a serious activity. Here I would like to underscore an important corollary of this notion of efficient mediation, namely the capacity of duration, the *enduring capacity*, that political institutions secure for every activity displayed within their field. Political activity may even be understood, according to the Aristotelian concept of *praxis*, as the action which aims at its own preservation. (It will be shown later that it is exactly upon this trend towards duration, in spite of all external and inner dangers, that the theme of hope may be grafted.) I hold this concern for the temporality proper to political action to be as important as the concern for efficiency. To be true, the former is implied in the latter, to the extent that efficiency requires duration, persistence.

Furthermore, the specificity of politics is assessed with still greater accuracy thanks to the recognition of a series of *paradoxes* which appear to be constitutive of political action, and which do not betray its weakness, but rather assert its risky seriousness. (These paradoxes will even appear as a source of strength when interpreted in terms of hope and not of despair, complacency, or resignation, as will be said later.) These are paradoxes in the sense that each of the political ingredients that will be taken into account appears to be at the same time a mediation, i.e. the promotion of freedom as a political achievement. The concept of *institution* is the one which seems the most closely linked to the concern for efficiency and duration: it is the enduring mediation *par excellence*; but at the same time institutions seem to imply something antithetic not only to arbitrariness but also to individual initiative. The next paradox is that of *author-*

ity: it seems impossible for the citizen to get full recognition by his/her peers – i.e. the kind of mutual confirmation by which Hegel, mainly in the writings of the Iena period, defined political liberty – without entering the kind of asymmetrical relationship which obtains of hegemony and subordination. *Sovereignty* in turn adds a specific acuteness to the previous paradox, to the extent that the multiplicity and the opaqueness of its sources prevents any claim to legitimacy from overcoming the conflict between fact and right. As to the concept of *law*, its major paradox results from the intricate relationship between the legislative initiative linked to positive law and the weight of customs and previous laws making the strength of prevailing traditions. But it is obviously toward the concept of *coercion* that all the previous paradoxes converge. An insuperable gap seems to separate the ideal of community consensus and the fact of obstruction on the part of private interests, to say nothing of the apparently irreducible margin of asocial behaviour. Without some minimal coercion, even tempered by restraint (we shall see later the critical role of this concept in connection with that of hope), no political action seems to be capable of efficiency and duration. These paradoxes are indeed the distinctive features of political action.

The reader will not fail to greet the total absence of angelism in a political thought which will nevertheless make room for hope. Yes, Bernard Dauenhauer takes politics *seriously*.

The author has a second way of taking politics seriously, namely by making it the major test of a well-articulated *philosophical anthropology*. As I said, the strength of the book lies in the convergence between a political analysis and a philosophical anthropology. Both together generate political *thought*. The present writer has chosen to start from the political pole and move toward the more philosophical one, in order to escape the temptation merely to summarize the book. The author has chosen the opposite strategy. He had his own reasons, mainly his insistence on marking the continuity between this new book and the previous one which he holds as a twin work: *Silence: The Phenomenon and its Ontological Significance*. Rather than start from this declared kinship between both works, I rejoin him later after a detour, in order to better underscore the complete absence of arbitrariness in this connection.

The philosophical anthropology advocated by Bernard Dauenhauer is summarized in a few recurring key words: intersubjectivity, historicality, finitude. I follow this order for two reasons. On the one hand, it is the first one which allows the most conspicuous implications of a philosophical anthropology for political thought to be displayed. On the other hand, it is at the level of the third one that the conjunction with the ontology of silence makes sense in the most forceful way.

That man is unconceivable in full solitude, that his humanity relies on others, and that not by accident, but by essence – this major thesis is common, in spite of important competing interpretations, to Hegel, Husserl, Merleau-Ponty, Arendt, Gadamer, and more generally to most phenomenological or hermeneutical trends of philosophy. What the author intends to do by resuming this well-known theme of *intersubjectivity* is to show its immediate impact on political thought. If man is never free alone, then any political philosophy which claims to define freedom by the autonomy of the will is basically wrong. What shows its radical falsity is the fact that it is condemned to hold all the specific features of politics as extrinsic, accidental, and deplorable. The *nemesis* which hits all these theories – including the contractual ones – is their impotence to give an account of the paradoxes which specify political activity. In this sense the theory of autonomy is antipolitical by principle. Only a *relational* conception of freedom can make sense of the irreducible conditions of an action efficient and durable.

The concept of *historicality* too is familiar to readers of Hegel and Heidegger and of all the thinkers who proceed from one or the other or from both. Bernard Dauenhauer puts it in new relief by bringing it directly to the test of political philosophy. To be historical indeed is not only to be submitted to change, but still more to be capable of imprinting on action the form of history. In order to give an account of historicality in this strong sense, the author borrows from Merleau-Ponty a powerful model, consisting in the expansion of Saussure's dialectic between *langue* and *parole* from discourse to action. Such is the major borrowing of Bernard Dauenhauer from Merleau-Ponty. In the same way any event of *parole* implies as its background an already established structure of *langue* – not only at the phonological, lexical, and syntactic level, but also at the level of traditionally established usages of language – in the same way an efficient action is the one which grafts initiative, the equivalent of *parole* on the plane of praxis, upon institution, the practical equivalent of *langue*. As is easy to see, this 'legacy of Merleau-Ponty to political thought' is of the utmost value. It provides the key to the phenomenon of institution which we held earlier as the first paradox with which political analysis has to come to terms. In a sense, all the other paradoxes – including the most intractable of all, that of coercion – may be considered as extensions of the basic paradox of institution, i.e. the kind of sedimented phenomenon which offers both a support and a resistance to action as it does to language.

I noted as the third key term the concept of *finitude*. It designates at once the point of opacity in all philosophical anthropology, the connecting link with the author's previous work, the ontology of silence, and the necessary condition for the notion of hope becoming a relevant concept in the political sphere. Finitude, says Bernard Dauenhauer, is no defect, no lack. It displays a positive constitution, whose full significance appears precisely both in the order of discourse and in that of action. In the order of discourse it means that there is no such thing as complete discourse, that there is no last word, and furthermore that language is not all, but leaves aside nonverbal expressions, and that, within language itself, there are levels and forms irreducible to one another. Now, it is this essential incompleteness of discourse which makes room for silence and that silence justifies. Silence, as the previous work of our author demonstrates, is the *other* of language, not an exterior other, but an immanent other. It consists in active interruptions which allow a phase, a form, a level of discourse to be initiated or terminated. An initial and terminal silence makes room for shifts from one phase, one form, one level of discourse to another one, as well as from language to nonlanguage and vice versa. Thanks to silence, the speaking subject may move freely within language and between language and nonlanguage. Now, if we assume Merleau-Ponty's model according to which action is constituted in the same way as discourse, we may be able to draw two consequences: first, the incompleteness of discourse has its equivalent in the imperfection of action, which means that all the paradoxes of political action are capable of assuming a positive significance, as the mark of the positive finitude of all action; second, silence must have its equivalent in the political field of action, and this equivalent is restraint: like silence, restraint allows the interception of one type of action for the sake of another, so that it may therefore move freely within the space of appearance of the *polis*; furthermore, like silence, restraint allows the paradoxes of political action to be dealt with in a constructive way, i.e. by preventing them from slipping to non-negotiable contradictions. This last remark provides us with the transition needed toward a relevant use of the concept of hope in politics.

II

The introduction of the concept of hope in the political field is unusual. It seems to imply either a category mistake, because of the religious connotations of the word, or an inappropriate synonymity with utopia, as the term is used by Ernst Bloch in *Das Prinzip Hoffnung*. Bernard Dauenhauer's use of the concept of hope is intended to reject both these alternatives. On the one hand, without denying the religious origin of the term, the claim of the author is to confine it to the political sphere, by tightly connecting it with the very structure of political action, as is delineated by the purpose of efficiency and of duration and by the network of paradoxes linked to the exercise of political action. The politics of hope relies on hope for the sake of politics as such. On the other hand, the notion of hope, in spite of the secular character that it shares with utopia, is intended to provide a clear alternative to utopia. Whereas utopia tends to elude the constraints of efficient and durable action and the hard paradoxes of institution, authority, sovereignty, law, and coercion, hope is addressed to the very possibility of dealing responsibly with these constraints and paradoxes. Religious hope and utopia seem to share a common presupposition, namely that a complete resolution of historical contradictions is possible above or beyond history. The politics of hope relies on the opposite presupposition, i.e. the recognition of the ultimate incompleteness of discourse and action. As the author likes to say and to repeat, man is politically *en route*.

Now, what does hope mean, if it is not the expectation of an historical resolution of the tensions of political action? What does it add to the mere statement that the paradoxes of political action are insuperable? The beginning of the answer resides in the assertion that hope is not a statement but an interpretation. The only transcendence that hope may claim is that of interpretation *vis-à-vis* description. To make sense of this decisive point, I should like to remind the reader of the three questions that Kant raises in the

Opus Postumum: what *can* I know? what *ought* I to do? what *may* be hoped? This third question is irreducible to the two former ones, to the extent that I need not hope in order to know, not even in order to do my duty. But I must hope in order to believe that I am able to act. This is why freedom appears as a Postulate in the *Dialectics of Practical Reason*. The postulate is of an existential kind. It postulates freedom as the power to act according to ethical demands, in other words the power to be efficient and to endure in time. In this way hope has to be interpreted in terms of routedness and routedness in terms of hope. Applied specifically to political action hope implies the confidence that a *responsible* political action can be conducted *in spite of* the perversions, the dangers, and the paradoxes of political action, and as a plausible alternative to some other interpretations which compete with hope on the basis of the same recognition of the incompleteness of political action.

Let me insist on the expression *in spite of . . .* which I borrow from Paul Tillich and which I hold as constitutive of any interpretation of action and discourse in terms of hope. In spite of what? Let us resume the previous series of assertions: in spite of perversions, of dangers, of paradoxes.

The *perversions* which keep recurring in the background of the author's political thought are too well known: their names are tyranny, anarchy, and totalitarianism. The possibility of these perversions is inscribed in the very nature of political action, to the extent that it relies on the distinction between rulers and ruled. It is always possible that this distinction collapses – then you get anarchy; or that it leads to the break of the link of mutual recognition between both parties – then you get tyranny; or that political action suppresses the free play of all other activities in the space of appearance delineated by political institutions – then you get totalitarianism. Hope then is the expectation that mediation between rulers and ruled *can* still be managed, that the situations of hegemony and of subordination are not necessarily incompatible with mutual recognition between the rulers and the ruled.

That the space of appearance is always in *danger* of being shattered results from the very nature of political action as aiming for efficiency and duration. Danger is always there coming from without and from within. In this sense, political action is risky. But thanks to hope, risks become bearable.

It is mainly in relation to the basic *paradoxes* of political action that hope makes sense. In the last chapters of his book, Bernard Dauenhauer takes in turn each of the paradoxes that we have sketched above, pertaining to authority and power, to sovereignty and coercion. Related to these concrete constraints of political action, hope implies that man may be the *mediator* required by the definition of freedom as a relational freedom. In spite of these specific paradoxes, the status of man as politically *en route* is feasible. Man as political animal is possible.

What is more difficult to assess is the claim that hope is a more plausible interpretation of political action than some other attitudes which seem too to take politics seriously. Bernard Dauenhauer considers three competing interpretations: presumption, resignation, containment. The first one, by overestimating human resources to cope with tensions, tends to trivialize danger. The second, by holding paradoxes as insuperable, tends to discourage action. The third one tends to encourage compromise for the sake of the *status quo*. To my mind, the author is at great pains to discard the claims of these competing interpretations, precisely because they are interpretations and because in the field of interpretation you get only probable arguments ('enthymemes'), not demonstrative proofs. The suggestion that the author makes only once, that hope could be held as the practical a priori of political action, cannot actually comply with the requirements of a genuine transcendental deduction of the form: *if* not hope, *then* no politics. The deduction should be demonstrative. But the claim would then violate the very argumentative and 'enthymemic' status of such an interpretive concept as hope. In this sense, the concept of hope remains as *risky* as that of responsible politics. A kind of hermeneutical circle between the interpretive and the practical levels is unavoidable. But this is not a sign of weakness, rather the genuine condition of political man, of man as politically *en route*. This is why Bernard Dauenhauer leaves open many more interpretive possibilities than he seems to exclude, possibilities ranging from active pessimism to tragic optimism.

Paul Ricoeur

Series editor's introduction

An earlier volume in this series, Andrew Levine's exceptional book *Arguing for Socialism*,[1] analyzed two of the most significant traditions in political theory. It compared the theoretical claims behind a variety of forms of capitalism and socialism according to two sets of principles, those articulated in the dominant perspective in political philosophy and those generated out of a more Marxist framework. At its center was a realization of the utter importance of reasoned debate about the efficacy of competing theories of justice and of the need to interrogate the received wisdom of political traditions that are all too often taken for granted.

With the growing tendency in modern society to concentrate most significant decisions exclusively in the hands of an elite, the political domain has become fragmented. In a period in which the very sense of the common good is atrophying,[2] in which technocratic solutions based solely on efficiency and/or profit have tended to reduce the political sphere to the actions of a mandarinate in a variety of political systems, the reintegration of the political as an elemental form of life for all of us is essential. Political philosophy that takes this task as a central part of its problematic is very necessary in the current situation. This is where Bernard Dauenhauer begins. While his arguments are of a different order than those of *Arguing for Socialism* – a volume that provided an immensely interesting and largely positive inquiry into the theoretical justifications underlying socialist political thought – they too are of considerable moment.

The central aim of *The Politics of Hope* is a vindication of politics, to show its irreplaceability. Dauenhauer's goal is deceptively simple. He wants to demonstrate that political thought and practice are not reducible to other forms of human action. Politics must not be seen as something to be eliminated, but instead is essential to the establishment of human well-being. It is to be fostered wherever possible. Yet he does not stop here. There is irresponsible politics and responsible politics. *The Politics of Hope* establishes a theory of the latter.

Political philosophy has had to grapple with a number of serious problems. Among the most significant have been the relationships between ruler and ruled, what the nature and scope of authority should be, the issue of social conflict and how it is to be resolved, and the proper objectives of political action. Along with other writers, Dauenhauer claims that to treat these problems adequately a responsible politics must embody four constitutive principles: intelligibility or reasonableness, effectiveness, justice, and freedom. In less abstract terms, this means that for a politics to be responsible, the following conditions should prevail: '(1) responsiveness and nonarbitrariness in the exercise of political rule, (2) adaptability of political policies and institutions to the prevailing circumstances, (3) the requirement that political benefits and burdens be shared widely, and (4) consent of the governed to the government.'

Unlike others, however, the author believes that these conditions can be met only if we recognize certain primordial facts about the human condition. And these can be understood best by turning to the tradition of more phenomenologically oriented political work that has evolved in Europe.

Dauenhauer recognizes that political philosophy is never 'innocent.' As an 'implicit critique of actual political practice, political theory necessarily seeks to affect the appreciation and assessment of that practice.' Yet he is dissatisfied both with the liberal democratic tradition and with aspects of the more Marxist positions here. Instead, he seeks a 'third way,' a way between what he has called the politics of vision and the politics of will. This he labels the politics of hope.

In the process, he must differentiate his proposals from those of other prominent political theorists. He provides interesting criticisms of Rawls and Habermas. The approach of the former is based on an ahistorical individualism. While perhaps somewhat stronger, the latter is incomplete and falls prey to an overly rationalist bent. Other positions, including those of Sartre, are also subject to close scrutiny.

Dauenhauer's own insights are drawn from a different heritage of political and conceptual work. The influences of Marcel, Heidegger, Gadamer, and Ricoeur will be evident. However, one figure stands as the most prominent. This is the French phenomenological and political philosopher, Maurice Merleau-Ponty.

The theory of politics argued for in this volume is a politics of ambiguity, a politics that eschews determinism and dogmatism. There can be no certainty. Following Merleau-Ponty, the author claims that politics is a permanently open interrogation. It is an 'open dialectic.' Closedness and certainty are not gains. They are indeed losses, for the essential character of 'political man' is to be *en route*. Thus, an adequate political theory must stress the finitude, historicality, and intersubjectivity of the human condition. These are the fundamental or irreducible elements of all human efficacy.

The idea that the person is *essentially en route* has implications for the prevailing concepts of freedom. It rejects much of the doctrine of freedom that has come to be associated with liberal democratic political theory. At the same time, it also opposes several of the elements that have underpinned Marxist thought, though as Dauenhauer states 'Marx's own doctrine of freedom is complex and not in all respects in conflict' with his position. Again basing his arguments on Merleau-Ponty's insightful discussions of intersubjectivity, discourse, and history and again arguing against determinism of any kind, Dauenhauer claims that in its fullest sense freedom:

> consists in both the possession and the exercise of the capacity
> simultaneously to both participate in and maintain oneself as a
> pole of different kinds of relationships involving either
> hegemony, equality, or subsumption in order to perform
> mediations which are reflectively and, in principle, mutually
> acceptable.

What does this imply? Freedom can never be settled, a previously known relation. It is an activity. It is a process that is marked by both continuity and change, one in which one's prior condition 'is both preserved and transformed.' Freedom is both a fact and a task and has *respect* as one of its essential conditions. For the author, freedom and respect are thoroughly relational concepts. They cannot exist without mutual agency and responsibility.

Dauenhauer goes on from there, establishing other elements of a responsible politics in refreshing ways. Then, after elaborating the basic principles that constitute a politics of hope, he turns to the question of whether they can yield a more appropriate account of institutions and power than their competitors do. He examines how one might determine the appropriate exercise of political power, law, and political education.[3] Thus, the author's interpretation of the irreducible characteristics of men and women not only has implications for how we should understand politics. It has consequences as well for how we should participate in concrete political practices.

The Politics of Hope is truly synoptic. It creatively brings together, criticizes, and rearticulates many of the most significant elements of Western political thought. These elements are reorganized around a theory that values a diversity of institutions and practices and, especially, mutual dialogue.[4] Aside from its always interesting conceptual arguments, the volume's stress on such diversity and mutuality and on the essentially dialogic nature of politics provides us with a context for much needed further debate on what constitutes a 'responsible politics.' Those persons of all political persuasions who are interested in political theories and in what principles should guide our polity, as well as those who are interested in political education, will find a good deal to reflect upon here.

Michael W. Apple
The University of Wisconsin, Madison

Notes

1 Andrew Levine, *Arguing for Socialism* (Boston: Routledge & Kegan Paul, 1984).

2 Marcus Raskin, *A Common Good* (New York: Routledge & Kegan Paul, in press).

3 Compare his position to those taken in Raskin, *A Common Good*. On how education is now already political, see Michael W. Apple, *Ideology and Curriculum* (Boston: Routledge & Kegan Paul, 1979) and Michael W. Apple, *Education and Power* (Boston: Routledge & Kegan Paul, 1982).

4 For a provocative position on the importance of dialogue in political interaction, see also Katerina Clark and Michael Holquist, *Mikhail Bakhtin* (Cambridge, Mass.: Harvard University Press, 1984).

Preface and acknowledgments

This book is the outcome of two lines of thought which have occupied me for at least ten years. One of these lines is a standing concern with issues in political philosophy. The other line is an abiding interest in the interplay between silence and speech. These lines intersect and interweave in the matter of both political discourse and that of the relation between that discourse and political action. My reflections have been nurtured by the works of several major contemporary thinkers. Among these, Merleau-Ponty deserves special mention.

In a nontrivial sense, this work is a sibling of my *Silence: The Phenomenon and Its Ontological Significance*. There I argued that there could be neither complete speech, speech to which nothing further need be added, nor perfect action. There is neither *le mot juste* nor *le geste juste*. Silence is the ineliminable other of speech. It is not merely the correlative opposite of speech but is a positive, complex phenomenon in its own right. It need not undercut speech. Rather, silence can enhance it.

The counterpart in the realm of action to silence is restraint. Restraint is ineliminable from genuinely efficacious action. As silence is able to enhance speech, so restraint need not undercut action but rather can enhance it. This restraint, in political matters, is of two sorts. On the one hand, there is restraint in embracing political programs and objectives. The man of restraint remains open to having his political objectives modified. On the other hand, there is restraint in asserting will or might. The man of restraint leaves room for the assertions of others.

The ineliminability of silence ultimately requires interpretation. What must Being be if silence is to make sense? Similarly, the ineliminability of restraint requires interpretation. On the interpretation I propose, restraint reflects man's essential condition, namely his being permanently *en route*. Neither this condition nor the restraint which it elicits bear witness to any deplorable flaw in man and his doings. Rather, these are conditions which make human efficacy possible. And when they are lived out in hope, they most vigorously promote this efficacy.

Substantial ramifications for political thought and practice follow from this interpretation. It is the task of this study to set forth the most salient of these ramifications.

In the course of developing this book, I have been greatly helped by the advice and criticism of a number of friends. Some of them will surely still find much here with which they disagree. And all will likely quarrel with some part. But the book is far better than it would have been without the distinctive help each of them gave me. Among these critic friends, let me mention David Carr, Fred Dallmayr, Robert Dostal, Charles Sherover, Robert Sokolowski, Joseph Walsh and Michael Zimmerman. Special thanks are due to William McBride and Tom Rockmore. And in the background, patiently and gently prodding, has been Herbert Spiegelberg. Finally, but hardly least, I thank Bruce Roig whose critical eye has examined every line of the text. I hope that all of these colleagues and friends will find that, in spite of the book's flaws, their help was not given in vain.

Finally, I thank Cambridge University Press for permission to quote a lengthy passage from Patrick Riley's translation of Leibniz's 'Portrait of the prince,' in *The Political Writings of Leibniz*, ed. Patrick Riley, 1972.

1
Initial demarcations

I

This study is an exercise in political philosophy. Though no concise, comprehensive definition of political philosophy is readily available, there is unquestionably a long, well-developed tradition of thought about the purpose, objectives, and conditions of the complex ways in which men order their activities with respect to one another.[1] This essay is both informed by that tradition and seeks to contribute to its further development.[2] On the one hand, it learns from the tradition both what the domain and characteristics of political thought are and the precious acquisitions of political thought. On the other hand, it seeks to think past persistent conundrums in this same history of thought.

The tradition shows that, even if no satisfactory definition of political philosophy is at hand, the central issues with which political philosophers have grappled are perennial. These issues, which are intimately intertwined with one another, include, among others, (a) the relationships between ruler and ruled, (b) the nature and source of authority, (c) the problem of social conflict and its resolution, and most fundamentally, (d) the very objectives of political action. These issues can be summarized in large part in terms of questions about the relationships between freedom and order or security on the one hand and between the individual and the community on the other.

The realities to which these issues refer constitute the domain of politics. Politics, then, can usefully be described as follows. It is: (1) a form of activity engaged in by groups of individuals or societies centering around the quest either to attain competitive advantage, to avoid competitive disadvantage, or to attain cooperative

1

enhancement; (2) a form of activity conditioned by the fact that it transpires in time, amid changing circumstances and relative scarcity; and (3) a form of activity which produces consequences which significantly affect at least a substantial portion of the people concerned.[3]

The tradition has also bequeathed to us substantial and abiding desiderata which any politics claiming to be responsible should acknowledge. Among these are the importance of (1) responsiveness and nonarbitrariness in the exercise of political rule, (2) adaptability of political policies and institutions to the prevailing circumstances, (3) the requirement that political benefits and burdens be shared widely, and (4) consent of the governed to the government. One might speak of these four desiderata respectively in terms of four principles, namely the intelligibility or reasonableness principle, the effectiveness principle, the justice principle, and the freedom principle.[4] With the tradition, I assume that a responsible politics will be one which honors in some recognizable form these four principles.

Though the tradition presents one with both a well-developed conception of the domain of politics and a substantial set of principles which any concrete politics claiming to be responsible must honor, it does not provide a compelling, coherent foundation either for these principles or for the distinctive characteristics of the political domain. In general, traditional political thought has been dominated by two tendencies. One tendency is that toward rationalism, toward a politics of vision. The other tendency is toward voluntarism, toward a politics of will. The former tendency is exemplified in utopian thought of various sorts. The latter tendency appears in conventionalist and contractualist thought. But not only are these tendencies at odds with each other. Each also displays fatal flaws within itself. Kant, with his doctrine of the rational will, attempts without success to synthesize these tendencies.[5] One mark of their common failure is their inability to preclude at the same time both tyranny and anarchy, the twin antitheses of responsible politics.

The proposal I present in this study is meant to serve as an alternative to both politics of vision and politics of will. The justification for my proposal is that it can (1) help us to deal with the conceptual puzzles and practical tensions involved in reconciling the apparently competing claims of freedom and order or security on the one hand and the individual and the community on the other, while (2) avoiding the flaws of both rationalism and voluntarism. My alternative, I will show, can accomplish this task while still preserving the four desiderata or principles mentioned above.

My proposal is rooted in the recognition of man's essential finitude and historicality. He has no vision of an atemporal order of the true and the good which he can then translate into unassailable prescriptions for political practice. Nor has he so thorough an independence of particular historical circumstance that he can construct a political order exclusively on his own terms, at his own discretion, and for his own purposes. Responsible politics, a politics which is in keeping with man's finitude and historicality, is rather a politics of hope. A politics of hope acknowledges both its indebtedness to the past, its opportunity in the present, and its supercession in the future. Reflection on man's condition yields elements of a responsible politics. These elements constitute a politics of hope.

I do not claim that this present study uncovers all of the elements of a responsible politics. But I do claim that a responsible politics must embody the elements uncovered here. The objective of this study is first to set forth these elements and then, second, to show how they contribute both to the understanding and to the assessment of central features of political life.

II

Further to clarify how this study is related to the tradition, let me explicitly acknowledge some of the ways in which it instructs the political inquirer. In addition to pointing out the subject-matter to be discussed and to presenting abiding desiderata, the tradition also shows that substantial contributions to political thought have generally shared three significant characteristics, whether their authors have explicitly adverted to them or not. First, they have been formulated in terms not of mere observational reports but fundamentally in terms of recommendations. Second, they have been responses not merely to perennial issues but responses to the distinctive cast in which these issues are presented in a particular era. Third, and perhaps most importantly, these responses have all, or almost all, rested upon some interpretation of what it is to be a human being. Any essay claiming to be attentive to the tradition must take note of and incorporate these characteristics as well as deal with the prescribed subject-matter.

A few remarks about each of these three characteristics are in order here. First, political philosophy always or for the most part articulates an *attitude* toward concrete political practice.[6] As a form of practical philosophy, it seeks not only understanding but also efficacy. It passes judgment upon political practice and seeks to affect that practice by shaping the judgments made about it. Political philosophy, then, is a political act, albeit one of a special sort.[7] Some notable philosophers have missed this point, but all significant politicians have recognized it. Political theorists, as Wolin helpfully points out, do not issue predictions. Rather, they both post warnings and try to discover the necessary and sufficient conditions for attaining ends considered good or desirable.[8] That is, political philosophy necessarily either embodies or seeks to contribute to a recommendation concerning both the way political relationships should be understood and assessed and the way political activity should be conducted. As at least an implicit critique of actual political practice, political theory necessarily seeks to affect the appreciation and assessment of that practice. Thus political philosophy is never innocent.

Given this lack of innocence, a positivism in political philosophy is impossible. Contrary to the positivist's own intentions, behind his back so to speak, the very articulation of even a positivist position has political consequences. It is bound to bear upon the way in which political practice is appreciated and engaged in.[9]

The second characteristic common to substantial contributions to the tradition of political philosophy is that they respond to perennial issues in the light of the special circumstances prevailing in their respective eras. These circumstances are of two sorts, namely (1) the specific state of intellectual debate about matters touching upon the political, and (2) the specific exigencies of the prevailing political practice. Indeed, as a matter of historical record, 'most of the great statements of political philosophy have been put forward in times of crisis; that is, when political phenomena are less effectively integrated by institutional forms.'[10] Contributions to the tradition of political thought, then, have something of the 'occasional' about them. They are evidently marked by history. To admit their occasional character is not to deny their subsequent relevance. It is to note their origin, not to deny their enduring significance. But, as will be discussed later, this 'occasionality' does bear upon what an author can legitimately claim about the definitiveness of his contribution.

The third common characteristic of substantial contributions to the tradition of political thought, namely the fact that they have all been developed on the basis of some interpretation of what it is to be a human being, does not need much comment. The warnings and recommendations proffered by political philosophers depend in no small part for their cogency upon an estimation of the capabilities of actual and potential political actors. Little could damage the acceptability of any specific warnings or recommendations so much as evidence that efforts to heed them would run afoul of what lies within human competence. Nonetheless, political philosophy cannot remain bound to mere observation of what people have done. It also requires the exercise of imagination. This exercise of imagination aims to illuminate political matters by relating what is or has been to what can be. The interpretation of what lies within human competence and what does not is the cornerstone of the imaginative enterprise called political philosophy.[11]

Since this present study is meant to contribute to the tradition of political discourse, it will be useful for me to sketch here the salient features of the context whence my proposal arises. To know what is being said, one must also know who speaks and from where he speaks. In Lucien Goldmann's words:

> It is necessary to know that one always speaks from within a world from which comes the structure of consciousness of the one who is speaking and who, in order to know what he is saying, must know this world and this structuration at the risk of otherwise remaining within an ideology.[12]

Three sorts of considerations are relevant here. First, what clue or clues prompt the interpretation of man which I will propose? Second, what peculiarities of the present political era elicit my proposal? And third, what is the connection between my proposal and other expressions of contemporary thought? These questions both impinge upon one another and defy comprehensive treatment.[13] But the sketch of a response to them will serve to locate the present work and clarify its import.

My interpretation of man, the political agent and patient, is prompted in no small measure by three considerations drawn from

Aristotle's *Politics*. Man, he says, is a naturally political being because he has the power of speech with which to set forth the just and the unjust as well as the expedient and the inexpedient. Second, nature makes nothing in vain. And finally, the state, the body politic is self-sufficing, whereas the individual, when isolated, is not self-sufficing.[14]

Politics, therefore, is both natural and necessary to man. It follows from his capacity to speak. In and through the exercise of speech, man acts. He initiates. Speech and action, then, are fundamental, if not the sole, constituents of politics.[15] But speech, as I have argued elsewhere, is essentially bound up with silence.[16] This fact precludes the possibility of definitive discourse or perfect speech, speech which would make further speech pointless. Further, silence serves to relate speech and action to one another. It both holds them apart and brings them together. It is that cut or interruption which paves the way for the transition from one to the other. But that such a transition is a permanent necessity for political practice which is efficacious, is genuinely political, shows that not only is perfect speech inpossible but so is perfect practice. It is not just a matter of a perfect practice becoming outdated. At no date can the practice be perfect. Of course, the impossibility of perfect speech also entails that no treatment, including this present one, of any topic, political or otherwise, can be definitive. That is, an exploration of the full range of possibilities inherent in speech and action will require a deployment of the full range of possible ways in which silence can occur.

The third clue drawn from Aristotle which bears upon my interpretation of man as agent and patient of politics is his claim that man, taken as an isolated individual, is not self-sufficient. He needs other men fully to be himself. His speech and action, his political activity, therefore cannot be aimed at detaching him from politics. If freedom is of positive worth, then exercises of that freedom cannot have as their ultimate objective the holding of their performer apart from his fellow men. Rather, their ultimate objective is to establish and maintain a community of men, for only a community of men can be self-sufficing.

The interpretation of man which I shall defend in this work unites these Aristotelian considerations with the aforementioned recognition of man's essential finitude and historicality. On this interpretation man is taken to be a wayfarer, to be *en route*. But rather than being destined to complete a route and arrive at some final resting place, his destiny is to the route itself, to remain *en route* so long as he is man.

Man is likewise essentially intertwined with other men. He is a wayfarer in the company of other wayfarers. As such he is essentially political. Further, he was introduced into this company of wayfarers by predecessors. And part of what it means to be *en route* is to introduce new members, successors, to the path.

But even if man is necessarily *en route*, whether he recognizes and embraces this necessity or pretends that escape from the route is possible makes a vast difference practically as well as conceptually. The interpretation of man which I propose has consequences for participation in concrete political practice as well as for understanding politics. The scope of this study, therefore, includes the task of showing these consequences for fundamental political phenomena such as authority, sovereignty, law and coercion.

III

In addition to these general considerations concerning what it is to be a man, significant peculiarities of the present political era and the works of major contemporary thinkers also form the backdrop against which my proposal is worked out. Let me turn first to some prominent features of contemporary life which give a unique cast to the political enterprise of our era. Two of these features require only brief treatment. A third feature will call for somewhat longer consideration.

A first, obvious, factor weighing heavily upon all dimensions of contemporary life, political and otherwise, is the present threat of global nuclear warfare and the developing threat of global biological and chemical warfare. Throughout history, war and threat of war has been a constant component of politics. But wars used to be fought either to conquer something valuable or to destroy those who threatened one's community or way of life. Such wars could succeed in accomplishing their objectives. The survivors would in some sufficiently determinate sense have gained something. Global nuclear warfare, at least in the form in which it is presently threatened,[17] can yield no such gain. But even if global nuclear warfare is irrational, its possibility cannot be rationally ignored in any responsible political practice. The ultimate task of a responsible politics, failure at which would negate all other successes, is to fend off a global conflagration.

The problem of global nuclear war points to a second, more general feature of the present world with which contemporary political thought and practice must cope. Now, and for the foreseeable future, all politics has an international dimension.[18] Marx and Engels, in the *Communist Manifesto*, pointed to the tendency of both capitalism and communism systematically to transgress, and thus to trivialize, national boundaries. European and American imperialism, even after its decline, has stamped a Western brand upon political practice over the entire earth. Economics, demographics, and communication possibilities reinforce this globalization of Western political practice and the theory which it embodies. These same factors have, of course, rebounded upon the politics of Europe and America.[19] But the general direction of this movement is from West to East and from North to South. The result of the movement is a globalized political arena.

To be sure, this movement does not tend to reduce nations to mere regions of one global political entity. But no nation today can effectively hold itself in radical isolation from all other nations.[20] As a consequence, what it is to be a nation today is something other than it was for Locke or Montesquieu. Likewise, what it is to be a citizen has also changed. These differences have ramifications for all the basic elements of both political thought and practice.

This fact can be exemplified by brief reflection on the notion of sovereignty. Consider a few widely accepted, well-supported convictions about important dimensions of international activity. First, multinational corporations are generally taken not to be fully under the jurisdiction of any individual political sovereign. Second, it is regularly conceded that creditor nations do not have debtor nations under their total control. The economic well-being of the creditor nation is apparently closely dependent upon its sustaining the debtor nation. Third, military alliances are no longer considered to be optional, to be merely matters of convenience or expressions of particular interests. They are regarded as essential.

These considerations do not show that the notion of sovereignty is now bankrupt. Domestic politics is not a merely derivative function of global political and economic activity. But sovereignty, whatever else it might be, cannot be absolute national autonomy.

The third general feature of contemporary life which poses a distinctive challenge to present contemporary thought is the tendency, in both thought and practice, to depreciate politics in the name of some supposedly more lofty enterprise. To be sure, there is nothing new about attempts to depreciate politics. Such efforts date at least back to the time of Plato. But this antipolitical tendency today takes on shapes peculiar to our era. Two of these shapes, which are not obviously contradictory to one another, are of particular interest.

The first of these shapes is nicely described by Wolin. The present era, he argues, is marked not so much by an antipoliticism as by a 'sublimation of the political into forms of association which earlier thought had believed to be non-political.'[21] In the Western tradition of political philosophy the political has been understood to pertain to that which is common to a society. The political society includes smaller social units. Recent political theory, to the contrary, has tended to segment society and treat its several pieces as though they had no natural affiliations with one another. In place of the general political society, recent political thought has concentrated on either the organizational efficiency of some particular group or the formation of specialized communities designed to foster its members' well-being over against a forbidding outer world. Each of these tendencies favors an elite whose action is free from external restraint.[22]

The fragmentation of the traditional political domain has been defended on grounds that it is a necessary bulwark against totalitarianism. Modern totalitarianism, one can argue, has reduced every form of human activity to political activity and then rigidly structured political activity so that there is no plausible alternative to political activity. To avoid totalitarianism, so this line of reasoning goes, one should promote the fragmentation of the political.

Wolin correctly, I believe, rejects this defense of fragmentation. Such fragmentation tends toward one of two equally pernicious perversions. Fragmentation sometimes tends to concentrate the power to make the crucial decisions concerning human life exclusively in the hands of an elite. This elite, willy nilly, has in effect only its own lights to guide it. Those outside the ruling elite, by reason of this fragmentation, are close to political impotence. On the other hand, fragmentation sometimes tends to disperse decision making power among so many agents pursuing particular goods that those

9

who are supposedly charged with care of the common good are reduced to near impotence. Impotent rulers guide no one beyond the confines of their narrow particular interests. Thus if all political initiative lies in the hands of a ruling elite, then there is tyranny. And if no genuine initiative is available to the titular rulers, then there is anarchy, either the anarchy of paralysis or the anarchy of unbridled acquisitiveness. But tyranny is itself the ultimate antipolitics. It is, as Aristotle says, either the worst of politics or no politics at all.[23] Anarchy is no better. Rather than either tyrannical or anarchical uniformity, then, a responsible politics fosters a unity in diversity.[24]

The second shape of antipolitics prevalent in the contemporary era is a manifestation of individualism. Whether or not Arendt is right in locating the roots of this view in the conjunction of Cartesianism, Protestantism, capitalism, and Galilean science,[25] it is clear that from the seventeenth century, there has been a strong tendency to understand man either as a self-sufficient entity, or one who, by his own devices, can and should make himself self-sufficient. French Enlightenment and Revolutionary thinking strongly shaped this tendency.

On the contemporary version of this view, each person is taken to be both free and autonomous. This autonomous freedom is understood either as an innate characteristic with which one is endowed or as a characteristic one is naturally destined to achieve and is capable of achieving independently of the collaboration of other men. In either case it is a freedom which is fundamentally independent of political activity or organization.[26] This characteristic, so construed, is taken to be the fundamental human attribute. It is taken as that which should be inviolable and as that which serves as the measure of the legitimacy of all human interaction.[27] Once possessed, human freedom, on this view, needs no external enhancement, though it may need protection from having its exercise impeded.

This understanding of freedom is regularly associated with an expansive, indeed extravagant, doctrine of equality. Equality among men is taken to make sense because all men are regarded as being in the same condition. Thus equality is, at bottom, not regarded as an achievement but rather as an initial condition.[28] Equality then would not necessarily involve a concrete relation among those who are equal to one another. Rather it would mean that any person whatever selected for consideration would possess the same fundamental characteristics.[29] This equality, at least in principle, is understood to extend synchronically to all of one's consociates and diachronically to all of one's predecessors and successors. If all men should indeed be, in all relevant respects, equal, then no one could rightfully impinge upon another's autonomy and freedom.

A capital consequence of such a view, whether expressly articulated or not, is that politics is either (a) a merely optional enterprise, one in which participation is fully discretionary, or (b) a strategy for harmonizing conflicts of interest, or (c) a temporary therapy. If one takes politics to be a necessary condition for the harmonization of conflicts of interest, then one has to admit that autonomous freedom must submit to restrictions if it is to be fully efficacious. But such an admission runs counter to the sense of the doctrine of the supremacy of individual autonomy. If, however, politics is taken to be only an aid to harmony of interests, then in the final analysis its significance is contingent and participation in it is fundamentally discretionary. Thus, on any of these views, in the last analysis, politics is either merely one of several possible ways of expressing one's autonomous freedom and equality or it is a remedy for previously contracted handicaps to the exercise of such freedom, a remedy destined to be discontinued once the handicap is removed. On either alternative, the primary political task would be to allow man's extrapolitical autonomous freedom to be displayed.

The practice of politics, on this general view, is necessarily of limited value. It is a means to an end lying outside itself. It is, indeed, a practice which is, at least in principle, unnecessary, a practice which can, without ascertainable loss, be abandoned either now or at least in some future. Insofar as the practice of politics, as Aristotle already saw,[30] necessarily involves a subordination of the ruled to some ruler, and insofar as the practice of politics is taken to be in principle eliminable, then the title to exercise political leadership is never completely clear. The title is in principle either revocable without reassignment or contingent upon a removable defect. The exercise of political rule, then, is either already eliminable without loss or is destined by its intrinsic *telos* to its own elimination. The view, then, that each person possesses autonomous freedom and is in all pertinent respects equal to any other person and that this freedom and equality are fundamentally

11

independent of political practice turns out to be an apolitical or antipolitical theory of politics.

It is not trivial to note that this sort of 'sublimation of the political' is to be found in classical communism as well as in Western 'democratic capitalism.' In classical communist theory, it is the Party which is autonomously free. The exercise of politics involving discriminations between rulers and ruled is supposedly a temporary remedy destined to become outmoded when classes are finally abolished. Then, in the classless society, the autonomous freedom and equality of each person will be simply displayed without political activity properly so called. Only routine administrative duties, capable of being discharged by anyone and thus giving eminence to no one, will have to be performed.

Unfortunately for this general view, history provides little to support it. Autonomous freedom and the expansive sense of equality, far from being readily synthesized, have persistently undercut one another when translated into practice.[31] Rather, the historical record shows that efficacious activity, activity whose consequences perdure beyond the time when the agent is acting or even present, depends upon a political context. That is, even if a person never deliberately performs a political act, whatever acts he does perform can attain efficacy only if they are performed within the context of political activity performed by others.[32] This efficacy appears to be inextricably bound up with, even if not reducible to a mere function of, the amassing of wealth, the capacity to use property,[33] and the concentration of both military and police force in the hands of rulers.

These tendencies to depreciate politics may well be seen as desperate reactions to the presently perceived incompatibility of central elements in modern democratic political thought. This thought on the one hand promoted an ideal of utilitarian, atomist social engineering. On the other, it fostered an ideal of absolute freedom and equality which was to be achieved through the realization of a Rousseauian general will. Hegel apparently discerned just how these ideals, when translated into practice, would beget two destructive forces which would threaten the very existence of modern states. Charles Taylor summarizes Hegel's description of these forces as follows:

The first is the force of private interest, inherent in civil society and its mode of production, which constantly threatens to overrun all limits, polarize the society between rich and poor, and dissolve the bonds of the state. The second is the diametrically opposed attempt to overcome this and all other divisions by sweeping away all differentiation in the name of the general will and the true society of equals, an attempt which must issue, Hegel thinks, in violence and the dictatorship of a revolutionary elite.[34]

Both of these forces suppose the modern trend toward a radical egalitarian homogenization. But this homogenization cuts men adrift from the traditional communities in which they could find identity. The only focus which homogenization could provide in practice is either a militant nationalism or a totalitarian ideology, both of which would depreciate or even eliminate diversity.[35] As Taylor himself rightly sees:

> One of the great needs of modern democratic polity is to recover a sense of significant differentiation, so that its partial communities, be they geographical, or cultural, or occupational, can become again important centres of concern and activity for their members in a way which connects them to the whole.[36]

This whole to which men are connected, on my view, must finally be coextensive with mankind.

The proposal I offer in this study seeks to establish that political thought and practice are not reducible without loss to some other form of human endeavor. But rather, politics, I will argue, is essential both to the establishment of and the maintenance of human well-being. Contemporary prescriptions for the elimination or truncation of politics notwithstanding, I will show that a responsible politics undercuts any tendency toward tyranny without at the same time engendering tendencies toward anarchy. Politics, then, on my proposal is to be fostered rather curbed.

IV

The penultimate task to be discharged in this Introduction is to provide an indication of how my proposal is related to the works of some important contemporary theorists. Then I will be able to fulfill the final task, namely the task of summarizing just what my proposal consists in, how I intend to articulate it, and why it should be adopted. I will satisfy the penultimate task first by offering brief criticisms of two prominent theories and then by taking note of sources of support on which I will draw. But since my study seeks primarily to present a distinctive contribution to my own, these remarks make no pretense of doing full justice to any other positions. Rather, they serve to locate for the reader my point of departure.

John Rawls and Jürgen Habermas are two contemporary thinkers whose works have made major contributions to contemporary political thought. Each of their positions, though, have limitations or defects – sometimes self-acknowledged and sometimes not – which are substantial enough to lead one to seek an alternative comprehensive position. Though my study is not developed as an explicit counterproposal to either of their positions, it does in effect serve as such an alternative.

Consider, first, Rawls's *A Theory of Justice*.[37] It suffers from several substantial weaknesses, two of which I wish to single out for attention. First, his doctrine of justice is intimately connected with that of the self, the moral subject. It is on his doctrine of the self that I wish to focus. For Rawls, 'the self is prior to the ends which are affirmed by it.'[38] This self is fundamentally distinct from all of its contingent attributes, i.e. its contingent desires, interests, and ends.[39] The unity of the self is not an achievement effected in the course of Time. Rather, 'the essential unity of the self is already provided by the conception of right,'[40] a conception which is radically independent of 'the contingencies and accidents of the world.'[41] Such a self is and necessarily remains so radically individuated that no experience, no decisions could decisively alter this self. Such a self is radically ahistorical. The Rawlsian self is so thoroughly independent that 'it rules out the possibility of a public life in which, for good or ill, the identity as well as the interests of the participants could be at stake.'[42] Thus the self is fully constituted prior to and independently of any intersubjective involvements. Rawls's conception of the self, in short, is radically voluntaristic.[43]

But there are good reasons to question whether Rawls's conception of the self can either account for its capacities for agency or support his theory of justice. Sandel shows that Rawls must regard the distribution of natural talents as an asset to society as a whole. But if Rawls continues to insist that all endowments are contingent and therefore in principle detachable from the self, then Rawls's self or subject apparently turns out to be radically disembodied. But Rawls himself rejects such as Kantianesque self.[44] To avoid such a consequence, Rawls would apparently have to qualify the distinction between the self and other selves. He would have to allow the description of the self to include essential reference to others. Thus the notion of common assets, essential to Rawls's theory of justice, is tied to 'the possibility of a common subject of possession'. It appeals, in short, to an intersubjective conception of the self.[45]

Rawls's radically individuated, self-contained self, further, fails to account for crucial features of common moral experience. On Rawls's view, one should regard oneself as fundamentally independent of one's family, nation, and era. One should regard such ties as either merely voluntary or as merely natural and so not basically distinct from those which link one to any human being whatsoever. On this view, the self is basically unaffected by long-lasting commitments and attachments.

But this conception both does violence to experience and undercuts much that Rawls wishes to preserve. As Sandel puts it:

> To imagine a person incapable of constitutive attachments . . .
> is not to conceive an ideally free and rational agent, but to
> imagine a person wholly without character, without moral
> depth. For to have character is to know that I move in a history I
> neither summon nor command, which carries consequences
> none the less for my choices and conduct. . . . As a self-
> interpreting being, I am able to reflect on my history and in this
> sense to distance myself from it, but the distance is always
> precarious and provisional, the point of reflection never finally
> secured outside history itself.[46]

In addition to the ahistorical character of his theory, Rawls's position is handicapped by the restricted scope of his inquiry. He expressly limits his effort to the task of formulating 'a reasonable conception of justice for the basic structures of society conceived for the time being as a closed system isolated from other societies.'[47] There is of course nothing in principle inappropriate about delimiting the scope of an inquiry. But how the limits are drawn affects the strength of the results secured. What Rawls in fact says about his expectations for how the results of his inquiry would relate to larger questions, specifically to questions about relations among nations, reveals a second substantial weakness of his approach.

Rawls says that, with suitable modifications, his theory should provide the key to some other problems of justice. One of these, an especially urgent one today, is the problem of a just international order. According to Rawls, the basic principle of what he calls the law of nations is a principle of equality which is analogous to the equal rights of citizens in a constitutional regime. 'One consequence,' he says, 'of this equality of nations is the principle of self-determination, the right of a people to settle its own affairs without the intervention of foreign powers.'[48]

On this view, just as the individual citizen is the self-sustaining unit of which nations are constituted, so each nation is such a unit of which the international order is constituted. The scope and content of the agreements into which each unit enters, so long as it acknowledges the self-sufficing of other units, is entirely at its own discretion.[49] National order and international order are simply the respective complexes of such agreements and the various forms of apparatus required for their implementation.

This ahistorical 'individualism' of nations is subject to the same sorts of criticism as is the ahistorical individualism of Rawls's view of the self. And once again, his view violates the experience of practical political life. Consider, first, the question of separatism, e.g. the Welsh or Scottish separatist movements. How does one determine the unit of self-determination in Great Britain? Or consider the question of resident aliens, legal or illegal. How would one sort out the units for self-determination?

A second practical, and no less relevant, objection to Rawls's position here is the fact that the interdependence among nations revealed by contemporary economic practice shows that the notion of self-determination, even if it is coherent, is inapplicable and irrelevant to crucial questions of justice. In economic terms, 'creditor' nations are no more independent of 'debtor' nations than the latter are on the former. And the caliber of that dependence does not rest exclusively upon the discretion of either.

Rawls's position, then, whether it is a question of the individual's relationship to his own community or whether it is a question of the relationship among political communities, shows itself to be substantially flawed. In both cases, the flaw is the outcome of interpreting man, the political agent, in terms of an ahistorical individualism. The flaw and its consequences make evident the need to develop a politics rooted in a more adequate conception of man.

The general position of Jürgen Habermas, itself intricate and often refined and revised, comes closer in many respects to providing a sound account of man upon which to base a responsible politics. Habermas clearly recognizes both that genuine human freedom is intersubjective and that freedom finds its most excellent expression in the context of discourse. Such discourse, he sees, cannot be bound by national or regional limits. Thus, human 'autonomy' is based upon full-fledged reciprocation in both discourse and action among all participants.[50] The reciprocal, unconstrained communication and the community in which it would be set is the outcome of a reciprocal trust or hope among speakers.[51] Thus, at least some of the basic objections to Rawls's theory cannot, without further ado, be transferred to Habermas's work.

Nonetheless, it is essential to note that Habermas seeks at least a qualified release from history. He aims to 'mitigate the radically situational character of understanding through the introduction of theoretical elements.'[52] Habermas calls for a community whose life is guided by a genuine consensus arrived at and maintained in an ideal speech situation. The ideal speech situation is one in which there is unlimited discussion free from all distortions arising either from domination, deliberate strategies, or the various forms of self-deception.[53]. Though this ideal speech situation is only rarely, if ever, achieved, it serves as a regulative ideal for all discourse.[54] The structure of this ideal allows it to function as a criterion by which concrete social interaction is judged.

Habermas's position can reasonably be interpreted as one which holds that both individual and social life can be understood in terms of a possible progressive cancellation of limitations and deficiencies. That is, linear progress of some sort is, if not necessary, at least natural and possible.[55] If the goal of the ideal speech situation is not in fact attainable, it is at least accessible as a guiding norm. Progress toward satisfying this norm involves a surpassing of the crippling factors of deficient institutions, organizational ineptness, and scientific immaturity. Some progress of this sort has, for Habermas, already occurred and thus the lines delineating the direction of future progress are evident.[56]

For all of its considerable merit, Habermas's position suffers from substantial flaws. Perhaps the root defect lies in Habermas's rationalist bent.[57] This bent leads Habermas to distorted views about discourse and its human participants. On the one hand, his concept of the ideal speech situation appears to be sheerly formal and thus seriously incomplete. Since the practical implications of his theory are undeveloped, it is not clear that his theory is applicable to any concrete situation.[58] To add, as Habermas does, that 'the principle of justification of norms is no longer the monologically applicable principle of generalizability but the commonly followed *procedure* of redeeming normative validity claims discursively'[59] is insufficient to overcome the excessive formalism. As John McCumber says, reflective discourse 'is too specialized in nature and too restricted in scope to have any clear or direct relation to ordinary speech, or to the concrete needs that people actually feel.'[60]

On the other hand, Habermas's position requires the assumption that there is or can be some uniquely privileged mode of discourse, a mode of discourse issuing from an interest in emancipation uncontaminated with either instrumental or practical interests. This discourse supposedly determines the ultimate worth and sense of all discourse. For such discourse to be possible, those who would participate in it would have to be effectively released from all the contingencies of historical circumstances.

But there is no good reason to grant this assumption. To the contrary, there are strong reasons to hold that any attempt to set history and enlightened reason in radical opposition to one another is artificial and abstract. 'If emancipation is to have more than an abstract meaning of "freeing (us) from," it has to be embedded in a hermeneutic interpretation of the "reason" already inherent in the historical positivity of traditions.'[61] Further, discourse taken as a whole is not self-sufficient. It calls for action. Though thought or discourse may appear to yield deductively established imperatives for action, action always refutes the pretension of thought to be the necessary and sufficient basis for action.[62] Or from a slightly different angle, one can appropriately challenge, as Paul Ricoeur does, the possibility of giving any concrete content to interest in emancipation without relating that interest to practical interests. In Ricoeur's words:

The interest in emancipation would be empty and anemic unless it received a concrete content from our practical interest in communication and, therefore, if it were not confirmed by our capacity to creatively reinterpret our cultural heritages.[63]

Whether it be source, consequence, or simple accompaniment of the claims made for an 'ideal speech situation,' Habermas's view of men, the participants in discourse, also shows a rationalist proclivity. The participants in discourse are taken to have a natural tendency toward an increasing individual autonomy set over against surrounding conditions.[64] That this autonomy will always be destined to be exercised in company with other autonomous egos in no way foreshortens the implicit rationalism. In the face of this purported definitive, extrahistorical norm for conduct, one must surely ask: Is Habermas's 'ideal speech situation' not tantamount to the absence of all situations? If so, what can that mean? If not, where and among whom could ideal communication take place and be recognized as such? Would such ideal participants and their speech still be human as that term is presently understood?[65] The rationalism of Habermas's position thus raises all the worries which regularly arise when any rationalist politics is proposed. To put the matter succinctly, if the notion of an ideal speech situation is to be taken as a regulative norm and if fully autonomous men are to uphold this norm, then how will they deal with those who are not yet ready to participate in the ideal speech situation? The model for the relationship between the autonomous and the 'heteronomous' would apparently be that of teachers (*cognoscenti*) working to lead pupils (*ignoranti*) into the light. Warranted practice would be only that which is sanctioned by the already instructed, by those who have achieved enlightenment. By definition, the enlightened can be taught nothing by the ignorant. Such a scheme, in effect, calls for an oligarchy of the *cognoscenti*. But such oligarchies, no less than oligarchies based on wealth, tend to tyranny.[66] Habermas, to be sure, would reject such oligarchies. But his position is so formal that it does not effectively block such an appropriation. Indeed, his claims concerning autonomy make such an appropriation plausible.

In summary, Habermas, like many others in the rationalist tradition, attempts to prove too much. His failure lies in his giving too little weight to the fact that all political theory, inasmuch as it can neither completely determine action nor be totally detached

19

from the full panoply of discourse, is necessarily incomplete.[67] My own proposal endeavors to do justice to this ineluctable fact.

V

This study, then, aims to provide, first, an alternative account of man, the political actor (Chapters 3 through 5). Then it will show how this new view of man affects one's understanding of central political phenomena, e.g. authority, law, coercion, etc.

The view of man that I will propose is at odds with the Prometheanism of the Enlightenment view of man, whether this Prometheanism be one of the intellect or one of the will. My account rather emphasizes man's essential finitude, historicality, and inter-subjectivity. Such an account does not require that one give oneself over either to quietism or to despair. Hope is also possible. Indeed, evidence in favor of hope outweighs that which would warrant resignation or despair.

The view of man which I will defend sheds new light upon the domain of politics (Chapters 4 through 8). It discloses both the limits and the possibilities of central political phenomena such as authority, law, coercion, etc. Though my interpretation stands opposed to doctrines of unequivocal progress and the perfectibility of man, it does show how the human condition can be ameliorated, even if the risk of stagnation or deterioration is not thereby cancelled. On my view, men can constitute a politics which in turn fosters their own appropriate understanding of themselves. Individuals, the community, and their political institutions can mutually strengthen one another, even if none of them can be brought to stable perfection. My interpretation of man and my account of political phenomena make no pretense of being exhaustive. For example, I will not give any significant treatment to the connection between politics and economics. But my study does, I claim, yield elements which must be found in any responsible politics. A responsible politics is one which both respects the human condition and at the same time takes optimal advantage of the opportunities available to men. A responsible politics, it will be seen, is a politics of hope instead of either a politics of vision or a politics of will.

Though this politics of hope rejects the Enlightenment interpretation of man, it does not repudiate all the achievements of the

Enlightenment. Enlightenment political thought provided a fresh, profound articulation of the desiderata and principles mentioned above and thus clarified cherished features of the Western political tradition. A politics of the sort I set forth in this study not only preserves these acquisitions but furnishes new support for them. In fact, on my interpretation of man, the observance of these principles or the pursuit of these desiderata is, if anything, shown to be more urgent than ever.

More generally, one of the merits of my account is its capacity to salvage numerous insights achieved by the major contributors to Western political thought. Their works do not merely serve as grist for the mill. Theirs are not merely shoulders to be stood upon. Even those whose positions would at first seem most at variance with my position, e.g. Hobbes, come to be seen not primarily as adversaries whose doctrine is to be refuted, but rather as great fellow workers, the fruit of whose efforts is integral to the worth, and even to the possibility, of the doctrine I develop.

Further, instructed by the efforts of previous thinkers, this study makes no pretense of eliminating all aporiae and ambiguities in political theory and practice. Rather, it accounts for these puzzles and their persistence in such a way that they can be seen as fertile rather than as consequences of sterility or impotence. My argument shows that these aporiae and ambiguities are not merely remediable flaws explicable solely in terms of the insufficiencies of previous political theorists and practitioners. Rather, it reveals them to be intrinsic features of any political theory or practice which perspicuously attends to the entire human condition.[68]

The position that I set forth here is not, of course, unprecedented. If it were, that fact alone would practically suffice to disqualify it from serious consideration. As will be evident in the course of my presentation, my debt to others, past and present, is heavily and happily admitted. Those who have read Gabriel Marcel will find frequent marks of his influence. Even more have Heidegger, Gadamer, and Ricoeur shaped my thinking.

But in a unique way, my study springs from a meditation on Merleau-Ponty's works. To be sure, I do not claim to present here Merleau-Ponty's political philosophy.[69] But his subtle, circumspect reflections upon numerous political themes have left a legacy important for any contemporary thought about politics. Attention to the principal aspects of that legacy will provide an appropriate *point d'appui* for my own efforts. Chapter 2, then, will be devoted to the exploration of Merleau-Ponty's bequest to subsequent political thought.

2
Merleau-Ponty's legacy to political thought

Merleau-Ponty's contribution to responsible political thought can be approached in two, complementary, ways. The first way is that which focuses on his reflections on Marxism. The second is that which considers the implications for politics of his philosophy of language. Both of these ways find in him a thought which consistently rejects, on the one hand, all metaphysical dualisms and, on the other hand, all standard versions of either empiricism or rationalism.

Further, Merleau-Ponty's political thought is always related to the prevailing patterns of contemporary political practice. It is a response to a debate which is already in progress when he joins it. This 'occasional' character of his political essays does not weaken his contribution. To the contrary, it gives an exemplary concreteness to his investigations. Throughout his political reflections his coherent aim is always to search for a 'third way' which would surpass the supposedly exhaustive alternatives posed by the antagonism between liberalism and Soviet communism. This third way, the way which he would come to speak of as that of a noncommunist left, would undertake the unrelenting task 'of evading antagonists' hostility, of springing the traps that the one prepares for the other, of thwarting the complicity of their pessimisms.'[1]

Whether one approaches Merleau-Ponty's political thought through his discussions of Marxism or through his philosophy of language, one always encounters Merleau-Ponty's thoroughgoing appreciation of the essentially finite, historical, intersubjective character of human existence.[2] This appreciation is the source of the distinctiveness of Merleau-Ponty's contribution to political philosophy. In this chapter I will show what that contribution is by taking up, in turn, his reflections on Marxism and the bearing of his

23

philosophy of language upon political thought. Then I will summarize in what respects Merleau-Ponty's work contributes to the formulation of a responsible politics.

I

It is well known that Merleau-Ponty, after having embraced and supported Marxist politics for several years, later came to reject that politics. My concern here is not to determine why Merleau-Ponty's allegiance shifted. Nor is it to assess the accuracy or adequacy of his understanding of Marxism.[3] Rather I wish to concentrate on those considerations which shaped his analysis of Marxism and Marxism's pertinence to the whole of contemporary politics. In important respects, his reasons for first embracing and for subsequently rejecting Marxism turn out to be much the same.

In *Humanism and Terror*, Merleau-Ponty writes:

> The decline of proletarian humanism is not a crucial experience
> which invalidates the whole of Marxism. It is still valid as a
> critique of the present world and alternative humanisms. In this
> respect, at least, *it cannot be surpassed*. Even if it is incapable of
> shaping world history, it remains powerful enough to discredit
> other solutions. . . . Marxism is not just any hypothesis that
> might be replaced tomorrow by some other. It is the simple
> statement of those conditions without which there would be
> neither any humanism, in the sense of a mutual relation between
> men, nor any rationality in history.[4]

Taken in this sense, he concludes, Marxism 'is *the* philosophy of history and to renounce it is to dig the grave of Reason in history.'[5]

The uniqueness of Marxism, then, consists in its insistence upon intersubjectivity on the one hand and a history which is open to reason on the other. Marxism, as presented in *Humanism and Terror*, does not pretend to guarantee the advent of either unimpeded intersubjectivity or a totally rational history. But it does, for Merleau-Ponty, invalidate any politics or putative humanism which neglects or slights either of these essential possibilities of human existence.

For Merleau-Ponty, Marxism further makes it clear that these two possibilities, namely unimpeded intersubjectivity and rational history, can only be actualized together. There is no ahistorical intersubjectivity. Nor is there any rationality in history which is not an intersubjective achievement. Because this is so, both intersubjectivity and rationality in history are necessarily fragile and finite.

These two possibilities are essentially linked with freedom. This freedom is not merely a question of choice. Nor is it an independence from circumstances. Rather, freedom is always situated. It exists only within a field of possible action. As situated, freedom wrestles with but does not cancel the weight of material circumstances. Nor does it destroy the sedimented weight of previous human activity. 'Our freedom,' Merleau-Ponty says, 'does not destroy our situation, but gears itself to it.'[6] Similarly, freedom contends with but does not subjugate the freedom of others. It heightens rather than attenuates intersubjectivity and independence. The very point of freedom is to foster human interaction.

Merleau-Ponty brings this view of freedom and its intercalation with history and circumstance to his analysis of the 1938 Moscow trial of Bukharin. Bukharin's life, trial, and condemnation reveal what Merleau-Ponty calls 'the real tragedy of historical contingency.'[7] Man, whatever his intentions, has to act without knowing exactly what he is doing. It is always possible that events or the action of others can so transform the thrust of a man's efforts that what comes about is the opposite of what he intended. And yet he remains responsible for what transpires. 'Only children,' Merleau-Ponty says, 'imagine that their lives are separable from the lives of others, that their responsibility is limited to what they themselves have done. . . .'[8] And yet one must act. Failure to act has its own consequences for which one is accountable. Thus man is willy-nilly responsible for the course of events even though he cannot control it.[9]

The political implications of the situated character of human freedom are substantial. One of the most important of these, as Merleau-Ponty sees, concerns the matter of political judgment. He asks:

What if our actions were neither necessary in the sense of natural necessity nor free in the sense of a decision *ex nihilo*? In particular, what if in the social order no one were innocent and no one absolutely guilty? What if it were the very essence of history to impute to us responsibilities which are never entirely ours? What if all freedom is a decision which is not chosen but assumed all the same?[10]

And he answers: 'We would then be in the painful situation of never being able to condemn with good conscience, although it is inevitable that we exercise condemnation.'[11]

Accordingly, Merleau-Ponty is led to repudiate the standard liberal charge that Soviet communism is invalidated by reason of its oppressive, violent policies. This charge, Merleau-Ponty claims, springs from a pharisaism blind to its own defects. It pretends to stand upon unshakable ahistorical principles which serve as justification for propaganda, violence, and war against communism.

Even though he himself has finally to conclude that Soviet communism is untenable, his evidence is historical, and historically corrigible. His rejection is not rooted in inflexible principle. Rather it is a contingent rejection based upon historical contingencies.[12] He sums up *Humanism and Terror's* assessment of Marxism as follows:

Thus we find ourselves in an inextricable situation. The Marxist critique of capitalism is still valid and it is clear that anti-Sovietism today resembles the brutality, hybris, vertigo, and anguish that already found expression in fascism. On the other side, the Revolution has come to a halt: it maintains and aggravates the dictatorial apparatus while renouncing the revolutionary liberty of the proletariat in the Soviets and its party and abandoning the humane control of the state. It is impossible to be anti-Communist and it is not possible to be a Communist.[13]

But what, in the face of such contingency and uncertainty in human affairs, can be said about the rationality of history? Such contingency does indeed rule out any metaphysical guarantee that history is rational. It also requires that one abandon the notion that reason is fundamentally impervious to history and independent of intersubjective validation. Truth is not to be sought only in solitary thought and a priori reflection. Rather it is achieved 'through the experience of concrete situations and in a living dialogue with others apart from which internal evidence cannot validate its universal right.'[14] Reason, then, is not inevitable but neither is chaos. Reason in history is a possibility and a task, an intersubjective task.

Thus Merleau-Ponty can sum up the sense of reason in history as follows:

> *The human world is an open or unfinished system and the same radical contingency which threatens it with discord also rescues it from the inevitability of disorder and prevents us from despairing of it*, providing only that one remembers its various machineries are actually men and tries to maintain and expand man's relations to man.[15]

As I mentioned above, Merleau-Ponty eventually concluded that, in the face of Soviet aggression in Korea in 1950, he could no longer give communism his 'critical support.' Further, between 1952 and 1954, he determined that the roots of the Soviet conduct were already contained in Marx's own writings and thus Marxist theory itself was fundamentally flawed.[16] But this shift in Merleau-Ponty's political position does not betoken a shift in his own fundamental political thought. That thought remained committed to the search for a 'third way' between a crude realism or historical positivism on the one hand and an abstract rationalism or idealism on the other.

Already in *Humanism and Terror*, Merleau-Ponty had written:

> Hegel said that Terror was Kant put into practice. Having started with liberty, virtue, and Reason, the men of '93 ended with pure authority because they believed they were *the bearers of truth*, that this truth, once embodied in men and in government, is immediately threatened by the freedom of others who as subjects are *suspect*. The Revolution of '93 is Terror because it is abstract and wished to proceed directly to the enforcement of its principles.[17]

At the time of *Humanism and Terror*, Merleau-Ponty thought that Marx, contrary to the later Hegel on the one hand and to Kant on the other hand, had recognized that truth emerged in history and was not the possession of any particular man or Party. His 1950s' re-reading of Marx convinced him that this was not the case.[18] This re-reading did not lead Merleau-Ponty to abandon his view that truth, like man, is historical, finite, and intersubjective, a view already found both in *The Structure of Behaviour* and *Phenomenology of Perception*.[19] Rather, it led him to maintain this view and to base his critique of Marxism in *Adventures of the Dialectic* on it.

II

Merleau-Ponty's emphasis on the essentially finite, historical, intersubjective character of human existence not only furnishes him with reasons to reject Marxist communism. It also leads to important positive conclusions about politics and its responsible practice. The sense and coherence of these conclusions appears when one follows Merleau-Ponty's rather clear suggestion that we understand politics in terms of discourse or parlance. In heeding his suggestion, I will divide my account into two parts. First, I will discuss the political counterparts of language (*langue*) and speech (*parole*), the two constitutive moments of parlance (*langage*). Second, and more briefly, I will draw attention to a crucial but largely unthematized feature of both his philosophy of language and his political thought. This feature is the connection between parlance as a whole and its Other. This Other turns out to be silence and its actional counterpart, namely restraint.

In the preface to *Signs*, Merleau-Ponty explicitly directs us to think history according to the model of parlance (*langage*) or of being. We are, he says, 'in the field of history as we are in the field of parlance or of being.'[20] That is, we are born into history just as we are born into both parlance and perceptual being. These fields are neither fully determinate nor are they sheerly chaotic. Rather they both manifest previously established structures and at the same time provide the resources and opportunities for the men of the present to make distinctive contributions of their own.

Less explicitly but no less clearly Merleau-Ponty takes politics to be a special case of history.[21] Since politics, like history, is constituted in its actuality by genuinely initiating agents who are, nonetheless, always tied to some specific situation, it is appropriately conceived according to the model of parlance.[22] On the one hand, the specific character of concrete political situations consists of the particular intertwining of men and things which obtains at some juncture of time and geography. On the other hand, political agency is the endeavor to preserve or modify *directly* the prevailing shape of this intertwining.

To be more specific about the consequences of thinking politics as a special case of both history and parlance, let me detail how the central elements of Merleau-Ponty's political thought are structurally comparable to the principal features of parlance which Merleau-Ponty appropriated from Saussurean linguistics. These features are: (1) the distinction between *langue* (language) and *parole* (speech), (2) the distinction between the synchronic and the diachronic dimensions of language, and (3) the essentially inter-subjective character of all parlance.[23]

First, one discovers a direct political counterpart to the distinction between language and speech. Just as no speech can be articulated apart from the background of the language in which it is uttered, so no political accomplishment can be achieved apart from the previously established background of things and institutions. The 'things' in question here are not, of course, mere things. They are things recognized as available or unavailable material or cultural resources. That is, they are institutionalized things. Thus, there can be no genuine political enterprises today which ignore the presence or absence of such cultural resources as well-established legal, educational and religious institutions. Nor can the relative availability of material resources such as oil, grain, cobalt, or copper be overlooked. And the same holds good for both the level of technology and industry and the quantity, quality, and distribution of military might. All these elements, and more, enter into the constitution of the political language which both makes possible and constrains the political speech. Any putative political initiative which pretends that the specific background whence it arises is irrelevant is mere babble.

But just as language neither dictates nor necessitates some specific speech, so neither does the political situation dictate or necessitate a specific political undertaking. No living politics simply acquiesces in the factual situation as it finds it. Every politics, Merleau-Ponty says, insists upon its right to alter the way in which its tasks and problems are posed.[24] Indeed, this alteration is not merely a right which a politician may exercise at his discretion. The transformation of the situation is constitutive of politics itself.

Precisely what Merleau-Ponty praises in Machiavelli is the latter's recognition that men need never be mere victims of *fortuna*, of some given political situation. Political action consists in a grasp of the concrete possibilities which the situation presents, coupled with a bold effort to actualize them.[25] Thus, genuine politics requires not merely the acknowledgment of the weight of the determinate political situation, the 'language' in which one finds oneself located, but also the risky endeavor to transform that situation, to revivify it by the exercise of *virtù*, the uttering of the new 'speech.'

Nothing, of course, guarantees ahead of time that the new

political endeavor will either succeed or be appropriate. Even if, as the Marxists have it, men make their own history, still they often do not and cannot know the history they are making.[26] In Merleau-Ponty's words: 'If everything counts in history we can no longer say as Marxists do that in the *last analysis* historical logic always finds its ways, that it alone has a *decisive* role, and that it is the *truth* of history.'[27] For one thing, there is no last analysis. For another, however much logic may find its way, contingency is ineliminable from human affairs. Political situation and political initiative, then, like language and speech, belong together. Each has its *sens*, its meaning and direction, only by reason of its reference to the other.

The ramifications of thinking politics according to the language-speech model become clearer when one takes note of the counterpart in Merleau-Ponty's political thought to the Saussurean distinction between the synchronic and the diachronic dimensions of language. Here I want to call particular attention to one feature of Merleau-Ponty's political thought which emphasizes the synchronic dimension of the political situation and to two features which emphasize the diachronic dimension.

First, the synchronic feature. For Merleau-Ponty, it makes no sense to attempt to divide the elements of the political situation into unqualified blessings and unmitigated curses. As is the case with language, in political situations there are no elements which have full sense apart from the context in which they are located. Every element of the political situation is simply a component of a whole. None is self-subsisting with an independent positive meaning. Any responsible political initiative, like any speech, must acknowledge the irreducible complexity of the context against which it arises. Responsible initiative must avoid what Merleau-Ponty calls, in a somewhat different setting, the cops and con-men conception of history and politics.[28] Thus, for example, capitalism cannot be regarded as unmitigated evil nor does Soviet communism deserve simplistic, virulent denunciation. Each has its meaning in function of the other.[29] Policy decisions and implementation of principles necessarily induce responses which alter the context in which initiatives are undertaken. For example, pressures in favor of human rights exerted by one nation upon another will evoke responses from other nations. These responses will affect the effectiveness of the initial pressure and will also set the stage for the next initiative.

The diachronic features of Merleau-Ponty's political thought, however, introduce subtle but substantial modifications into this apparently neat system. First, however systematically intertwined the elements of the political situation may be, none of them is so definitively fixed in its meaning and bearing that it preserves some identical sense regardless of all temporal considerations.[30] This fact is, of course, a necessary condition for any political initiative. But more to the present point, this fact requires that political initiative not attempt either to reverse history or to annihilate the effective weight of anything brought by history to the present situation. To make such attempts would amount to pining for an imagined world which can no longer exist.

For example, Western and Third World peoples have already come into contact with one another. Even though the terms of this contact have been nothing for either side to boast about, that is not sufficient reason for either side to try to withdraw and perhaps start afresh. It makes no sense to consider this contact simply evil. And, as Merleau-Ponty puts it: 'In any case, it is something settled; there can be no question of recreating archaism; we are all embarked and it is no small matter to have begun this game.'[31] But, of course, as Merleau-Ponty makes clear in his essay on Indo-China, this does not mean that a failed specific policy must be clung to simply because it has been the policy.[32]

But even the initiative which acknowledges both the synchrony of the elements in the political situation and the uniqueness of the temporal moment which each of the elements inhabits cannot be guaranteed in advance to succeed and thus be preserved intact as part of a new situation, a new political language. This is a second diachronic feature. All shifts in the situation are indeed brought about by external influences, here specific initiatives. But the outcome of these influences is always not only particular but also beyond full prediction or control. What Merleau-Ponty says of history is likewise applicable to politics. Politics 'works on a question that is confusedly posed and is not sheltered from regressions and setbacks.'[33] As a consequence, neither a science nor an intuition can prescribe an undertaking whose outcome can be guaranteed. This fact disappoints those who believe in a definitive salvation and a single means to that salvation. But this fact does not make initiative absurd. To the contrary, it calls for unending initiative, *virtù* without resignation of any sort.[34]

That there can be neither a science nor an intuition which can guarantee the full outcome of a specific political undertaking is the political counterpart of the essential incompleteness of all perception, thought, expression, and action. There is no perfect moment of any of these.[35] Two of Merleau-Ponty's remarks concerning the incompleteness of language are of special interest. He says:

Now if we rid our minds of the idea that our language is the translation or cipher of an original text, we shall see that the idea of *complete* expression is nonsensical, and that all language is indirect or allusive – that is, if you wish, silence.[36]

And again:

Language is not the servant of meaning and does not govern meaning. There is no subordination or anything but a secondary distinction between them. . . . In speaking or writing, we do not refer to some *thing to say* which is before us distinct from any speech. What we have to say is only the excess of what we live over what has already been said.[37]

These texts emphasize the historical character of all human performances. Whatever truth or goodness men achieve is reached not in spite of but rather by virtue of their inherence in history. The point of origin of all truth, including philosophical and scientific truth, is man's interaction with other men in history.[38]

The thoroughgoing historicality of all human performances, when considered both synchronically and diachronically, provides the basis for two further significant dimensions of Merleau-Ponty's political thought. First, he sees that timeliness is an essential feature of all efficacious political initiative. Though there is no ideal or perfect moment for initiating some specific action, there are timely and untimely ones. What once could have been a solution to a problem ceases to be a possible solution. Or a problem which once had a likely solution no longer does but may in the future again do so. From another standpoint, a particular agent's capacities to engender solutions can both wax and wane. And do what one may, neither the appropriateness of the solution nor its timeliness can be guaranteed in advance.[39]

Second, and of major importance for Merleau-Ponty, the consideration of both the diachronic and the synchronic dimensions of the political situation leads to a distinctive view of the institutions which men inhabit. Institutions, he insists, are not inert. With Marx, Merleau-Ponty holds that there is a coming-to-be of meaning in institutions.[40] Sartre notwithstanding, institutions, as social apparatuses, are human and cannot be set over against man as something less than human.[41] Rather, institutions endow men's experiences with durable dimensions and allow them to form a history. At the same time, they invite men to further experience and thus make possible a future.[42] Indeed, far from regarding institutions as obstacles to freedom and political creativity, Merleau-Ponty maintains that one of the most crucial political tasks for our era is 'to find institutions which implant this practice of freedom in our customs.'[43]

The recognition of the importance and positive potential of institutions refines the sense of political initiative. Genuine initiative does not necessarily introduce discontinuity. The maintenance or preservation of some pattern of political thought or practice can itself be the outcome of initiative. Initiative, new 'speech' can at times be precisely that which reaffirms the old. The different has no intrinsic superiority to the same, even though the same, because of its historicality, is destined some time, if not now, to be superseded.[44]

Finally, serious attention to the synchronic and diachronic dimensions of all parlance shows that there is no unequivocally privileged type of discourse or action. From the standpoint of form or structure, Merleau-Ponty's claim concerning artistic activity, namely that there is no means of expression which, once mastered, can resolve the problems of painting or transform painting into a technique, can properly be generalized to apply to all types of discourse and action.[45]

Similarly, there is no unequivocally preeminent topic or perspective on topics. Thus there are discourse and deeds which are properly characterized as political, scientific, religious, etc. And there is philosophical discourse. But none of them is either totally self-sufficient nor, without qualification, architectonic. 'Somehow politics and culture, anthropology and sociology, psychology and philosophy are all related, intertwined with one another, together disclosing the unity and meaning in the lives of men.'[46] Thus no type of discourse or deed can properly lay claim to dominate or to regulate completely the field of human performances.[47]

The third dimension of the Saussurean analysis of parlance which bears upon Merleau-Ponty's political thought is, as was mentioned above, the essentially intersubjective character of all parlance. There is no isolated individual speech.[48] Parlance necessarily involves a historical community of speakers. Genuinely to speak is likewise to hear.[49]

The structural counterpart in politics of this feature of parlance is that all politics, whether domestic or international, is necessarily intersubjective. Political leaders and the people they lead are ordained to one another. They meet and address each other by virtue of the 'interworld' constituted by institutions and the cultural and material resources which the institutions provide. No one, Merleau-Ponty says, either commands or obeys absolutely.[50]

When one attends to the fact that political activity is not only intersubjective but is also embedded in some unique situation which involves institutions, he realizes that politics is essentially dialectical. This dialectic, of course, neither moves toward some preestablished terminus nor does it subsume everything under itself. Contingency is never banished.[51] In politics, as in history, there is no immunity from error. The rational always remains to be imagined and created. It never gains the power of simply replacing the false with the true.[52]

Given its essentially intersubjective and dialectical character, political discourse and conduct are fundamentally to be measured, as I mentioned above, against the standard of whether they acknowledge and sustain an interrogative dialectic. Only an unremitting interrogative dialectic allows men, if not to achieve fixed truths, at least to slough off errors.

Politics, then, like history, is a permanently open interrogation.[53] Merleau-Ponty, already in *Humanism and Terror*, had recognized the danger of the dialectic collapsing into a nondialectical positivism.[54] In *Adventures of the Dialectic* his justification for a noncommunist left is precisely that such a 'third force' would keep open dialectical interrogation, keep open self-criticism.[55] Through the power of interrupting standardized, sedimented discourse and practice, through the power of refusal, both the sheer gratuitousness of voluntarism and the rationalistic exaltation of some putative ideal political terminus or goal disappear.[56] The living interrogatory dialectic is the manifestation of their banishment.

One consequence of the open dialectic which constitutes genuine politics is that it is always appropriate to consider complicating or altering the terms of the prevailing dialectic precisely to further the dialectic. Thus it could make sense for Merleau-Ponty to promote a new left force. Such a force is not finally hostile to the practitioners of either liberalism or orthodox communism. Rather, it seeks to rescue them from the stultifying encrustations of dogmatically embraced ideologies and thus free them for participation in genuinely dialectical politics.[57]

This consequence entails that genuine politics requires tolerance. It necessarily takes people as they are, with their prejudices, fears, and aspirations.[58] Tolerance is not a matter of mere strategy. It is required because no agent can be a pure presence either to itself or to some object.[59] No one, alone, can possess the truth either about himself or about the world.

Dialectical politics thus demands an opposition which is free. Truth and action can never come together, Merleau-Ponty says, 'if there are not, along with those who act, those who observe them, who confront them with the truth of their action, and who can aspire to replace them in power.'[60] These and similar considerations lead Merleau-Ponty to his well-known endorsement of parliaments. Whatever its limitations, and clearly it has limitations, parliament is the one significant institution, a proven element in the political situation, against which fresh, free and living political initiative, political speech, can stand forth. 'Parliament,' according to Merleau-Ponty, 'is the only known institution that guarantees a minimum of opposition and truth.'[61] It likewise preserves the opposition needed to insure an intersubjectivity worthy of the name.

However tolerant and dialectical politics may be, it still involves the amassing and wielding of power. There can be no effective freedom, the freedom necessary for dialectical politics, without power.[62] Those who amass this power do so without the benefit of some unimpeachable prior title to it. Their power can only find its legitimation in their exercise of it.[63] In wielding power one necessarily impinges upon others. But political abstention is no solution. It simply yields the initiative to others. Merleau-Ponty therefore concludes: 'I would rather be a part of a country which does something in history than of a country which submits to it.'[64] Unless people risk the revitalizing 'speech' of political initiative, the institutions from which they have drawn their sustenance will either ossify or grant their opportunities to others, others who will be left without the benefit of appropriate opposition.

What has thus far been said about politics, on the basis of thinking it according to the model of parlance, takes on another dimension when one attends to the fact that there is no universal parlance. There is only a multiplicity of parlances which undergo translation into one another. Similarly, there is no universal politics. There are only multiple concrete politics. Different times and lands have different institutions and stocks of cultural and material resources. These differences call for and make possible different initiatives. It is idle to weigh situations against some abstract standard. Situations are to be lived through, not judged from some putatively independent spectator's vantage point.[65]

But even if the appropriate political initiative, the concrete political speech, is always geared to a specific, more or less local, situation, Merleau-Ponty holds that today all responsible politics must be resolutely international. 'The main concern of our time is going to be to reconcile the old world and the new.'[66] This intertwining of the local and the global is not the achieving of a teleologically ordained ideal. It is simply a contingent fact of our era. But it is a fact of consummate contemporary importance.

These two considerations, namely that there is no single universal politics but that today responsible politics must be international, are summarized by Merleau-Ponty in this way:

> There is no universal clock, but local histories take form
> beneath our eyes, and begin to regulate themselves, and
> haltingly link themselves to one another and demand to live,
> and confirm the powerful in the wisdom which the immensity of
> the risks and the consciousness of their own disorder had given
> them. The world is more present to itself in all its parts than it
> ever was.[67]

Politics, like parlance then, is not a seamless, stable whole. Rather, it is a vibrating, moving complex.

The emphasis upon the open, interrogatory, dialectical character of genuine politics does not, however, pit politics against morality. Even if politics is not reducible to morality, it is not contrary to morality. Rather, Merleau-Ponty says, there must be a positive relationship between them.[68] Granted that values and principles are insufficient for genuine politics, they are nonetheless necessary. There must be, Merleau-Ponty recognizes, a guideline to distinguish between political *virtù*, the excellence in acquiring and wielding power to make the most of the opportunities provided by *fortuna*, and political opportunism, which is no more than the makeshift accommodation to prevailing pressures aiming merely at survival.[69]

For Merleau-Ponty, this guideline apparently consists in making the preservation and extension of the dialectic the overarching objective of all political initiatives.[70] Political judgments, however attentive they are to the uniqueness of the situation to which they are inextricably linked, must all issue in action which has this as its ultimate objective. This guideline warrants Merleau-Ponty's conclusion that reform, far from being outmoded, 'alone is the order of the day.'[71] This conclusion in turn provides the basis for Merleau-Ponty's support for parliamentarianism as the best candidate for that form or institution which can keep power in reins without annulling it.

In brief, then, political judgment inhabits an interworld. It draws upon and oscillates between imperatives of will and acknowledgment of facts. Thus, on the one hand, it itself has structural features like those of parlance. On the other hand, the specific content of genuine political judgments reveals that they refer to a world which is itself appropriately thought according to the model of parlance.

III

Substantial light is shed on politics when one thinks it, as Merleau-Ponty's work encourages, in terms of the interplay between language (*langue*) and speech (*parole*). Further illumination is achieved by reflecting upon the finite, historical, intersubjective character of discourse as a whole.

Throughout his work Merleau-Ponty rejected the notion that there could be either a pure thought or an ideal discourse, a discourse, that is, which would supposedly capture some pure disembodied thought and be completely under the control of the speaker. As I mentioned above, he denies both that language 'translates' some more original 'thought' and that there is any sense to the notion of 'complete expression.'

And in the same vein, he says in *The Prose of the World*:

There is indeed an interior to language, a signifying intention which animates linguistic events and, at each moment, makes language a system capable of its own self-recovery and self-confirmation. But this intention exhausts itself to the extent that it is fulfilled. *For its aim to be realized, it must not be completely realized, and for something to be said, it must not be said absolutely.*[72]

For Merleau-Ponty, then, there is neither some ideal moment of discourse nor any definitively complete discourse. Similarly, and directly to the point of political thought, just as there is neither pure thought nor perfect expression, neither is there pure action, action released from the exigencies of circumstances and fully in control of its agents. Moments of pure action, perfect moments, would be those in which constraint is totally absent and restraint is unnecessary. In such moments all would do and want to do the same thing.[73]

It may be, Merleau-Ponty grants, that there are privileged moments, moments of unusual opportunity for initiative when constraint is minimal. But these moments can neither last nor be reproduced at will. And even in these privileged moments there remain traces of constraint which herald the institutions of constraint which necessarily follow.[74] Thus Merleau-Ponty does not deny that there are uniquely propitious moments for political action. But he does deny that these moments are absolutely privileged.

As a consequence, Merleau-Ponty can conclude in *Adventures of the Dialectic* that there is no such thing as permanent revolution. The idea of a permanent revolution, which Merleau-Ponty finds at work in Trotsky and Sartre, among others, is, he says, a chimera just as is the idea of pure action.[75] Successful revolutions, when they become regimes, inevitably degenerate. They 'are true as movements and false as regimes.'[76]

But for Merleau-Ponty, the ineluctably partial character of discourse and the constrained character of action is no defect or flaw. Far from either seeking or pining for detachment from the constraints of situations, the free agent appreciates that the situation, including as it does other agents, makes possible his own freedom. Freedoms do indeed impinge upon one another. But they also require one another. No man 'by himself is subject nor is he free.'[77]

For responsible politics, freedom is always bound up with commitment. Genuine commitment to the situation in which one is located does not consist simply in acquiescing to the *status quo*. Rather, it involves unremitting inquiry into that to which one commits himself. This inquiry is accomplished not by pretending to become total master either of oneself or of the situation, 'not by deciding to give my life this or that meaning; rather it is by attempting simply to live what is offered me, without playing tricks with the logic of the enterprise, without enclosing it beforehand inside the limits of a premeditated meaning.'[78] Free commitment, then, requires waiting as well as initiating.

For Merleau-Ponty, then, political action is always action with others in a determinate context. It is necessarily constrained by the impossibility of either perfect discourse or pure action. Responsible politics is constituted by taking this constraint to be more than just a brute fact to be endured, by taking it to be normative. It is normative inasmuch as, against multiple attempts to deny the situated character of all human existence, its acknowledgment promotes a proper assessment of one's transactions with one's fellows in the historical context they inhabit.

In summary, then, the model according to which Merleau-Ponty would have us think politics involves not just the dialectic between language (*langue*) and speech (*parole*). It also involves a positive interplay between parlance as a whole (*langage*) and its Other. This Other, Merleau-Ponty suggests in several ways, is silence. And the counterpart of silence, in the domain of action, is restraint. Though he himself left the questions of silence largely unthematized, Merleau-Ponty's work rather clearly hints that, if appropriately thematized, the issue of silence would fill out in important respects the conditions for responsible politics.[79] In Chapter 3, I will make silence thematic and show its bearing upon political matters.

IV

It would be an exaggeration to claim that Merleau-Ponty has articulated a comprehensive doctrine of politics. And it would be misleading not to acknowledge that significant challenges can be raised against his position.[80] Nonetheless, he has made a rich contribution to contemporary political thought. From his works, one can extract a substantial number of positive, logically overlapping constituents of a responsible politics.

First, in no particular order, every political theory, on the one hand, and all political conduct and institutions, on the other hand, are essentially historical. All attempts to claim for any of them any sort of atemporal legitimacy or validity are fundamentally nonsensical.

Second, politics always involves the old. Any politics which attempts either to cancel, disregard, or decide definitely the weight of the past out of which it arises is blind to its own possibilities. Such a blind politics, when armed with modern weaponry, threatens man's very existence. Genuine politics, to be sure, involves volition and decision. But this volition never pretends to radical independence from a past which alone makes volition possible.

Third, by reason of a necessity belonging specifically to the political realm, as opposed to some non political realm, the distinction between the rulers and the ruled is irreducible. The irreducibility of this distinction does not, of course, presuppose some 'natural' oligarchy or aristocracy. On the contrary, any presupposition which would imply that legitimate exercise of command amounts simply to having the so-called true will or true insight of the body politic express itself to itself is a concoction which rests on a fiction. Nonetheless, whatever political rights may be ascribed to each member of the community, it is simply not the case that all have equal title to rule. All may indeed have the right to obey through critical response rather than through mere compliance. But initiative always resides with some rather than with all. Some must be prepared to listen so that others can speak.

Fourth, those who have the right to command hold this right by reason of their political virtuosity, and not by reason of some putative radical autonomy. Virtuosity consists in grasping the opportunities of the historical moment and handling them dexterously to stamp the moment with the virtuoso's own distinctive mark. Any concrete right of command presupposes a field of play constituted in great part by the factual fears, hopes, and resources of the ruled.[81] But without the virtuoso's play, the field is prepolitical. Should the virtuoso lose his virtuosity, for whatever reason, he thereby loses his right to command.

Fifth, whatever political correctness is, it comes to be in the actual doing of political deeds. Thus political undertakings are intrinsically risky. Neither the ruler nor the ruled can know in advance that what they are embarked upon is unmistakably correct. There are hopeless, and therefore surely wrong, political endeavors, e.g. endeavors which deny some of the elements of responsible politics. But the sole assurance that one can have in embarking upon some specific political activity is that there is a prospect that once the deed is underway, it can persuasively be said that 'things are going well,' and that subsequent generations may be able to look back on the deed and say that 'things worked out well.'

Sixth, the task of political conduct is not to redeem men from their historicality. Rather, it is so to respond to the opportunities afforded by the present moment that a space is opened and preserved in which future opportunities for all sorts of human achievements, political and nonpolitical, can arise. Politics, then, aims at effecting a displacement away from the repetitious performance of routines towards performances which respond to the ever distinctive proximate and remote possibilities granted by each historical moment. But even so, there is always the danger that the political deed will be untimely. And untimeliness in politics, no less than hopelessness, thoroughly vitiates the deed.

Seventh, the political domain, however distinctive it is, cannot be self-sufficient. It and the activity appropriate to it make sense only in conjunction with other domains, with other ways of discourse and action. Its own institutions and 'things' are inextricably intertwined with the practices, institutions, and 'things' belonging to other domains (artistic, religious, scientific, etc.). And all of these domains, taken singly or together, necessarily remain on the hither side of complete speech or perfect action. Their finitude is essential. It both makes the isolation of any domain impossible and at the same time precludes the stasis of any domain. There is, then, no such things as the unqualifiedly 'pre-political' or 'extra-political.' But neither is there nothing but the political.

Eighth, and finally, Merleau-Ponty emphasizes an apparent paradox of the contemporary political scene. On the one hand, there is no universal politics, only multiple concrete politics. Yet all responsible contemporary and foreseeable politics must be resolutely international. Isolationism is indefensible. He says:

There is no serious humanism except the one which looks for man's effective recognition by his fellow man throughout the

world. Consequently, it [serious humanism] could not precede
the moment when humanity gives itself its means of
communication and communion. Today these means
exist. . . .[82]

Apparently, Merleau-Ponty holds that both communism and
economico-political liberalism are political phenomena whose day
is essentially over. But what they have bequeathed to us is the
opportunity for a world politics. This world politics cannot be
homogeneous. But its heterogenity cannot be of the sort that
sustains parochialism. Whatever is henceforth to count as legitimate political conduct must be judged in global terms.

In summary, then, Merleau-Ponty's political thought gives full
scope to the finite, historical, intersubjective character of human
existence. It is true that his position is marked by ambiguity. But
that ambiguity is a faithful reflection of the ambiguity intrinsic to all
concrete political practice. His thought, then, stands in opposition
to both rationalist and voluntarist approaches to politics,
approaches which claim either a preeminent vision or a preeminent
title to will. Over against both pretexts to vision and resorts to sheer
will, Merleau-Ponty explores a 'third' way, a way of restraint. This
way, a way which avoids the enervation of skepticism as well as
dogmatism, lies open to him because he has thought politics according to the model of parlance.

Merleau-Ponty's political thought, taken as a whole, then,
opposes both politics of vision and politics of sheer will or might.
His critique, however, does not yield only negative results. His
work positively points toward what I call a politics of hope.[83] In the
rest of this study, I will develop my own proposal in the light of the
positive accomplishments of his political reflections.

3
Speech, silence, and being human

Merleau-Ponty's reflections on parlance and politics yield one fundamental criterion for determining responsible political activity. Political activity is responsible precisely to the extent that it fosters and maintains an open dialectic among men. This conclusion is congruent with two staples of traditional Western political thought, namely that men are essentially speakers and that without speech there is no politics. Speech, both for the tradition and for Merleau-Ponty, is not merely one of man's many possibilities or capabilities. It is that without which there would be no man. Similarly, both for the tradition and for Merleau-Ponty, though there is speech which is not political, there is no politics without speech. Politics may indeed involve fabrication and action. But without speech, fabrication and action would remain extra-political.[1] Politics is 'the correlation, in broad daylight, of speech, of acting, and of a practical state of affairs.'[2]

For Merleau-Ponty, man's speaking, and indeed his entire way of being, is at bottom interrogatory.[3] But there is no complete, no definitive speech. Nor is there any perfect action or fabrication. Further, no domain of human activity, political or otherwise, is either radically closed or self-sufficient. Responsible politics must acknowledge these facts. And the way these facts are properly to be acknowledged is by establishing and maintaining an open dialectic among men, a dialectic from which, at least in principle, no living person is ever excluded. Hence Merleau-Ponty comes to endorse parliamentary forms of government.

The eight considerations educed in Chapter 2 from Merleau-Ponty's political reflections clarify in important respects the condition of man, the political agent. Nonetheless, his works leave man's essentially interrogatory character underinterpreted. To the extent

43

that it remains underinterpreted, the force of his call for an open dialectic is left vague.

My own endeavor to determine the basic elements of responsible politics, instructed as it is both by the tradition in general and by Merleau-Ponty in particular, acknowledges both that men are essentially speakers and interrogators and that there is no politics without speech. In this chapter, taking up where Merleau-Ponty left off, I want to consider in more detail speech and action in their basic incompleteness. By doing so, I will be able to bring to light what the possibilities and limits of discourse reveal about man, the political actor. These possibilities and limits obviously affect what concrete political enterprises can achieve. Thus any satisfactory theory of politics must acknowledge them.

To set forth these possibilities and limits, I will make thematic the relationship between discourse and silence. The discussion of this relationship, to which Merleau-Ponty not infrequently alluded but which he left mostly unthematized, lays the groundwork for my interpretation of what it is to be human. To be human, I will then argue, is to be *en route*. If this is so, then political man is one who is *en route* politically.

Substantial consequences for politics follow from the admission that discourse and silence are essentially intertwined and from the interpretation of man as one who is radically *en route*. A politics which denies, either in word or in deed, the limits intrinsic to and constitutive of man's routedness is irresponsible. Observation of these limits, in effect, is a necessary condition for any politics at all. But as there is a difference between mere discourse and excellent discourse, so there is a difference between mere politics and excellent politics. A large part of my task in this work is to set forth conditions for excellent politics. Attention to the connection between discourse and silence will also contribute to the determination of these latter conditions.

Arguments concerning the necessary conditions for politics can be, in the Aristotelian sense, demonstrative. From them, categorical commands can be generated. But arguments concerning what constitutes excellent politics deal with future contingencies, with the likely. These arguments can at best be enthymematic.[4] From them, only recommendations, counsels, and cautions can be generated. As Paul Ricoeur points out in discussing Aristotle's *Rhetoric*: 'The kind of proof appropriate to oratory is not the necessary but the probable, because the human affairs over which tribunals and asssemblies deliberate and decide are not subject to the sort of necessity, or intellectual constraint, that geometry and first philosophy demand.'[5] These considerations guarantee that my proposal cannot, with any more legitimacy than any others, claim to give an exhaustive account of responsible politics. But that fact in no way counts against it.

I

In my study, *Silence: The Phenomenon and Its Ontological Significance*,[6] I have shown that silence is more than a mere absence of speech. It is, rather, a positive phenomenon in its own right. Further, silence is not simply the correlative opposite of speech. It is not an alternative to speech. Rather, it brings about and maintains a tension both among multiple levels and shapes of discourse on the one hand and between the realm of signification and other realms of experience, e.g. perception and fabrication, on the other.

The positive phenomenon of silence is the outcome of an active, not merely spontaneous, human performance. Among the most salient features of this kind of performance is that *pure* occurrences of these performances do not intend already fully determinate objects of any sort. Silence can of course be deployed as part of a tactic or strategy geared toward the achievement of some already determined objective. Jones can keep silent about Smith's theft so that Smith will not be dismissed from his job. But not all performances of silence are so bound. In its pure occurrences, silence loosens the grip which previously constituted objects and objectives have on a person and on how he deals with them. Such performances of silence interrupt or cut some already instituted stream of performances which do intend well-defined possible or actual objects or states of affairs.[7] Jones silences his own talk about cattle so that Smith or anyone may say something about cattle or about any other topic or even so that no more – for now – be said by anyone about anything.

The phenomenon of silence, nonetheless, is never wholly divorced from discourse and, like discourse, it takes on multiple shapes. To see something of its complexity, consider, first, performances of silence which occur inside the bounds of the realm of discursive activity. These performances make possible highly variegated sorts of relationships among speakers, hearers, and the subject matter of the discourse. All discourse has the form: A says p about x to B. Discoursing, then, is a double-rayed act. Because discourse is double-rayed, there can be a shifting of emphasis between its two general regions. If the primary ray is directed toward the subject matter, the x, then the utterance is topic-centered and both the speaker and the hearer take their task to be primarily that of ensuring that the subject matter is appropriately expressed. If the primary ray is directed toward the audience, the B, then the utterance is interlocutor-centered and the primary task for the participants is to care for one another's aspirations and needs. One ray, so far as I can tell, is always predominant. They are never of equal primacy.[8] It is through performances of silence that shifts between topic-centered and interlocutor-centered discourse can occur. Silence interrupts the stream of discourse of one sort, a stream which in principle need never be interrupted, and opens the way for discourse of the other sort.

Topic-centered discourse is itself variegated. And performances of silence enter into the constitution of these different forms of topic-centered discourse. One can distinguish scientific discourse, technological discourse, moral discourse, artistic discourse, religious discourse, as well as political discourse. Each of these forms of discourse is marked by a specific sort of temporality, of temporal sequence. But few, if any, topics can be uniquely assigned to one and only one of these forms of discourse. A form of topic-centered discourse then is constituted by a specific emphasis given to the objects with which it deals and the relationships recognized among those objects. This emphasis is correlated with a specific sort of temporality. Specific sorts of performances of silence mark these several forms of discourse and enter into their distinctive constitutions.[9]

Not only does silence bear upon the relationship between speakers and hearers on the one hand and their topics on the other. It also bears upon the relationships among the participants in discourse themselves. An important aspect of the complexity of the realm of discourse which is particularly relevant to political thought is the fact that there are distinct levels of interpersonal involvement in discourse. Each particular level of involvement is intimately correlated with the sort of responsibility which one can take for what is actually said.[10] Consider, for example, the discourse transpiring in a political meeting. There can be a monological lecture in which the speaker is well distinguished from the audience and for which the speaker can and often does assume primary if not exclusive responsibility for what is said. There can also be a dialogue of question and answer, of joint exploration in which all assembled participate or not at their discretion and thus all bear roughly equal responsibility for what is said. And there can be 'we' sayings in which all participants affirm together allegiance or fidelity to that person or political program they all esteem. It is performances of silence which make possible the shifts from one of these levels to another. The possibility of such shifts is inherent in all discourse and is thus, in principle, never definitively eliminable from it. Actual and possible shifts of this sort are obviously important to politics.

In addition to those forms of silence which effect diversifications within the realm of discourse, there are two forms of silence which serve to distinguish the realm of discourse as a whole from other realms of human experience.[11] I will call these two forms of silence inaugural silence and terminal silence. On the one hand, these two forms of silence frame the realm of discourse and thus contribute to its distinctiveness. On the other hand, they serve to link it with other realms of experience. Discourse neither comes from nowhere nor, once begun, takes on the character of a latter day *Ens a se*, i.e. a speech saying only itself to itself.

Inaugural silence opens the way for discourse. It makes possible the shift from nonsignitive experience to signitive experience. This shift is, in Husserlian terms, motivated already by nonsignitive experience but inaugural silence is a necessary condition for its accomplishment.

The nonsignitive experience which motivates the shift to discourse is itself complex. It includes perception, imagination, memory, and the associations they achieve in their multiple interwoven moments.[12] It includes appetition and desire.[13] It includes nonsignitive doings and makings, e.g. walkings, poundings, etc., which do not aim to signify anything determinate.

Nonsignitive experience, in its several dimensions, binds the person to the particularity of his situation. Inaugural silence, though it does not reduce the grip of the particular to nothing, slackens it. Inaugural silence thus makes possible a shift from an absorption in the features of one's immediate spatiotemporal context

47

to that distance from particulars which it required if there is to be room for signitive mediation.[14] Here then one finds grounds for holding the correlative opposite of Merleau-Ponty's famous remark that the greatest lesson of Husserl's reduction is the impossibility of a complete reduction.[15] That is, the greatest lesson of the encounter with the most absorbing of particulars is the impossibility of complete absorption. There is always room for silence to slacken the grip which particulars have on the person involved with them.[16]

Important as inaugural silence is, it is perhaps much more urgent to give proper attention in one's understanding of the human condition and its political possibilities to terminal silence.[17] Terminal silence reveals the limits of all signification. It thereby shows the limited character of any mediation of any sort. Though signification, and discourse, can, in principle, go on interminably, the entire realm of discourse is widely experienced as either insufficient or incomplete, as unable to cope definitively with some dimension of extrasignitive experience. Sometimes discourse has been felt to be too wedded to sensuous experience and so people have sought an 'ideal discourse,' a discourse unencumbered by the vagaries of perception and appetition. But other times discourse has been felt to be too divorced from perception and desire and so people have searched for 'a genuinely concrete' discourse, a discourse corresponding fully to the particularity of the moment of perception and desire.[18] Though such searches have proven fruitless, and indeed countersensical, these quests, and the experiences which prompted them, show that the realm of discourse in its actual constitution does not present itself as a self-sufficient realm, a realm whose resources satisfy the full range of human experience. Terminal silence is motivated by the experience of the nonsufficiency of the realm of discourse. But even though terminal silence interrupts the entire set of performances belonging to the realm of discourse, it remains essentially linked to that realm. Together with inaugural silence it bounds the realm of discourse. The former establishes the gap between nonsignitive experience and signification. The latter confirms the uncancellability of that gap now that the gap has been established.

Of itself, terminal silence does not impede further discourse of any sort. Just as inaugural silence is compatible with subsequent nonsignitive experience so is terminal silence compatible with subsequent discourse. But in bringing closure to the realm of signification, terminal silence reveals both that the scope and power of discourse are limited and that discourse is a well-defined, irreducible realm. Discourse there must be. Complete discourse there cannot be. Thus, terminal silence 'changes the sign' of all discourse. It transforms discourse by distancing it from its pretensions to completeness or adequacy. Terminal silence shows the uncancellability of the gap between what is in fact said and what ought to be said.

Terminal silence thereby sheds light in turn upon the specific play among perception, inaugural silence, and discourse. It shows that this play is not the play of a unidirectional movement. Discourse does not supersede perception, but abides in dialectical tension with it. All perception is indeed worded perception. But all discourse is also perception-laced discourse. Discourse and perception perpetually prompt one another. They are two moments in an unending dialectic, each either clarifying or beclouding the other. This play, as terminal silence shows, can have no definitive culmination.[19]

Terminal silence, then, so long as it holds sway, modifies the meaning of all other mediations. As such, it can be said to hold a preeminence over all other mediations. But this preeminence is only a qualified preeminence because terminal silence could neither occur nor make sense without other kinds of mediational performances.[20]

Together, inaugural silence and terminal silence modalize the entire range of both nonsignitive and signitive experience. But the character of that modalization is not immediately transparent. At least at first glance, any number of interpretations of the fact that discourse, though necessary, is necessarily incomplete suggest themselves. What is transparent is that the experienced need to engage in performances of silence requires some interpretation.

Before proffering an interpretation of why it is that silence is ineliminable, let me point out one crucial feature of experienced temporality which shows up when one pays close attention to silence. This feature, and its interpretation, bear directly upon the sense which is to be made of the intrinsic incompleteness of discourse.

Perhaps the best way to make this feature clear is to look back at the phenomenon of desire. Desire involves some absence which is taken to be transformable into a presence. Desire thus shows a temporal spread. It points to a future which is not only distant from the present but which also can be different from it. When desire is itself transformed by inaugural silence, and indeed by any mediational performance, then the dimensions of the possible difference between the present and the future are shown to be much more ample than would otherwise appear. The recognized flow of things, events, and the web of experience in which they are encountered is recognized as being open to multiple and repeated interruptions and alterations.

Terminal silence, for its part, along with the unsuppressed residue of desire, always directed as it is toward particulars, shows the ineliminability of the new. No set of interruptions, modifications, or mediations of what has already come to pass can forestall the emergence of the new. Nothing can cancel the possibility of its own alteration. And this possibility of the new is no mere logical possibility. It is a possibility motivated by the entire range of human experience.

The ineliminability of the new, which can always arise either in man or in his Other, shows that time is not all of a piece, that temporal moments are experienced as qualitatively differentiated. This ineliminability of the new itself calls for interpretation. Is the ineliminability of the new to be construed as evidence that mediations are ultimately pointless? Sartre's *No Exit* would suggest this interpretation. Or does the inevitability of the new reveal more explicitly the positive sense of mediations? The new, when seen in the light of both desire and silence – inaugural and terminal – shows that the world cannot appear as a *plenum*, as that which is in all significant respects finished. It also shows that man cannot find permanent release from the transformations he necessarily both undergoes and effects by reason of his worldliness in a fluid world. Is this condition of man a weakness or is it a strength?

In short, how is man the mediator to be understood? It is to this question that I now turn. How man the mediator is in fact understood will obviously bear heavily upon how politics and its responsible practice is understood.

II

Man, on my interpretation, is essentially a mediator. He is so and can be so because he dwells effectively 'in the middle' of experience.

He dwells with an Other which he has not established, with which he can at least partially cope and maintain himself, but whose Otherness he cannot finally domesticate.[21] His performances, whether spontaneous or active, are neither pointless nor make just precisely only the point he aims to make.

To mediate is to modify. To modify is both to build upon what is already in place and to bring some new thing or state of affairs into being. More generally, to modify is to affect the prevailing patterns of stability or determinateness and instability or nondeterminateness in which one is involved. These patterns are affected either by being preserved, by being altered, by being generated, or by being eliminated.[22] Desire already points toward this kind of essential mediation. The work of silence makes clear that the stream of mediations is essentially interminable. The concept of a definitive mediation makes no sense.[23]

Closer inspection reveals that mediation always involves a striving and that striving, or struggle, necessarily works within a context of harmony and strife. Striving does not beget this context. It presupposes such a context. Indeed, the context somehow elicits or provokes the striving. But without the striving the context remains nondescript. At its point of departure, striving depends for its sense upon some configuration of forces[24] already proportionately bound together or harmonized and on the fact that this configuration is neither definitive nor comprehensive. At its point of arrival, whether achieved or only sought, striving issues in a configuration whose perdurance cannot be fully assured. Striving does not aim exhaustively to reduce harmony to strife or vice versa. It also aims to preserve the tension between them which makes striving itself possible. Striving thus removes its context from the realm of the nondescript without pretending to have given it a unique, definitive description.

Striving, then, has characteristics comparable to those which Hans-Georg Gadamer ascribes to play. Play has a certain primacy over the players, though without the players there is no play. Players are constituted as such by the play. It is more the play which puts the players to the test than the players who try the play. All play is characterized by a to-and-fro movement. Play is nothing but the performance of this movement, of this striving. This movement, this play 'has no goal which brings it to an end; rather it renews itself in constant repetition.'[25] And, Gadamer continues, 'we can say that man too plays. His playing is a natural process. The meaning of his play, precisely because – and insofar as – he is a part of nature, is a pure self-presentation.'[26]

But even if man is necessarily a player, he fully plays only if he takes his play seriously. Play puts the player himself at risk. He who does not play seriously, nonetheless plays. But whether his trifling be thoughtless or cynical, the nonserious player is a spoilsport.[27] There is, then, a crucial difference between merely playing and playing well.

The play of stability or determinateness and instability or non-determinateness provides the leeway without which there could be no striving. If striving is required for mediation and mediation is an essential human activity, then the termination of striving, and hence the termination of man, can hardly be the goal or even the acceptable foreseen side effect of any particular striving.[28] That is, the striving cannot intelligibly either aim at or accept as its consequences the elimination of the play or tension between the determinate and the nondeterminate. Nonetheless, the distinction between mere striving and serious striving is not abrogated. He who merely strives dissembles the sense of striving. He who strives seriously clarifies, either in word or in deed, that sense.[29]

It is evident, of course, that man's striving and mediating do not work exclusively on the Other. They also work upon the mediator himself. Whether the direct focus of a particular mediation is upon the mediator or rather is on his Other, both the mediator and his Other are affected in some way by all actual mediations. Man, then, however individualized he is, is never a closed, fixed system. He meets himself as one who is constituted by the play of the determinate and the nondeterminate, as one who embodies the tension between harmony and strife.

To meet himself is to be near himself. But nearness implies some distance, a distance which is beyond exhaustive cancellation. Without this nearness – distance, performances of neither memory nor imagination could have either the scope or the tenuousness which they in fact do have in man. Man, then, is the sort of being who necessarily figures in both the stabilization and the nonstabilization of both himself and the Other he encounters.

The mediations whereby he exercises his efficacy are always, in the last analysis, performed in connection with the interplay of discourse and silence. Indeed, it is this interplay between discourse and silence which ultimately allows his mediations to have enduring efficacy and specific weight. Thus, through his mediations he both achieves and preserves self-definition and at the same time keeps that self-definition partial and liquid.

In other terms, man is 'eccentric.' Though he is a product of nature, he interrogates nature. Though he is bound to a physical habitat, he reshapes his habitat to his own ends. He is thus neither a mere segment of cosmic order nor an arbitrary, rootless adventurer. Similarly, he is always involved with other men but is not exhaustively bound to already established social constraints. Though he learns about himself only through encountering other men, he goes beyond habitual attachments and contacts. Men question one another and in so doing achieve a self-exegesis.[30]

But how is this nonrigid eccentricity to be interpreted? Is his inability to achieve definitive self-coincidence to be regarded as an ultimate defeat? If so, then human life would have to be said to be fundamentally futile and absurd. His mediations, whatever their apparent outcome – successful or otherwise – would all turn out to be pointless. Or is his inability to achieve definitive self-coincidence to be interpreted as the consequence of a 'fall' from which he can somehow be redeemed either in some future[31] or in another world? If so, then present human life finds justification only in that for which it prepares, in that which is fundamentally and radically other than itself.

It is hard to see, as the latter view would have one see, that anything done in present human life could be a preparation for a condition which, by definition, is radically different. These two views, i.e. the defeatist view and the redemptive view, appear to collapse into one, namely into the position that actual human mediations are ultimately pointless.

Be that as it may, neither of these interpretations is demonstrably false. But both outrun the available or anticipatable evidence. If man in fact happens to be radically absurd, then none of his performances, mediational or otherwise, could furnish conclusive evidence showing his absurdity. Or, on the other hand, if man is destined for a redemption in which his eccentricity will give way to rigid, fixed self-identity, then again nothing that he can experience in this life could provide him with conclusive grounds for recognizing that this eventuality awaits him.

Reflection on the experience of mediation, with special emphasis upon performances of discourse and silence, suggests a third, more 'modest,' interpretation of the inevitable incompleteness of every mediation. Consider these two pieces of evidence. First, all mediations do not show themselves to have the same relative potency. The *Psalms*, the *Tao Te Ching*, Euclid's *Elements*, Alexander the Great's military feats, and Chartres Cathedral may not be definitive achievements. But they are surely long-lasting ones. They are strikingly different from the ephemeral sayings, doings, and makings of thirty years ago reported in the *West Bank Shopper's Guide.*[32] Though all sayings, doings, and makings are interrupted by silence, and are supplemented by further mediations, they are not all thereby necessarily rendered equivalent, equivalently trivial. Nor do they point to some ultimate source of All-sense, upon which they exhaustively depend for their worth.

Second, silence does not merely restrict the scope and efficacy of other mediations. It serves to link them into patterns of rhythms. If one focuses not on individual mediations but on substantial sequences of mediations, one finds that those sequences which are genuinely efficacious exhibit a complex pattern or rhythm. Alternations among sayings, doings, and makings are not haphazard. They are actively ordered. Silence, especially terminal silence, is the dominant constituent of this patterning. It makes possible the shifts from one sort of mediation to another. And it is the possibility of patterns or rhythms of mediations which allows for the possibility of both history and tradition, those two conjoined manifestations of efficacious mediations.

If these two pieces of evidence are joined to the assumption that every *type* of human mediation makes sense, then a different interpretation of mediational activity than those claiming either ultimate futility or ultimate transformation into immediacy, ultimate 'redemption,' is warranted.

The assumption that every type of human mediation makes sense is a restricted version of the general assumption that every type of human performance, whether mediational or not, makes sense. This assumption, in its unrestricted as well as in its restricted version, is neither original nor extravagant. Nonetheless, a brief justification and clarification of it is not out of place. For present purposes, I will discuss the assumption only in the restricted version mentioned above. This assumption does not, of course, claim that each and every concrete human mediation makes sense. Pointless and erroneous undertakings surely occur. Nor does the assumption claim that each and every human being, sometime or other, makes sense. There can be consummate madmen or fools. Rather, the assumption takes note of the fact that normal people engage in different types of mediations, sayings, doings, and makings, and claims that each of these types of activity is intelligible and senseful and is at least sometimes an appropriate way for men to inhabit the world.

Aristotle implicitly sanctioned this assumption when he enunciated the doctrines that human desire always aims at the good and that the true and the just have a natural tendency to prevail over their opposites.[33] Philosophers since Aristotle, admittedly with some exceptions, have regularly either held or at least employed the view that man and his characteristic types of acts are not fundamentally and radically baseless or absurd. However flawed or wanting acts of these types may be, whether taken singly or as a group, they are not all either sheerly chaotic or whimsical. At least some of the acts even of the insane are sufficiently intelligible to make the discipline of psychoanalysis possible. The only available evidence for the claim that men, in all their mediational performances of any particular type, are necessarily acting absurdly is the mere formal logical possibility that such is the case. There is no conceivable material evidence to buttress this logical possibility.

The occurrence of errors and mistakes in no way undercuts the assumption that all types of mediations make sense. Particular defective mediations of any sort are deviations from normal or appropriate mediations either of the same sort or of some other sort.[34] A defective saying is rectified by an appropriate saying. Or a saying is misplaced if it is deployed where and when the performance of a deed or of silence is called for. There is, then, no particular type of mediational performance which is always appropriate. But there is likewise no type of mediational performance which is in principle always inappropriate. They are all, in principle, appropriate ways to respond to the world and to others.

Discourse, as I showed above, is essentially capable of being either topic-centered or interlocutor-centered. It is also essentially capable of being deployed either monologically, dialogically, or in we-sayings. Silence shows itself in various ways in connection with these possibilities of discourse. It also appears as inaugural silence and as terminal silence. On the assumption just discussed, each of these discursive possibilities and each way in which silence can appear is a type of performance which in principle is appropriate to the world in which man dwells and thus makes sense. If it is indeed the case that man's basic types of mediations are appropriate types of responses to the world and others and if, more specifically, the fact that silence interrupts all mediations and streams of mediations other than itself and even holds a certain preeminence over other types of mediation does not make these other types equivalently trivial, then one can develop a 'modest' interpretation of the inevitable stamping of each mediation and sequence of mediations as nondefinitive.

The interpretation I propose understands man's mediations, his play, to be responses to the Other by a wayfarer who is already *en route*. This interpretation acknowledges (1) the nondefinitive character of all mediations, (2) the relative preeminence of signification or discourse over action or fabrication, and (3) the relative preeminence of silence over discourse.

My interpretation maintains that man, in his mediational activity, is neither condemned to pointless ambling nor furnished with secure grounds for holding that there is or could be some ultimate union with the Other which would bring his wayfaring, during his life, to a definitive conclusion. This interpretation stands in contrast, on the one hand, to those interpretations of human mediations which attribute their nondefinitive character either to immaturity or flaw in the agent. This lack, on these interpretations, is to be either cured, or at worst assuaged, by achieving or at least finding accessible a complete and perfect mediation or to be remedied by going beyond mediation as we know it into some alleged higher immediacy. On the other hand, my interpretation opposes those interpretations which conclude that human mediations, however inevitable they may be, are finally doomed to futility.

To say that man is essentially *en route* is to say that he is always involved with other men and with the nonhuman world.[35] The context he inhabits always presents itself as essentially articulated into other men and entities which are not human. All of these, himself included, have their own specific weights, or 'gravitational pulls,' each of which is, at least in large part, reciprocally correlated with the others.

To say that man is *en route* is not, however, to say that he has a clear cut destination which is fundamentally distinct from himself and his context and which he either misses or unqualifiedly reaches or at least draws near to. It is not to say that his *terminus ad quem* is a condition whose achievement would eliminate his routedness. The specific *telos* of man, on my interpretation, is to persevere willingly, in thought and deed, in his essential routedness. His aspiration is to be faithful to his essential routedness. Thus to be *en route* is to tread and tend the route itself. A man fails to achieve his *telos* if he insists upon pursuing a destination which supposedly would end his routedness. But even such an insistence presupposes one's recognition that he is indeed *en route*. Even if in fact there is some ultimate *terminus ad quem*, some higher immediacy, if one insists that only such a well-defined culmination can either justify concrete mediational performances or explain the fundamental absurdity of mediation he effectively deprecates mediation in all of its forms. This kind of deprecation is tantamount to nihilism.[36] It is a denial that human life as presently constituted is of *intrinsic* worth. To be *en route* is to walk a path, to be a path dweller. To walk a path is not only to follow it. It is also to break it. It is to effect something new while simultaneously preserving something old.

To be a path dweller is to live out the play, the indissoluble tension, between determinateness and nondeterminateness. This tension, as I noted above, is to be found in all dimensions of experience both of oneself and of the Other. That is, man strives both with himself and with the Other for harmony. This striving is a rending which at the same time binds together.[37] One finds, on the one hand, that this tension is rooted in his essential constitution and, on the other hand, that he himself both maintains this tension and instigates transformations of it.

The polyvalency of the experience of this tension between the determinate and the nondeterminate requires that the interpretation of man as one who is essentially *en route* be pushed further. Still mindful of the relative preeminence of signification over action and fabrication and of silence over discourse, I propose to understand the man who is *en route* as he who both innovates and renews a world which elicits his interventions. Thus time matters. His routedness is not that of a Sisyphus. Both man and his route are temporal. Both what he is and what it is can show themselves by virtue of time.[38]

Man in plying his path is constantly confronted by a confluence of the old and the new. This confluence constitutes his unique present.

His fundamental response to this confluence is renewing innovation. By his response, man renews the force of that which has already come to be. Maintaining and preserving are modes of innovating just as much as are inaugurating, changing, and terminating. That which enables a person to respond to this confluence most efficaciously is signification. Signification gives every human response of any sort its maximal duration. It allows other sorts of responses to perdure beyond the span of their actual effectuation. It allows them to be inscribed into a memorable narrative and thus to be joined with other responses both of his own devising and of others. Within the signitive domain, silence both makes room for new discursive performances of various sorts and insures that the new discourse in its own clamor does not drown out what is to be heard of the old. Man's mediation, then, effectively transforms the path. For this transformation to occur, and to occur on the basis of man's mediation, it is appropriate to interpret man's kind of being as that in which nondeterminateness enjoys a certain preeminence, a preeminence sufficient to permit him to claim these mediational performances as his own.

In short, man's essential renewing innovation is that which constitutes human historicality. Historicality encompasses both history and tradition. In all of its aspects historicality appears as that which has on the one hand cut or interrupted the established flow of nature. And on the other hand, historicality appears as that whose fruit has been rejoined to nature's flow, to have been inscribed back into nature. Through his renewing innovation, man both severs and joins. He lives out the play of strife and harmony as the one whose destiny it is to renew by innovating, the one in whom nondeterminateness enjoys a relative preeminence.

But however thoroughgoing are the results of man's mediational performances, he remains a pathdweller who has not so subjugated the path he walks that it mirrors or even can mirror nothing but his mediations. Man's performances always involve at least a lateral, if not a focal, reference to that which is given as Other, namely the world and other men. The world is given as that which elicits and receives mediations, sustaining some and sloughing off others. Other men are given simultaneously as fellow mediators and as those in whom mediations can be inscribed. To admit this does not entail that one embraces a thoroughgoing realism in which full-fledged determinations and differentiations are already in place

58

prior to any human performances. But it does entail that the world is sufficiently articulated that some human responses, some mediations, are appropriate or proper and others are not. The Other, both human and nonhuman, may not legitimate just one and only one appropriate response. But it does not legitimate just any differentiations which a man or group of men might chance to propose. The Other, then, is experienced both as pliable to man and as imposing constraints upon man's plying of it.

However hospitable the Other may be to human mediations, it sustains them in its own fashion. The mediator is not totally free to have the mediation he performs sustained just as and for so long as he wishes. Once his mediation is performed it escapes from his control into that of the Other. Then only in and through the Other can the author, like any other member of his audience, return to it. Thus men do not completely control the perdurance or decay of specific concrete mediations. The Other's efficacy is also at play.[39] This interplay is attested to, for example, by man's struggle with the world to preserve the buildings of the Acropolis against the corrosive forces of the elements and by the struggle of the French Academy with its fellow French users to preserve a form of linguistic purity.

Let me shift the focus now to the nonhuman Other, the world. The world, too, presents itself as not all of a piece. The revelation of the world is a temporally distended revelation. It presents itself as having some aspects which are enduring, perhaps omnitemporal, and others which are fleeting, perhaps only instantaneous. Nothing about the mediations referring either to the enduring or to the fleeting provides grounds for ascribing unqualified preeminence to either of them.

As the path which men ply, the path by virtue of which men can be said to be *en route*, the world itself can also be appropriately interpreted as a play of the determinate and the nondeterminate. In this play, in contrast to the play which is man, there is a certain preeminence of the determinate. There is a preeminence of that which has already come to be and endures as a determinate process. This preeminence, for instance, makes causal accounts of worldly things and events so persuasive. The world shows itself as that which, though pliable by men, plys its own course in ways beyond man's influence. Men, even when they effect mediations, are always running to catch up with both the not yet mediated and the unexpected twists resulting from mediations. From another stand-point, unlike men, the world in its self-transformations does not effect historicality. Rather, it effects the continuation of determinate sequences which, however subject they are to mediation, have a persistence of their own.

When, then, one considers the interplay of these two plays, one finds a certain preeminence of the world. To be sure, the world can make no sense without man.[40] But it is still less misleading to say that man is for the world than it is to say that the world is for man.

Support for this contention comes from reflection upon mediation. Mediations spring from an interrogative endeavor either to introduce something new or to educe into presence that which was either absent or latent. Though this interrogative mediation can, as Heidegger and others have pointed out, attempt to summon the world to answer to man as its master, such an interrogation misunderstands the interrogator himself. Interrogation does not proceed from a man who is first self-possessed and transparent to himself and who then, on this secure basis, investigates that which is radically discrete from himself. Rather, interrogative mediation is a process in which the sense of the interrogator, as well as that of the world, is unfolded.

Mediation, as was shown above, presupposes desire. Both components of desire, namely emotion and interest, attest to the relative preeminence of the world over man. On the one hand, man awakens to himself as inhabiting a world which solicits his attention and his mediation. He also awakens to a world populated with other people whose interest the world also engages. On the other hand, he finds himself and his fellows inhabiting a world on terms which he and they cannot fully set. The world comes bearing pains as well as pleasures, sickening stenches as well as fragrant scents. Not only does the world support a man's life. It also ensures his death. It both allows man time to achieve his mediations and withdraws that allowance without consulting him. Desire, then, in both of its components, makes a mockery of any claim that man is fundamentally autonomous.[41]

Interrogation, then, is instigated and guided by interest and emotion which in turn spring from man's perceptual encounter with the world. Thus mediational performances spring from an exclamatory interrogation.[42] Exclamatory interrogation is a wonder engendered by the recognition that man struggles and plays in a world, treads a path, which simultaneously both invites his interrogative mediations and nonetheless reserves to itself the authentication of particular interrogations and that which they elicit.

Thus, to say that man is essentially *en route* is to say that he necessarily replies to the path that the world itself plies. His reply cares for the world's path. Willy-nilly, all of man's replying both springs from and responds to the path plied by the world. The world, as path which has been plied and is still to be plied, is that which man's replying, his mediational activity, is destined to serve. Whether a particular man recognizes it or not, tending the world's path is the intelligible point of performing mediations of any sort.

To say that man is *en route* is to say that man is for the world. This does not mean that the world dominates man. He can be for the world only insofar as he is the world's other. The world allows, at least for a time, man to be its other. It is in maintaining his otherness that man remains for the world. His otherness from the world is finally for the world.

Let me conclude this sketch of the interpretation of man as he who is *en route* by briefly noting, first, how this interpretation respects the evidence drawn from the signitive realm, the realm of discourse and silence, which is distinct from both action and fabrication. Then let me indicate something of what this interpretation entails for one's understanding of man's finitude, historicality and intersubjectivity.

The intertwining of silence and discourse reveals that no single type of performance, either extrasignitive or signitive, is alone sufficient to respond adequately to the Other – other men and the world – which man encounters. Further, there is no antecedently establishable pattern of performances of different types which fully satisfies the exigencies engendered by the encounter with the Other. There is always room for silence in some one of its facets either to interrupt a stream of performances in favor of other possible performances or, through terminal silence, to bend human performances back upon themselves by revealing that they have no ideal culmination. This state of affairs shows the uncancellable absence of perfect fit between any set of human performances and that Other with which man is always involved. But at the same time, silence notwithstanding, mediations of all sorts never appear as unquestionably and definitively pointless. The Other cannot be encompassed but it is always there to be dealt with. Thus, to say that man is essentially *en route* is to say that in human life mediation never loses its point nor does the need for shifts in types of mediation ever lapse. Silence is never done with. But neither are other types of human performances, whether signitive or extrasignitive, ever done with.

The interpretation of man as one who is essentially *en route* in a pliable world entails a distinctive understanding of the sense of the finite, historical, intersubjective character of human existence. Finitude, on this interpretation, is not something imposed upon man either by external or by biological factors. Rather, by reason of a finitude belonging to his very essence, no matter what he does he can never either fully merge with the Other or fully immunize himself to it. No human performance can preclude other performances, either by oneself or by others, which have genuine efficacy upon oneself and one's doings. The world, too, shows itself as finite. Though it plies its own way, the world is always permeable to man's plying. It is neither finished nor complete. It neither is nor can be, in the etymological sense, perfect. Indeed, it is the world itself which sustains men in their physical and biological characteristics in such a way that they can ply the world in both old and new ways.

Both the world and men, then, are thoroughly temporal. Temporality makes the interplay between man and world possible by eliminating the possibility that either determinateness or nondeterminateness enjoy unrestricted sway. Further, by synthesizing the multiple moments of this interplay, temporality saves these moments from both ossification and sheer evanescence. Ossification would transmute these moments into a rigid unmodifiable sequence. Evanescence would rob them of their efficacy. Within man, temporality makes possible biography. Within the world, temporality makes possible both phylogenic and ontogenic development. These two together constitute man as essentially historical and make history possible. Man and his temporality, therefore, is not set over against a world inhospitable to him and his mediations. The temporality of the world, rather, gives point to man's historical character.

Finally, the interpretation of man as one who is essentially *en route* makes clear that men meet one another on the basis of a world not of their own making. The world both makes their meeting possible but also gives point and texture to this meeting. Men do not find surcease in each other from the claims of the world. But it is the world which, while claiming them, makes possible both their individual and their joint transformations of the world. As the mediator who is essentially *en route*, then, man finds his finitude, historicality, and intersubjectivity not conditions to be overcome or regretted but rather conditions which permit him to engage in efficacious mediation, conditions which permit him to be responsible.[43]

III

The interpretation of man as one who is essentially *en route* has consequences of capital importance for both the theory and the practice of politics. It effects substantial clarification of the bounds of responsible politics. By emphasizing the finitude, historicality, and intersubjectivity of the human condition, this interpretation, on the one hand, sheds light upon the distinguishing features of politics itself. On the other hand, it furnishes bases both for assessing specific political doctrines, programs, and problems and for formulating responsible political recommendations and cautions.

Consider, first, the contribution which this interpretation makes to the clarification of just what politics is and can be. As I noted in Chapter 1, politics can usefully be described as a specific form of activity engaged in by groups of individuals or societies. It is distinguished by three characteristics. First, this activity centers around the quest either to attain competitive advantage, to avoid competitive disadvantage, or to attain cooperative enhancement. Second, this sort of activity is conditioned by the fact that it transpires in time amid changing, relatively scarce, material and cultural resources. And third, it yields consequences which significantly affect the subsequent way of living of at least a substantial portion of the people concerned. The interpretation of man as a mediator who is essentially *en route* shows how this description of politics should properly be filled out.

Man's mediational activities are not all of a piece. During the performance of mediations of any particular type, there is motivation for mediations of other types. Given the interplay among men and between men and the world, there is room for a type of mediational activity which both allots to other types of mediations space in which to appear and at the same time preserves its own capacity to make this allotment. Politics is the name of this alloting activity.[44] Thus Arendt's account of the Greek *polis*, whether the Greeks understood it so or not, accurately portrays a central feature of politics. The *polis*, she says, is not a physical location.

> It is the organization of the people as it arises out of acting and speaking together, and its true space lies between people living together for this purpose. . . . It is the space of appearance in the widest sense of the word, namely the space where I appear to others as others appear to me, where men exist not merely like other living or inanimate things but make their appearance explicitly.[45]

As such, the *polis* seeks to provide men with a permanent context within which to share words and deeds and to make it possible for their words and deeds to endure, to be remembered.[46]

Politics, then, can properly be construed as that type of mediation which aims to establish and preserve opportunities for the members of a community to perform mediations of different sorts and which seeks to provide these opportunities precisely for man's earthly well-being. The possibility and pertinence of such a politics with the three characteristics previously mentioned is readily accounted for by the interpretation of man as a mediator who is essentially *en route*.

The life of one who is *en route* is one of unremitting striving. This striving is provoked, in part, by adversity. Politics is a definite type of striving, a distinct way of responding to adversity. It springs from the need to overcome disasters, whether natural or man-made, which threaten men and their achievements. Adversity is permanently possible, on the one hand, because world and men have opposite relative preeminences between determinateness and nondeterminateness. On the other hand, adversity is possible because men, among themselves, even though sharing the same structural preeminence of nondeterminateness over determinateness, need not effect mutually compatible mediations. Adversity from either source can threaten disaster. Scarcity, on this view, is a species of adversity. So is alienation. Both tend to stifle a man's capacity to mediate efficaciously, to be responsible for what he does. As Sartre, with his characteristic boldness, and some overstatement, says:

> [T]he geographical givens (or any other kind) can act only within the compass of a given society, in conformity with its

structures, its economic regime, the institutions which it has given itself. What does this mean if not that the necessity of fact can be grasped only by means of human constructions? The indissoluble unity of these 'apparatus,' these monstrous constructions with no author, in which man loses himself and which forever escape him, with their rigorous functioning, their reversed finality (which should be called, I think, a *counter-finality*), with their pure or 'natural' necessities and the furious struggle of alienated men – this indissoluble unity must appear to every inquirer who wants to comprehend the social world.[47]

Thus, man is born into and lives both within and against a language, a kinship pattern, a legal system, an economy, etc. All of his encounters with the world are thus infected by the residue of other human performances inscribed in material and cultural things.

But striving is not exclusively the result of adversity. If it were, politics, and indeed all of human life, would be a sorry affair. Striving is likewise provoked by the experienced synergy transpiring between man and his human and nonhuman Others. Politics, at the same time as it is a response to adversity, is also a response to this synergy. Politics springs from the aspiration to preserve and amplify this synergy. Man does not merely undergo the impact of the world and other men. He modifies the context into which they are thrust. Alone or with others, he lends support to or undermines the presently prevailing political order. To cite Sartre again: 'Our comprehension of the Other is never contemplative; it is only a moment of our *praxis*, a way of living – in struggle or in complicity – the concrete human relation which unites us to him.'[48] 'Counter-finality' never definitely quashes effective initiative.

The interpretation of political man as one who is politically *en route* gives due recognition to the essential ambivalence of human striving. It recognizes, on the one hand, that politics is doomed to inefficacy if the nonhuman Other, the material and cultural factors entwined in man's existence, should be either slighted or misconstrued.[49] Politics will emasculate itself should it take these crucial kinds of interaction with the nonhuman less than seriously. On the other hand, this interpretation calls for a politics which lays emphasis upon the human capacity to engage in multiple types of intervention into the world. Politics of this sort can properly be called anthropic.[50] The *telos* of such politics is both the preservation of men and their flourishing, their well-being.[51]

Conversely, since both the world and other men can give rise either to adversity or to synergy, nothing is, in principle, *absolutely* irrelevant to the political domain. This fact does not imply that everything is in all respects political. But it does imply that a politics which would systematically exclude from its concerns any part of man's transactions with the world cannot be a responsible politics.

Politics, then, is essentially a risky enterprise. And it never comes to possess the resources to eliminate this riskiness. Indeed, the very existence of a political domain is not guaranteed. It may be that there is a time without politics.[52] But there is no time without the motivated possibility of and need for politics. To regard, either explicitly or implicitly, politics as no more than one among many options in which men can engage is untenable. The interpretation of man as one who is essentially *en route* makes clear why politics, tenuous as it is, is both possible and needed.

Besides shedding light upon the distinguishing features of politics, the interpretation of man as one who is *en route* furnishes bases for demonstrating that a number of significant, influential doctrines or programs which have been advanced as political solutions are neither conceptually defensible nor practically accomplishable *as politics*. That is, to whatever extent they are implemented, they eliminate politics. Among these doctrines are those which would install tyranny, anarchy, and totalitarianism.

Alexandre Kojève has defined tyranny as the condition in which

> a fraction of the citizens (it matters little whether it be a majority
> or a minority) imposes its idea and acts on all the other citizens,
> which are determined by an authority which it recognizes
> spontaneously but which it has not succeeded in making the
> others recognize; and where it does so without 'coming to terms'
> with these others, without seeking any 'compromises' with them,
> and without taking into account their ideas and desires
> (determined by another authority recognized by these others).[53]

In short, tyranny is the systematic reservation of all initiative, political or otherwise, to the tyrant. Though the tyrant may delegate or permit others to introduce innovations, they do so only by his leave. Their initiative is derived from that of the tyrant.

As I noted in Chapter 1, one tendency growing out of the fragmentation of the political domain is that which tends to concentrate all the crucial decisions concerning human life exclusively in the hands of an elite. Those outside of the ruling elite tend to be reduced to impotence.[54] This tendency is explicitly endorsed and encouraged by those who would make organizational efficacy the ultimate standard for human conduct. On this view, which can be described as the technocratic depreciation of politics, freedom is either an illusion or simply another name for disorganization. Organization is to rearrange human limitations and disorganization so that rational decision and action result. It does so by defining the individual's functions and duties, specifying limits to his choices, and shaping his attitudes so that he has a sense of belonging to the whole. The point of organization is to achieve efficacy. And efficiency consists in having its members make those decisions and undertake those actions which best serve the organization's ends and needs.

> Human rationality, then, gets its higher goals and integrations from the institutional setting in which it operates and by which it is moulded. . . . The rational individual is, and must be, an organized and institutionalized individual.[55]

But, if man is indeed essentially routed, then no individual man or group of men, no elite or administrative cadre, can defensibly claim to have bases for initiative so sufficient that these bases would render idle initiative arising from any other source. Every mediation, from whatever source, by reason of man's finitude, historicality, and intersubjectivity, intrinsically calls for a response from another. Genuine responses are not mere echoes. Nothing precludes their arising from different bases.

The tyrant, by his tyranny, undercuts the responsiveness which his own mediations require if they are to make full sense and to endure. How, without the responsive support of others, could the tyrant's initiatives achieve efficacy beyond his own reach? How could he refrain from eliciting the active support of others in maintaining his own tyranny? How, conversely, could his subjects admit that all initiative belongs to the tyrant? Either this acknowledgment is genuinely initiated by them or there has been, properly speaking, no response.[56]

Further, the sense of all mediations culminates in discourse. But monologic discourse is not able to so preempt or dominate the whole discursive domain that it would make other sorts of discourse idle. Monologue itself makes full sense only in conjunction with other sorts of discourse. Without these other sorts, monologue tends to drift into sterile soliloquy. In short, then, tyranny is false to the intrinsic structure of one's encounter with other men. This encounter is always marked by a striving which presupposes the other's capacity for efficacious mediation. But neither the tyrant nor the willingly tyrannized admit the essential conditions of their own meeting.[57] Tyranny, therefore, even if it is supposedly benevolent, is inherently unstable and tends to its own dissolution.[58]

Anarchy, too, is fundamentally nonsensical. At bottom, it treats all mediations as essentially ephemeral. On the one hand, the anarchist repudiates the established order and, at least implicitly, claims that his mediations owe nothing positive to prior mediations. On the other hand, he seeks to prevent his own mediations from instigating an abiding order.[59] Such a program, in the final analysis, either denies the essential intersubjectivity of human existence or at least denies that men play out their mutual involvement within the context of a world which makes claims on them. On the one hand, for one to adopt anarchism is to fail to recognize the force of the world in the essential constitution of politics. On the other hand, for one who is not himself an anarchist to admit the defensibility of anarchy is at least to imply that all inscribing of mediations into one or another cultural order in the world is ultimately arbitrary, the mere outcome of the exercise of might which has no intelligible ground.

Somewhat less obviously, but no less certainly, the interpretation of political man as one who is essentially *en route* yields the conclusion that totalitarianism is indefensible. Totalitarianism is the doctrine which claims that the political domain is in all respects the supreme domain and that the justification for whatever rationally transpires in any domain is rooted ultimately in the political domain. Totalitarianism consists, then, in the subordination of all forms of human activity to just one of these forms, namely political activity.[60] Ultimately, totalitarianism reserves to politics the right to suppress any sort of activity which fails to acknowledge the unqualified supremacy of the political order. Suppression of religion and of artistic expression are common manifestations of totalitarian conduct. But so is any conduct or line of reasoning which is based upon the principle that, in the final analysis, *raisons d'état* must always prevail.

But, as I have shown above, no particular domain of human activity enjoys unqualified preeminence over other domains. Motivation to shift from one sort of mediational performance to another is always available. Totalitarianism, history shows, can be attempted and even largely achieved. But it rests on essentially nonsensical claims and is thus inherently unstable.[61]

The interpretation of political man as one who is politically *en route* does not, however, only yield arguments against some deviant political doctrines and programs. By virtue of the light which it brings to the constituent features of the domain of politics, this interpretation also provides resources for rethinking some persistent conundra in political debate. And further, it furnishes grounds for formulating positive proposals concerning both the understanding of and the participation in the central components of political life.

To see how this interpretation leads to the rethinking of persistent conundra, consider two examples, first the question of the relation between personal rights and property rights, and second the question of the relation between religion and politics.[62] My interpretation of political man shows that if one disjunctively contrasts personal rights and property rights and assigns unequivocal priority to one over the other, then one has posed the issue in an ill-formed way. Insofar as politics emphasizes human interaction and the preservation of space for enduring mediations, insofar as politics is 'anthropic,'[63] there is always a presumption in favor of each man being granted the material and cultural resources with which to engage in effective mediation. But in the concrete living out of the exchanges among men, the world, with its constraints and supports, substantially shapes what can be done at any particular time. This worldly element is not merely an accidental circumstance. It belongs to the very possibility of human interaction. In many respects, human interaction transpires across some distribution of material resources, across property. No attempt to acknowledge personal rights can make sense unless it recognizes the history of the people involved and the property distributions ingredient in that history. The worldly character of their lives is bound up with property and titles to property. The worldly character of their lives is constitutive of what they can accomplish in their involvement with each other. No personal right, then, can be said to be so absolute that failure to yield to its claims is unquestionably wrong. But, of course, even less absolute is any claim to property rights. The upshot of this situation is that the competition between claims to personal rights and claims to property rights cannot be definitively settled. Political discussions concerning where, how, and by whom the competition between rights is to be addressed is interminable. Political decisions concerning them are always subject to revision or revocation.[64]

Consider next the question of the relation between religion and politics, a question with a long and often ugly history. Confessional states, states which purportedly both are ruled by the doctrines of some specific religion and exist primarily to promote that doctrine, have been proposed.[65] Such proposals, insofar as they rest on the claim that one domain of discourse, here religious discourse, enjoys unqualified preeminence over all other domains of discourse and indeed holds unrestricted title to regulate all mediational activity, runs squarely counter to the interpretation of man as one who is *en route*. No domain of discourse, in principle, can possess such preeminence. Political man, recognizing his essential routedness, cannot acknowledge any such claim to preeminence. To do so would be to ignore the finitude and historicality intrinsic both to each domain of discourse and to discourse as a whole.

By the same token, political attempts either to eliminate religious discourse or to render it in all respects subservient to political objectives are likewise unwarranted. To do so would be tantamount to claiming that the discourse of one domain, here politics, can have the 'last word' about the sense of discourse in other possible domains. For man who is *en route*, there is no last word in any domain. Thus such a claim is totally without warrant.

Since the English and French Enlightenments, there have been attempts, particularly in the Western hemisphere, to achieve a total separation between religion and politics. Such a separation, it is often alleged, is needed so that the integrity of each domain will be respected. But the interpretation of man as *en route* shows that attempts to achieve a total separation between any two domains of discourse are doomed. Though it is not inconceivable that at some time in history there would be no political domain or no religious domain properly so called, it is always possible for there to be one. Motivation for the move to such a domain is always resident in whatever sort of discourse men in fact engage in. These motivations, in part, consist in the recognized incompleteness of the domain of discourse presently being inhabited. So long as there are both political and religious domains, there will be ample reasons for men to alternate their mediational activity between these domains. Thus, when the frailty of human vision and resolution is seen in detail, prayers for military victory or political peace can make sense. Similarly, political safeguards against unfettered religious proselytizing can make sense because self-styled religiously prophetic claims and injunctions, when they go wrong, can threaten human survival itself. Thus, civil laws against religious practices which jeopardize the health of immature individuals or of the community at large can surely be justified. But conversely, comments by religious leaders concerning political policies and their bearing upon either religion and its practice or on the welfare of the community as a whole are likewise defensible. For political man who is *en route*, the domains of religion and politics remain permanently in tension. There is no political warrant for any attempt to bring this tension to an end. To the contrary, it is part of his responsibility as one who is intrinsically routed to work for the preservation of this tension.

Thus, the interpretation of political man as one who is politically *en route* both furnishes arguments showing that some nontrivial political doctrines and programs are neither defensible in thought nor accomplishable in practice and sheds light upon significant persistent political conundra. This interpretation, therefore, is clearly not sterile.

But the scope of its fertility becomes more evident when one finds that this interpretation provides grounds for developing positive proposals concerning how central dimensions of political life are to be understood and participated in. As I argued above, no one type of human performance either has unqualified preeminence over other types or can make it senseless for men to engage in other types of performance. I have also shown that no type of mediation, no basic way in which people can present themselves to others, is essentially senseless. In principle, each type of mediation, though not of course each particular mediation of any type, is an appropriate type of response to otherness. Politics at its worst would deny all of these claims. Politics at its best, I propose, will not merely acknowledge them but will seek to promote optimally variegated ways of appearing by and for as many men as possible. Politics, on this view, aims equiprimordially both at living and at living well.

Neither objective need be nor should be either sacrificed or unqualifiedly subordinated to the other.

The proposals I will advance do not go so far as to recommend or caution against specific political policies or actions. Recommendations and cautions of that sort lie outside the field of political philosophy. But my proposals do bear upon how political practice is to be construed and assessed. Thus they do aim to set forth conditions under which politics will be conducive to living well. In effect, my proposals set forth elements which any political policy or action must acknowledge and embody if it is to be responsible and ultimately defensible. These same elements, I hold, are conducive to optimally variegated activity and thus promote living well.[66]

Though my proposal for the best of politics, thoroughly defensible politics, cannot be deductively demonstrated, it can be enthymematically defended. This defense consists in setting forth the implications of my interpretation of political man as one who is politically *en route* for crucial features of political life. The remainder of this study will be devoted to this task. In the next two chapters, I will further develop my interpretation of political man by showing how one should understand such a man's agency and the conditions of its exercise. Thereafter, I will explore just how this interpretation is to be inscribed in the world in which human agency transpires.

To begin the defense of my proposal let me turn to a topic which has long been at the center of political reflections, discussions, and enterprises, namely the matter of freedom. If man is one who is essentially *en route* then, if he can be said to be free, how is his freedom to be construed?

4
Freedom, being *en route*, and respect

Man, as one who is essentially *en route*, is necessarily engaged in a constant interplay with the Other, including other men. Among the fundamental questions raised by this interplay are (a) what sense of freedom, if any, is compatible with this interplay? and (b) what stance toward other men is called for by this interplay? The fact of man's essential routedness flies squarely in the face of the doctrine of freedom which has historically underpinned liberal democratic political theory. It also stands opposed to important strands of Marxist thought, though Marx's own doctrine of freedom is complex and not in all respects in conflict with the admission of this essential interplay.[1] In this chapter, I will show that the prevalent Western doctrine of freedom is untenable and that precisely the evidence which undercuts it provides the warrant for the alternate account of freedom which I will propose.

I will further argue that for freedom to be politically efficacious, the relationship between men must be one of respect. Respect, it turns out, is the cardinal virtue of both moral and political conduct which is genuinely responsible.

In the process of proposing and defending this alternate doctrine of freedom and the respect associated with it, I will flesh out more fully just what it means to understand man as one who is essentially *en route* and political man as one who is politically *en route*.

I

The pervasive doctrine of freedom today is one whose roots extend back at least to Descartes and Hobbes. But it came to full flower in the Enlightenment and continues to dominate both popular and

73

scholarly thought. According to this dominant doctrine, the principal characteristic and measure of freedom is *autonomy*. That is, a man is said to be free precisely to the extent that he is independent of every Other.[2]

So prevalent is the doctrine that it is regularly presented as obvious and noncontroversial. Consider, for example, the entry entitled 'Freedom' in the *Encyclopedia of Philosophy*. With no hint of perplexities or conundrums, P. H. Partridge sets forth the doctrine of freedom as autonomy in terms of the widely utilized distinction, perhaps most effectively articulated by Isaiah Berlin, between negative freedom and positive freedom.[3] Partridge describes negative freedom as a condition characterized by the absence of constraint or coercion. A man is to be counted as free just to the extent that he can select his own goals and course of conduct from the set of available alternatives and is neither compelled to act nor prevented from acting as he chooses by the decision of any person, state, or other authority. Positive freedom, on the other hand, is understood as the activity or process of making one's own choices and acting on the basis of one's own initiative.[4]

On this view, man is free only if he is under no coercion. Coercion, as Partridge says explicitly, encompasses not only commands and prohibitions backed by sanctions or superior power. It also includes the indirect forms of control whereby some mold or manipulate the conditions which determine or affect the alternatives available to other persons.

This general view of freedom, taken in both its negative and positive aspects, clearly rests upon the assumption that it is both possible and desirable for men either to achieve or to approximate radical independence from one another. Such independence is properly called autonomy. Further, this doctrine of freedom as autonomy usually has as its foundation a view of man as a discrete individual who is fundamentally self-contained and complete in himself.[5] For classical communism, of course, the Party is that which is self-contained, complete and autonomous.

The doctrine of freedom as autonomy lies at the root of a substantial segment of contemporary political and ethical claims advanced both in theoretical argument and in popular practice. On the one hand, negative freedom serves to support claims to the effect that participation in the work and objectives of social institutions is, at bottom, optional. Only if, through his own choice, a man derives personal benefit from a social institution is he obligated to take part in its work and objectives. Once such benefits cease and he has somehow paid for them, his obligation to participate lapses. Positive freedom, on the other hand, can and has been used to justify the contention that men, or at least some men, are to be the lords and possessors of nature.[6] A man's first responsibility, then, would be to preserve as unfettered as possible his own course of conduct.

The political ramifications of the doctrine of freedom as autonomy are of capital importance. For example, there is good reason to claim that proponents of modern democratic theory, with its insistence upon the claim that supreme power rests with the people and that the governmental power finds its legitimacy in the consent of the people, presupposes the doctrine of autonomous freedom in both its negative and positive aspects.[7] The tendency to link autonomous freedom and democratic theory culminates in the various contract theories of the state. On such theories, as espoused, for example, by Hobbes, Rousseau and, today, Rawls, men, of their own initiative and at their own discretion, establish and circumscribe all political power. They do so on the basis of resources belonging to them prior to their political engagements. As Taylor notes, a substantial part of the Hobbesian legacy consists in the conviction that

> political obligation was grounded in a decision, to submit to a sovereign, dictated by prudence (calculating reason). For a self-defining subject obligation could only be created by his own will. Hence the great importance of the myth of the original contract.[8]

But perhaps the spirit which animates the understanding of freedom as autonomy is best contained in Descartes's remark that among the extremes to be avoided are 'all promises by which one restricts something of his own liberty.'[9] Social contract theorists have gone to great pains to try to rule out the dissolution of the purported contract establishing the state once it has been instituted. But their efforts have not met with resounding success. The modern spirit has taken, and continues to take, the social contract to be ultimately revocable at will. That is, the contractors are not admitted to have ceded their basic sovereignty or autonomy. One finds this spirit expressed in terms of positive freedom, for example, in

Freedom, being en route, *and respect*

the unqualified preeminence which Sartre assigns to what he calls the group-in-fusion over the other two forms of communal life, over the pledged group and the serial collective or the organization.[10]

A pertinent consequence of the insistence upon unmitigated autonomy is that the only defensible use of coercion is retaliatory or rectificatory. Coercion could not, on this view, be legitimately employed to stimulate someone to act. That is, the only legitimate use of coercion against a man is in response to some exercise of his positive freedom. It would not be legitimate to coerce a person to act instead of abstaining from acting. One who refrains from acting or contracting to act could not, on this doctrine, be held to have thereby infringed upon anyone else's autonomy. In the absence of such infringement, retaliatory or rectificatory coercion could not be justified.

But if coercion is understood, as Partridge, for example, would have it, to encompass the shaping of conditions which affect the alternatives available to others, then any institutional pressure exerted to enlist a man's participation in its works would be unwarranted. Institutions, in this view, have no abiding authority. They are, and need to be, constantly given new legitimation by the unfettered choice of those who left to establish and maintain them. From the standpoint of autonomous freedom, to elect to establish or continue them or not to choose to do so is a matter of indifference.[11]

The primary ethical consequence of adopting the doctrine of freedom as autonomy is that one would have a fundamental, uncancellable right and quite possibly a basic duty to insist upon maintaining one's own unencumbered freedom. The proper object of freedom is to be nothing short of autonomy itself. A man would then be bound to preserve himself free from anything which would prevent him from being lord and possessor not only of nature but also of himself. One can interpret this basic ethical requirement as implying that though it is possible so to conduct oneself that fundamental rule is ceded to something – persons or circumstances – other than oneself, one is never obligated, and perhaps is morally forbidden, to do so. Or one might understand this ethical requirement to imply, as for example in Sartre's doctrine concerning bad faith, that since it is actually impossible to yield fundamental rule over oneself to any other person or group all claims to have yielded one's freedom are necessarily fraudulent.[12] On either of these interpretations, though, an essential condition for justifiable conduct is that it either preserves intact or promotes the agent's autonomy. It is therefore clear that if autonomy is the principal characteristic and measure of freedom, then a man must, at bottom, either actually be or be called to become a radically independent individual. If it belongs to man's very being to be radically independent, then he is a social being only derivatively or *per accidens*. If it belongs to his *telos* to become radically independent, then his initial sociality is something to be shed and whatever sociality he engaged in subsequent to his becoming radically independent is sheerly discretionary.[13] Sociality, then, would make no positive contribution to human freedom. Man either is or is to become a radically atomic individual.

But however widespread the doctrine of freedom as autonomy has been, it has proved extraordinarily difficult, if not impossible, to give a formulation to this doctrine which does not break down when tested. One man's autonomous freedom is perpetually poised over and against every other man's freedom. When he expresses his freedom in the world, he necessarily impinges upon his fellow men who inhabit that same world. Multiple attempts to manage such conundra have been attempted. None has been markedly successful.[14]

The lack of success in formulating a conceptually satisfactory account of autonomous freedom is not surprising when one attends to the experiential evidence which testifies to man's essential sociality. The phenomena of intersubjectivity, discourse, and history provide grounds for claiming that, far from men being fundamentally independent individuals whose interaction is contingent and derivative, they are equiprimordially both social and individual.[15] These three phenomena, then, lend small support to the contention that autonomy is the primary characteristic and measure of freedom.

In all three of these phenomena – intersubjectivity, discourse, and history – the individual does indeed appear as an agent, as one who exercises his initiative in circumstances not of his own making. Whatever truth there is in the claim that 'the greater one's ability the less one needs in the way of opportunity,'[16] the need for opportunity never falls to the zero point. In fact, the evidence suggests rather that increases in ability themselves depend upon both circumstances and others. They depend upon opportunities made available to the agent from outside of himself.

Husserl and Merleau-Ponty, among others, have argued that a man can be fully human, and consequently genuinely free, only to the extent that he is involved with other men. On this general view, a view which bears nontrivial similarities to classical Greek thought concerning human excellence, freedom necessarily involves interaction with other, and different, persons. No one, alone, can be free. Freedom requires a support which others must provide precisely by their otherness. Freedom, then, is not a fully constituted property of isolated individual entities.

Husserl, for example, shows that a wakeful person is essentially related to his surrounding world. He necessarily comports himself towards objects appearing in that world. Other human beings occupy uniquely privileged positions in this world. Some of them may, in fact, be thematized only as objects among other objects in the surrounding world. But at least some persons in the surrounding world are recognized as other persons like oneself, and not merely as objects. They are recognized as co-subjects. With his co-subjects, a person constitutes a community in acting, thinking, making, and perceiving. Though a person may retain his own distinctive activity in the world, he nonetheless always also shares in common activity with others. This common activity constitutes his surrounding world as a common world. In turn, this common world is foundational for the development of enduring cultures and civilizations and for undertaking the enterprise of natural science itself.[17]

One of the things shown by this analysis of Husserl's is that most, if not all, human achievements generally accounted as positive accomplishments require a person's involvement in the lives of others. Involvement with others is at the foundation of literature and the arts, of techniques and sciences, of laws and customs. Each person does indeed keep his individual praxis as his own. But individual praxis is not something held out of or preserved from communal praxis. Nor is it the preestablished basis for communal praxis. Communal and individual activity or praxis mutually involve each other. Neither sort of activity can be identified for what it is except by differentiating it from the other. On this view, if radical human autonomy were actually realized, it would be a defeat for him in whom it is realized and not a triumph.

One finds this same general theme of essential human intersubjectivity pursued in several ways by Merleau-Ponty. One of these ways springs from his analysis of language in terms of his adaptation of the Saussurean distinction between language (*langue*) and speech (*parole*). Merleau-Ponty emphasizes that men are always born into a preestablished language. No one is born alingual. Further, to speak at all is to speak a received language. This insight is of central importance for Merleau-Ponty's discussion of dialogue. In dialogue, the participants seek for and reach each other's meanings. Whatever struggle there is is not a struggle for independence. Nor is it necessarily a struggle for preeminence. To the contrary, the participants recognize that they are as active when they hear as they are when they speak. Dialogue, involving as it does both speaking and hearing, is a joint effort to bring to light something that makes sense. In fact, dialogue not only brings to light something which makes sense but, Merleau-Ponty implies, it brings forth a sense which no participant, acting alone, could have achieved. Further, the participants experience this common effort as one which they have not, strictly speaking, created *ab initio*. They conduct their dialogue in an already established language and they refer to a world that is Other. Thus they acknowledge, at least implicitly, that their dialogue continues a movement which has been underway long before their own utterances began.[18]

Something of the same sort can be said about writing and reading. At least in principle, there is no struggle for unqualified supremacy. Their enterprise, and the struggle indigenous in it, is a common one. Neither speaking nor writing makes full sense without an audience capable of some initiative.[19]

Merleau-Ponty further maintains that the intersubjectivity which is presupposed for dialogue is not a characteristic peculiar to discourse. The same kind of intertwining of participants is a precondition for concrete experiences of perception, thought, and action.[20] But perception, thought, action, and discourse are precisely the distinguishing characteristics which constitute man. Man is that open-textured unity whose fundamental moments are perception, thought, action, and signification. Therefore if all of these characteristics presupposes intersubjectivity, and if, as appears evident, every discernible exercise of freedom – and there is no point to trying to discuss indiscernibles – must manifest itself in some one or several of these moments, then there is no experiential foundation for claiming that radical autonomy is the primary characteristic and measure of freedom.

The force of this conclusion is enhanced when it is linked to another of Merleau-Ponty's theses. Every distinctively human performance, he holds, is at bottom interrogative. Interrogations, as I noted in Chapter 2, respond to that which elicits the questioning. Therefore, man, in his very being as human, is essentially a respondent.[21] He responds both to other men and to the world they jointly inhabit.

These considerations serve to show that from the outset all specifically human performances are social in character. More radically, one is led to conclude that, since to respond is not merely to react but is rather to amplify and to extend by introducing something distinctively one's own, something novel, then all human performances are at one and the same time both free and ineluctably bound not only to other persons but also to the world.

This conclusion is reinforced by a more detailed examination of the phenomenon of silence. As I showed in Chapter 3, discourse is, in all of its moments, essentially intertwined with silence. As a positive, active human performance, silence involves initiative just as much as discourse does. And like discourse, silence occurs in a variety of ways. Through the diverse ways in which silence is performed the domain of discourse is differentiated into a number of irreducible levels and shapes.[22]

What is of particular relevance here is the fact that within the domain of discourse one can and should distinguish bipolar discourse or dialogue properly so called from monologue on the one hand and co-discourse on the other. Monologue, which, unlike soliloquy, requires an audience which is distinct from the author, is characterized by the fact that the author retains maximal control over the content of what is uttered. He makes the content of the discourse as fully his own as he possibly can. When a speaker engages in monologue he aims for maximal independence from his audience. He fundamentally aims for some form of autonomy.

Nonetheless, the monologist necessarily acknowledges his essential involvement with an Other. Even if he claims to have privileged access to the world, he still has to admit that he has other persons associated with him as his audience. Similarly, he must recognize the commonality of the world to which his discourse refers.

In dialogue, unlike monologue, the roles of speaker and hearer are, in principle, interchangeable at any appropriate time. For a person to engage in dialogue, he must relinquish some but not all of his individual control over the content of the discourse. Responsibility for what is said in dialogue can be distributed in various ways, though it probably cannot be distributed with great precision. But each of the participants in a dialogue must bear some responsibility for what is said in the dialogue as a whole as well as a special responsibility for a determinable part of what is said. In dialogue, then, each participant yields all claims to maximal independence. But he nonetheless preserves his option to exercise his own initiative in the course of the dialogue.

Co-discourse differs from both monologue and dialogue. On the one hand, it eliminates the distinction within the ranks of the participants between author and audience. On the other hand, all the participants surrender their option to exercise individual initiative for the duration of the co-discourse. Thus co-discourse requires the maximal relinquishing of control over the discourse in favor of a saying of that which is not initiated basically at the pleasure of one or more participants. This relinquishing of control is not tantamount to a lapse into what is usually meant by heteronomy. Rather, it is a yielding which allows one to share in an intersubjective relationship which is taken to be capable of achieving or articulating something which could not be accomplished alone.[23]

Both bipolar discourse and co-discourse show more than attenuations of individual control over the content of the discourse. Like all discourse, they show at least implicitly the commonality of the world to which what they utter refers. Further, they show, unlike monologue, that no individual has an unequivocally privileged access to the world.[24]

An investigation of the intertwining of silence and discourse also shows that there is no justification for assigning unequivocal primacy to any particular level or shape of discourse. If one is to explore the full range of discursive power, he must, in the course of his life, periodically shift from one kind of discourse to another. Monologue, dialogue, and co-discourse each have their distinctive potency. They are irreducible. Of his own initiative, a man sometimes asserts control over his discourse and sometimes relinquishes it. Both to assert and to relinquish control involve freedom. Neither is more basic than the other, but neither is a manifestation of autonomy properly so called.

The considerations concerning the various shapes and levels of discourse point to a further reason for rejecting the doctrine of freedom as autonomy. If freedom is esteemed and cherished, then it must be something more than that to which a person is condemned.[25] Freedom is in fact desirable and desired because of what it allows one to accomplish. It is honored because of its capacity to make one's efforts efficacious in the world. The efficacy intrinsically belonging to freedom is of two sorts. It is that which, on the one hand, permits one to transcend the press of presently prevailing circumstances upon him. And on the other hand, it is that which enables one to stamp the prevailing circumstances with his own abiding mark. These two sorts of efficacy do not both necessarily show up in each free human performance. But if one considers a span of human activity which is esteemed by reason of the freedom manifest there, then both sorts of efficacy do show up. For example, playing tennis or dancing may show only a transcendence of preoccupation with life's necessities. But if the only free activities a man performed were of this sort which have no consequences perduring beyond the duration of the performance itself, then he would be considered to have led an impoverished life, a life which was trivial or insignificant.

The doctrine of freedom as autonomy captures only the first sort of efficacy, that which concerns transcendence of prevailing circumstances. Its failure to capture the second sort of efficacy does not merely leave a gap in that to which it applies. This failure in fact leads the doctrine to a distorted representation of even the sort of efficacy it does recognize. It leads to the view that freedom consists in an exemption from full-fledged interaction with the world with others. It fails to appreciate man's thoroughly historical character.

II

This doctrine of freedom as autonomy is of rather recent vintage.[26] It in fact amounts to a foreshortening of the traditional understanding of freedom. As Hannah Arendt has shown, freedom presupposes liberation from necessity. But mere liberation is insufficient for freedom. Freedom requires a politically organized world, a world in which at least some of men's deeds can have perduring efficacy.[27] Political freedom consists precisely in bringing it about that tomorrow is not just like today.[28]

Even within the modern era one finds intimations that a conception of freedom exclusively in terms of transcendence is inadequate. Montesquieu, for example, recognized that political liberty is distinct from independence.[29] And Hobbes before him had seen that fruitfulness was somehow connected with any worthwhile freedom.

Hobbes writes:

> Every man indeed out of the state of civil government hath a most
> entire, but *unfruitful* liberty: because he who by reason of his own
> liberty acts all at his own will, must also by reason of the same
> liberty in others suffer all at another's will.[30]

In Marx's work, the two sorts of efficacy belonging to any
freedom worthy of esteem and cultivation are clearly in evidence.
For him, freedom as a whole has two essential moments, namely
capacity for purposeful activity and realization of freedom in self-
transformation.[31] Freedom, then, is a temporally distended process. As Gould puts it, for Marx 'self-transcendence is not a process
merely of consciousness nor of the individual within him or herself
alone, but is self-transcendence through transforming the world.'[32]

In this respect Marx's doctrine is consonant with the Hegelian
recognition that freedom involves efficacy. Charles Taylor has
nicely summarized the Hegelian insight as follows:

> A purely inner freedom is only a wish, a shadow. It is an
> important stage of human development when man comes to
> have this wish, this idea, but it must not be confused with the
> real thing. Freedom is only real (*wirklich*) when expressed in a
> form of life; and since man cannot live on his own, this must be a
> collective form of life. . . .[33]

One need not adopt the Hegelian system as a whole to appreciate
his insistence upon freedom as something more than a characteristic
of one's inner life. It is surely correct to notice that people would
hardly esteem that which amounts to no more than a mere wish or
fantasy.

But if real freedom does indeed necessarily embody the two-fold
efficacy discussed above, then this freedom must show itself in one
or more of the ways in which man mediates his encounter with the
Other. Men mediate this encounter in performances of discourse
and silence, action, and fabrication-destruction. Every person is born
and reared into a world in which each of these kinds of mediations
has long been exercised. There is a history of mediations. Everyone learns to perform these kinds of mediation. He learns from
others and from his own earlier mediations. He does not simply
repeat mediations, but neither does he invent them from whole cloth.

If a person's mediations are to be fully efficacious, he must take up some mediational pattern as he finds it, contribute something of his own to it, and leave it available to others. That is, a necessary condition for fully efficacious mediation on the part of any man is the joint requirement that the mediator both employ a mediational pattern already somewhat familiar to others and yield to others some control over the consequences following upon his mediation. In short, if his stream of mediations is to be efficacious, is really to matter, then the agent cannot be radically autonomous from the outset of this stream. Nor can the stream culminate in his radical autonomy. For a stream of performances to achieve the two-fold efficacy described above, an efficacy which is not restricted to the specific moments of each particular performance, some control over at least some consequences of the stream must pass from the author to his audience.[34]

In summary, the three phenomena of intersubjectivity, discourse, and history are generally experienced as at least partially positive human accomplishments. Involvement in any of them is not experienced exclusively as being symptomatic of weakness. Even though they all undercut any pretense to radical autonomy, even though they involve an acknowledgment of human finitude, they are also to be counted as expressions of freedom. These phenomena, which show that man is essentially finite, further show that finitude is not a restriction of human freedom, but is rather a condition of its possibility.[35]

Finitude and freedom, then, are twin conditions for the efficacy of one who is *en route*. There is no freedom except that which is exercised in the struggle-play with the Other. Unless a man is engaged with other men in common projects in a common world, his words, deeds, and efforts are ephemeral. Unless he accepts and embraces others as co-agents, an individual man cannot achieve full agenthood. Nonetheless, complete absorption into the aims and projects already established by others would also eliminate agenthood. Unless a man preserves his capacity for initiative in the face of pre-established aims and projects, his words, deeds, and products become irrelevant.[36]

The foregoing considerations, both conceptual and empirical, seriously undermine the attempt to uphold a doctrine of freedom which insists upon autonomy as its primary characteristic and measure. These same considerations serve to reconfirm Aristotle's observations that 'every man should be responsible to others, nor should any one be allowed to do just as he pleases; for where absolute freedom is allowed there is nothing to restrain the evil which is inherent in every man,'[37] and that some men think 'that freedom means the doing what a man likes. . . . But this is all wrong; men should not think it slavery to live according to the rule of the constitution: for it is their salvation.'[38]

Nonetheless, it is still true that the autonomy doctrine is widely and vigorously pressed in the contemporary era, an era which in large measure remains under the aegis of the Enlightenment. The conflict between the urgent claim of autonomous freedom and the substantial evidence showing that such freedom is impossible makes, to borrow Taylor's words, 'the search for a situated subjectivity all the more vital. And the need grows more acute today under the impact of an ecological crisis which is being increasingly dramatized in the public consciousness.'[39]

The requisite search for a more responsible account of human freedom is substantially facilitated by the same evidence which I have adduced against the doctrine of freedom as autonomy. When this evidence is linked with clues drawn from Merleau-Ponty, a concept of freedom which more faithfully represents human experience can be articulated. This reformulation of the concept of freedom has considerable ethical and political ramifications.

To begin the positive development of an alternate account of freedom, let me return briefly to Merleau-Ponty's work, particularly to his discussion of freedom in his *Phenomenology of Perception*. In opposition to the Sartre of *Being and Nothingness*, among others, Merleau-Ponty insists that the very concept of freedom includes efficacy as one of its necessary features and therefore that every exercise of freedom impinges upon the future. Further, freedom interrupts a flow already in progress. Freedom is exercised in an already established field into which one is born. Thus freedom is thoroughly temporal. It always has a past. In Merleau-Ponty's words:

> The rationalist's dilemma: either the free act is possible, or it is not – either the event originates in me or is imposed on me from outside, does not apply to our relations with the world and with our past. Our freedom does not destroy our situation, but gears itself to it: as long as we are alive, our situation is open, which implies both that it calls up specially favoured modes of

resolution, and also that it is powerless to bring one into being by itself.[40]

Freedom, then, does not consist in withdrawing from the Other. One simply interrupts one form of involvement with the Other to commit himself to another form of involvement. Freedom's 'power of perpetually tearing itself away finds its fulcrum in my universal commitment in the world. My actual freedom is not on the hither side of my being, but before me, in things.'[41] These experienced facts allow Merleau-Ponty to conclude:

> What then is freedom? To be born is both to be born of the world and to be born into the world. The world is already constituted, but also never completely constituted; in the first case we are acted upon, in the second we are open to an infinite number of possibilities. But this analysis is still abstract, for we exist in both ways *at once*. There is, therefore, never determinism and never absolute choice. . . .[42]

On the strength of the evidence adduced concerning the phenomena of intersubjectivity, discourse, and history, and supported by Merleau-Ponty's work, I can now propose a responsible alternate understanding of freedom. Baldly, I propose that freedom be understood as follows. Freedom in its full sense consists in *both the possession and the exercise of the capacity simultaneously to both participate in and maintain oneself as a pole of different kinds of relationships involving either hegemony, equality, or subsumption in order to perform mediations which are reflectively and, in principle, mutually acceptable.*[43] Freedom, then, is an activity, a process, rather than merely a settled property or a relation. It is a process marked by both continuity and constant change. It is a process in which a prior condition is both preserved and transformed.

This understanding of freedom is, of course, not without precedent. In many respects, it is akin to important aspects of classical Greek thought. And it obviously has affinities with some themes stemming from Hegelianism.[44] But the basic justification for my proposal is that it respects the phenomena of history, discourse, and intersubjectivity, phenomena which are fundamental, irreducible constituents of all human efficacy.

Let me explain my proposal. Freedom, as a possessed capacity, can be exercised well or badly. As the capacity for sight can be either well used or abused so can the capacity for relationships be well used or abused. Similarly, as the capacity to see can wax and wane, so can freedom wax and wane. How the capacity for freedom is exercised rebounds to affect the quality and strength of the capacity. Though freedom can neither wax to the point of its apotheosis, its radical exemption from situations, nor wane to the point of its annihilation, its absolute impotence in the face of situations, the capacity for freedom is not immutable. If this is so, and if freedom is indeed of positive worth, then it makes sense to speak of responsibilities and duties to freedom itself, which are to be discharged in the course of the exercise of this capacity.[45] A man, then, can be duty bound to preserve or develop his freedom. In short, freedom is both a fact and a task.

The proposal I advance takes freedom to be a kind of oscillation. Freedom has a centrifugal aspect by virtue of which men can reach beyond themselves to participate in relationships which can achieve richer results than any of them could bring about in isolation from one another. But freedom also has a centripetal aspect by virtue of which he can reinforce and maintain himself as a distinct pole having resources of his own with which to enrich what is to be effected. By virtue of his freedom, then, man is 'eccentric.'[46]

The term 'oscillation' does not imply here a mechanical alternation. Rather it points to a two-fold emphasis in the unitary movement which is freedom, an emphasis on participation and an emphasis on self-maintenance. Neither emphasis can be consistently neglected without the favored one suffering as well. In a rather opaque way, each emphasis can serve to strengthen the other, but only if there are sufficient shifts in emphasis. The kind of oscillation intended here is, in important ways, similar to that which St Thomas Aquinas noted in a different context. In discussing three sorts of religious life, he distinguished the active life of helping other people (here the basically centrifugal thrust) from the contemplative life of prayer and solitude (here the basically centripetal thrust) and from the mixed life which blends periods of the other two (here the life with shifting emphases). The mixed life, he said, is the most perfect. In a similar fashion, on my proposal the maximally free life is one with appropriate shifts of emphasis.

This understanding of freedom does not include the claim that a man *absolutely* originates his participation in relationships. It does not assert that he begins his career of freedom as an already well-defined pole which he then either seeks or should seek to maintain. Freedom, rather, is in every respect both individual and communal from the outset. There can be no freedom which is not simultaneously both individual and communal. Man is an individual only in a social context. He can only be social as an individual among other individuals. Thus, if he is indeed free, man is free just to the extent that he can shift between emphasizing his participation in that which is richer or more efficacious than he alone can be and emphasizing his self-maintenance as one who has a unique contribution to make to relationships.

There is, clearly, no set of rules to determine precisely what sort of shifts of emphasis are sufficient and appropriate for maximal freedom. But that lack poses no insuperable obstacle. Even though concrete experience does not supply formulas for appropriate shifting, both exemplars and traditional practical wisdom do serve as guides. Paraphrasing Aristotle, one can say that appropriate shifting of emphasis is the kind of shifting in which the eminently free man engages. To be sure, neither exemplars nor traditional practical wisdom supply precise norms. But they do furnish just the sort of testimony which a person can both receive and accept while still maintaining himself as a distinctive pole in relationships with other persons.[47] If precise, comprehensive norms for shifting emphasis could be specified, then the maximally free man would merely be one who followed a script.

Correlatively, the object of freedom is not some attribute or trait which an individual agent acquires or maintains. Rather, the object of freedom is activity which is, at least in principle, acceptable to all who come to know of it. A necessary condition for rationally endorsing some particular activity is that it does not foreshorten the field of endorsable activity.[48] The proper object of freedom, then, is concrete activity in a maximally extensive field of activity.

On my account, then, the object of freedom is inseparable from its performance. In Husserlian terms, it is the noematic moment whose counterpart is the agent's performance of reflectively involving himself in relationships with others. Freedom, in short, is constituted by its object as well as by its performance.

Relationships involving freedom are of three distinct kinds, namely, hegemonious, egalitarian, and subsumptive relationships. In each of these kinds, there can be multiple more or less well defined roles. In all relationships involving freedom, participants can periodically swap at least some of these roles. Each of these kinds of relationships is distinguished by the type of connection holding among the several roles within it. Thus, in hegemonious relationships the roles are organized hierarchially. In egalitarian relationships all the roles have a fundamentally equal status. They are linked horizontally, not vertically. In subsumptive relationships, all roles are subordinated to some principle or norm freely acknowledged by the participants as already established and not subject to the discretion of the participants. Since this principle or norm is not itself a role, no participant can aspire to hold its place. This principle or norm assigns weight to the subsumed roles. It may also, but need not, assign participants to their specific roles.[49]

Not all relationships among people, however, manifest freedom. Neither genetic nor geographical relationships, for example, require freedom on the part of their participants. Only those human relationships which are participated in so as to engage in mediational activity which is reflectively and, in principle mutually, acceptable embody freedom.[50] Thus want of freedom in any participant in mediational activity is either a regrettable or a deplorable deficiency calling for rectification. There can be a relationship involving freedom when only some of the participants engage in reflective activity. But the relationship is deficient until the other participants can engage in such activity. For example, the physician – patient relationship is a free relationship even if the patient is unconscious. But the physician's activity is aimed ultimately toward bringing the patient back into conscious participation.[51]

Saying that the free relationship exists for the sake of some activity which is reflectively and mutually acceptable does not entail that the relationship must be taken as a means to some extrinsic end. To the contrary, there are good reasons for holding that the relationships most esteemed as manifestations of freedom are, as Aristotle suggested, precisely those whose activity primarily consists in enjoying the relationship. Further, to say that the activity aimed at is mutually acceptable is obviously not to say that it is mutually accepted. But a person's claim to be a member of a relationship, the aim of which is an activity he reflectively accepts, has two consequences. It entails, first, that the activity ought to be accepted by those with whom he is so related. And second, it entails that, if these others do not accept this activity, they fail to do so because their freedom is either culpably or nonculpably impaired.

None of this, of course, implies that any specific claim about what is acceptable in one set of circumstances claims that it is always acceptable. But it does entail that whatever is acceptable is so because it fits the relevant circumstances.

This relational understanding of freedom which I propose is consonant with all the evidence adduced above to show the insufficiency of the doctrine of freedom as autonomy. It is likewise supported by the sort of reflection on concrete practice which embraces not merely one or a few performances but a substantial stretch of a person's life. Such reflection confirms the existence and the necessity for the sort of shifting which I claim belongs to the very constitution of freedom. If a relationship is a genuine manifestation of freedom, and if it is sustained for a long enough time for the relevant surrounding circumstances to undergo significant modifications, then the relationship must be permeable to moments or stretches of time in which some other kind of relationship holds sway.

Consider the hegemonious relationship between the political ruler and the ruled. For this relationship to be a genuine manifestation of freedom there must be occasions when the ruler and the ruled are related in either an egalitarian or a subsumptive relationship. This requirement might be satisfied, for example, if there are occasions when all participants have equal voting rights. Or they may join together to respond to some natural disaster in a way approximating Sartre's group-in-fusion. Aristotle, in fact, appears correct when he says that, given the fact that no discernible class of people is so markedly superior to other classes of people that its members can undisputedly claim title to permanent rule, 'it is obviously necessary on many grounds that all the citizens alike should take their turn of governing and being governed.'[52] For, he asks, how could people who have no share in government be loyal citizens?[53]

Much the same requirement of permeability holds for egalitarian and subsumptive types of relationship as holds for the hegemonious type. Without this permeability, no type of relationship can be anything more than an impoverished manifestation of freedom. But there can be no such permeability so long as pretensions to autonomy are clung to.

If, however, freedom is understood in relational terms, then it is recognized as the capacity to sustain both relationships and their permeability. Freedom so understood is at the root of both initiative and acquiescence in the face of the Other. It is the capacity to be *en route* as one who is never totally lost in nor lost from the Other.

The doctrine of relational freedom as opposed to that of autonomous freedom is not only supported by the evidence concerning the historical, discursive, intersubjective character of human existence. It is also commended by its fruitfulness when applied to the political domain. Here I will confine myself to its implications for the constitution of the political domain itself. I will reserve for Chapters 6 to 8 the detailing of its bearing upon salient elements ingredient in politics.

In Chapter 3, I showed how the interpretation of political man as one who is politically *en route* ruled out the legitimacy of tyranny, anarchy, and totalitarianism. The doctrine of relational freedom reinforces this conclusion. Insofar as both tyranny and totalitarianism, each in its own way, exaggerate the emphasis on the centripetality of the ruler's activity and the centrifugality of the ruled's activity at the expense of their respective correlates, they both impoverish the freedom of both ruler and ruled. Anarchy exaggerates the centripetality of everyone's activity at the expense of centrifugality and thus likewise impoverishes freedom.

Substantial as is the amplification which the doctrine of relational freedom provides for the interpretation of man's essential routedness and the corroboration which this doctrine gives to arguments excluding tyranny, anarchy, and totalitarianism from the domain of responsible politics, let me now point to a second, more complex, and no less important application of this doctrine. It is often said that moral requirements stand apart from, and sometimes stand in opposition to, political requirements. Thus one hears talk of a supposedly acceptable *Realpolitik* which is amoral, if not immoral. One can hear that moral claims cannot, in principle, be given specific political application because they are necessarily universal whereas politics has to do with the particular and the expedient.

The consequences of this purported scission between the moral and the practical domains have been and remain severe both in conceptual and in practical terms. But the concept of relational freedom provides resources for eliminating this scission.

As I noted above, freedom is a process which can be either developed or allowed to degenerate. The sort of involvement which nurtures and develops freedom is one which is characterized by respect. Respect is an essential condition for all moral and political manifestations of efficacious freedom.[54]

Respect is not merely an attitude. Nor is it necessarily linked to an emotion. It is a relation marked and observed by established social practices.[55] It is associated with dignity and deference. The relation of respect is not exclusive and the practices associated with it are not competitive. If A respects B, either or both can still respect C. Respect, then, is a relation in which all people can share.[56]

Respect, unlike esteem, is a normative concept. It depends upon a specific understanding of persons and their social places.[57] When man is seen as one who is essentially *en route*, as one who is finite, historical, and inextricably linked with other men, and when he is acknowledged to engage in mediations by virtue of relational freedom, then he is seen as a member of a community from which, in principle, no one is definitively excluded. The appropriate way to acknowledge this general condition is by respect. Such respect would not be dependent upon any particular social position. Respect springs from what a man is and his standing in the community. It is accorded to a man 'not as a person simply but as a person *effective* in such and such a setting, a full and equal member, an active participant.'[58] The conditions for respect for others are the same as those for self-respect. 'Self-respect can not be an idiosyncracy; it is not a matter of will. In any substantive sense, it is a function of membership, though always a complex function, and depends upon equal respect among the members.'[59] In the relation of respect, men recognize themselves as mutually recognizing each other. And in this recognition there are intimations of cooperation rather than competition.[60] Mutual respect, then, entails mutual agency and responsibility. And since all respect is to some extent a shared respect, then respect is incompatible with tyranny. The tyrant cannot respect even himself.

The opposite of respect is contempt. He who is held in contempt either accepts his sentence and grovels or rejects it with resentment and sometimes retaliation.[61] In neither case is he who is held in contempt in a position to enhance the efficacy of the mediational activity engaged in by his disparager. Contempt, then, is always at cross purposes with efficacious freedom.

But the fact that respect is essentially ingredient in all political manifestations of efficacious freedom does not require that all political relationships be of the same type. Through the analysis of discourse, I showed above that mediation can transpire in any of three basic types of relationship among people. Each of these types is compatible with and indeed calls for respect. In fact, it is by virtue of respect for man's fundamental condition, for his being *en route*, that each of these three basic types of relationship is recognized both as having its own distinctive worth and as being in need of supplementation by relationships of other types. Respect does not preclude the legitimacy of any of these types of relationship. Nor does it assign unqualified preeminence to any one of these types.

Thus, hegemonious manifestations of freedom call for mutual respect between and among rulers and ruled. The power, efficacy, and need which each brings to the relationship warrants respect. The distinction between ruler and ruled thus rests upon differences among sorts of capabilities for efficacy and not upon a division between the capable and the incapable. Precisely for this reason the distribution of roles in nontyrannical relationships is subject to periodic reallocation.

Respect is essential to subsumptive relationships also. Without respect, subsumption betrays contempt and breeds groveling or resentment and retaliation. Witness the persecutions of the religiously or politically heterodox. Efficacious subsumptive relationships require devotion which is freely given by others as well as by oneself. No one's devotion makes that of others idle. Rather, the presence of the devotion of others is seen to enhance the efficacy of one's own devotion whereas its absence is taken to weaken that efficacy.

Egalitarian relationships, if they are manifestations of freedom, seek mutually accepted activity. Respect is prerequisite for such activity. Mere tolerance of the activity of others is not enough. The activity aimed at is not that which is merely unopposed. It is that which is positively endorsed.

Further, respect is at the root of invitations to new or lapsed members to participate in the relevant relationships. New members are recognized as those who can enhance the relationship. Otherwise, there is no point to inviting their participation. Similarly, the opportunity to participate is held open to lapsed members. Whether they are present enemies or simply uninterested former members, they are seen as people who can contribute positively to the relationship and the accomplishments of its participants. Thus, there is nothing essentially condescending about forgiveness.

Forgiveness presupposes the positive worth of the one pardoned. It is not, therefore, exclusively a moral act. It is an eminently sensible political act as well.[62]

The central role of respect in efficacious relationships appears even in such perverted forms as extorted confessions. Consider, for example, the Moscow Trials of the 1930s. The prosecutors sought the confessions as crucial, irreplaceable testimonies to the mutual acceptability of the activity they aimed at. Though disdain may mask respect, it is nonetheless regularly compelled to pay it.

Respect need not be reserved only for contemporaries. Since it is in the service of freedom, it is concerned with efficacy. On the one hand, if there is to be maximal efficacy, one's successors must be solicited to endorse and to continue the activity which one's performances either initiate or sustain. That is, to be maximally efficacious, one must so behave that others, including successors, can join the activity without loss of respect for either themselves or others. On the other hand, maximal efficacy requires respect for one's predecessors as well. Everyone has been reared in a world largely furnished by the efficacious performances of his predecessors. Insofar as they have bequeathed that furniture with respect, insofar as they have not attempted to preclude initiative by contemporary agents, they have provided the present person with opportunities to join his own performances with earlier performances of demonstrated efficacy.[63]

A man is not, therefore, necessarily shackled by attending to and respecting the activities of predecessors and successors. The contributions they can make to relational freedom are important to all. To give respect to others' contributions to freedom elicits a reciprocal respect from others for one's own activities.

Respect is at the root of even what are called we-relationships. We-relationships, under one description or another, are often taken to stand at the apex of all possible human relationships. They are often said to be either those at which all positive relationships aim or those from which all lesser relationships decline. Recall, for example, Sartre's account of groups-in-fusion. Such relationships, in their purported excellence, are sometimes mistakenly thought to embody a love which obviates the need for respect.

But, as I showed above, no particular type of relationship enjoys unequivocal primacy. To uphold we-relationships as either panacea for or last desperate therapy for contemporary political ills is simply unwarranted. For one thing, it is simply a matter of fact that membership in any we-relationship is always small. The very exclusiveness which characterizes we-relationships necessarily curtails their efficacy.

The exclusiveness ingredient in we-relationships does not, of course, vitiate we-relationships. Unquestionably, they are of major positive worth. But this is the case precisely because they too instantiate respect. In we-relationships, perhaps more clearly than in other relationships, the participational character of freedom is most trenchantly acknowledged. But at the same time minimal expression is given to the pole-maintaining character of freedom. For freedom to be fully displayed and fully efficacious, both of these characters must be in evidence. Respect on the one hand insists upon the pertinence of both of these characters and on the other hand prevents a person from assigning unequivocal primacy to any relationship whether such an assignment be made, in pride, to a relationship in which he participates or, in envy or despair, to a relationship in which he has no part.

Respect, then, stands as the cardinal virtue in both the political and the moral domains.[64] What is done or sought in either domain is to be measured by the respect which it involves, for it is respect which acknowledges the full scope and complexity of freedom. On the one hand, respect takes cognizance of the capacity which people possess to participate in multiple sorts of relationships as distinct poles. On the other hand, it admits that human performances can be either efficacious or inefficacious. It admits that freedom must be developed if it is not to atrophy.

Thus, for example, in the domain of morality respect measures both norms and excuses. It is true both that norms can and should be observed and that excuses can be acceptable. In brief, mercy and justice, whether distributive or rectificatory, do not compete with each other. Both are called for by respect. Respect prevents both the unequivocal subordination either of the concrete person to some general idea or program of activity and the unqualified subjection of all common requirements to the idiosyncracies of the individual person's condition or preference at the moment.

Similarly, respect ranges over the length and breadth of the domain of politics. For example, in domestic politics, respect measures both law and custom. Though laws can and should be devised and obeyed, not everything is to be brought under the law.

95

Custom is not in all cases an unacceptable guide. Respect calls for the cherishing of law while at the same time it prevents the radical dissociation of the present lawmaker's performances from the efficacious performances of predecessors which are embodied in custom.

In international politics, respect measures treaties and alliances on the one hand and the prerogatives of self-determination on the other. Treaties and alliances cannot justifiably disregard the concerns of those who are not signatories. Nor can a policy or program of self-determination justifiably include isolationism.

In all of these instances, political as well as moral, respect requires one to take both himself and others seriously. That is, respect requires both individual people and political bodies to acknowledge both their riches and their poverty, their strength and their importance, their knowledge and their ignorance. Respect likewise requires that all others be acknowledged to be blessed and burdened in comparable ways. As Walzer correctly suggests, the deepest purpose of distributive justice is to promote mutual respect or, in his terms, self-respect for all. 'When all social goods, from membership to political power, are distributed for the right reasons, then the conditions of self-respect will have been established as best they can be.'[65] But, he continues, even after any distribution there will still be men and women lacking in the respect they deserve. There is no perfect distribution. The respectful man will acknowledge that whatever blessings are effected by human doings, these same doings never fail to bring burdens as well. And he will also admit, as Herbert Spiegelberg has emphasized, that there is another distribution of benefits and burdens which man does not control. This distribution is simply an accident of birth.[66]

Through respect, then, the basic requirements of the moral and the political domains can be harmonized. Respect can play this central role in both morals and politics because it acknowledges man's finitude as well as his freedom. The doctrine of autonomous freedom, however, does not demand such an admission. Whatever sense respect could have within the doctrine of autonomous freedom would be insufficient to insure that at least some elementary political demands would be met. For example, the respect required by such a doctrine would not necessarily insist that a man expend efforts to preserve the political community into which he has been inducted. But no viable political community could fail to insist upon such effort. Thus, on the doctrine of freedom as autonomy at least some basic moral and political demands are prone to compete. Such difficulties do not beset the concept of relational freedom.

The doctrine of relational freedom defended here meshes well with both the leads furnished by Merleau-Ponty and the evidence drawn from the phenomena of intersubjectivity, discourse, and history.[67] It also clarifies what is meant by the interpretation of man as one who is essentially *en route*. As Aristotle said, man is by nature political.[68] He is so because he is always and necessarily *en route* with others in a common world.

To be *en route*, however, is, as I have shown, to struggle. It is to struggle with oneself and others for efficacy. It is to acknowledge that freedom is essentially both a fact and a task and that the gap between these two aspects of freedom is irreducible. Precisely this gap between the fact and the task of freedom is the field within which politics is played. This view is opposed then to those views which urge either that freedom is an illusion to be dispelled or a disadvantage to be overcome.[69] It is also opposed to the view, espoused sometimes by Marx and Sartre, that, at least in principle, the gap between the fact and the task of freedom can be definitively closed.[70] On my view, to seek either of these sorts of terminations of man's routedness is either murderous or suicidal, or is doomed to failure. Short of the annihilation of man, always now a threat, neither of these enterprises can reach its goal of closing the gap in and of freedom.

But if man is essentially *en route* and if the gap between the fact and the task of his freedom cannot be closed, then a further issue for interpretation thrusts itself forward. How is man to assess his complex condition? The assessment called for is no mere disinterested appraisal of some self-standing state of affairs. It is a practical assessment concerning how he should bear himself. Is his condition one to which he is, for want of alternatives, to give simple stoical acquiescence? Is it a condition which is ultimately devoid of sense? If so, is his respect for himself and his fellow men to be lived out as a kind of universal compassion for those who are essentially victims, conscious but impotent counters in a pointless game? Or may he, alone or with associates of his own selection, establish a benevolent tyranny, a tyranny in the spirit of the Grand Inquisitor, to spare others from the hardship of facing the implications of their condition of finite freedom?

Or, on the contrary, can man assess his complex condition as one of hope? I will argue in the next chapter that hope is not only possible but that it is required for maximally responsible political conduct. Responsible political conduct must acknowledge that man is essentially *en route*. When men hope that this being *en route* is as such of positive worth, then they are capable of maximally responsible politics. Men need not hope but they can hope. This hope has, in fact, been regularly exhibited. Such a hope provides the strongest bulwark against tyranny, anarchy, and totalitarianism. And only such a hope can insure that respect does not degenerate into mere pity. Hope, then, makes for the best of politics.

5
Hope and responsible politics

Richard Bernstein's *Beyond Objectivism and Relativism*, as I noted in Chapter 4, has helpfully drawn attention to Gadamer's recent emphasis on the solidarity and freedom which embrace all of humanity. In Gadamer's words, 'Practice is conducting oneself and acting in solidarity. Solidarity . . . is the decisive condition and basis of all social reason.'[1] And therefore, 'genuine solidarity, authentic community, should be realized.'[2]

Further in discussing that freedom which is realized only in and through mutual 'recognition' among men, Gadamer claims:

There is no higher principle of reason than that of freedom . . . No higher principle is thinkable than that of freedom of all, and we understand actual history from the perspective of this principle: as the ever-to-be-renewed and never-ending struggle for this freedom.[3]

And again, Gadamer writes:

The principle that all are free never again can be shaken. But does this mean that on account of this history has come to an end? Are all human beings actually free? Has not history since then [since Hegel] been a matter of just this, that the historical conduct of man has to translate the principle of freedom into reality? Obviously this points to the unending march of world history into the openness of its future tasks and gives no becalming assurance that everything is already in order.[4]

These claims of Gadamer's, which flow directly from his doctrine of the essentially dialogical character of human existence, are obviously in harmony with my interpretation of man as one who is essentially *en route* and is characterized by relational rather than autonomous freedom.[5] And both his claims and mine obviously have substantial political import. What Bernstein observes in the case of Gadamer holds, *mutatis mutandis*, for my position as well.

> If we think out what is required for such a dialogue based on mutual understanding, respect, a willingness to listen and risk one's opinions and prejudices, a mutual seeking of the correctness of what is said, we will have defined a powerful regulative ideal that can orient our practical and political lives.[6]

Nonetheless, however powerful such a 'regulative' ideal may be, it leaves open one further issue of capital importance. To put the matter in Gadamer's terms, what sense is to be made of the fact that the struggle for freedom and solidarity is 'ever-to-be-renewed and never-ending'? Or to put the matter in my own terms, if man is one who is essentially *en route* and relationally free, then how is he to interpret his condition? How is he to interpret his ordination to the route itself rather than to a route-ending destination? How is he to interpret his inexorable connection with things and other men?

The question of interpretation at stake here is both practical and theoretical. It is a question both of how he will live out and how he will think through his condition. It is a question of how he will assess and cope with being such a one that his very existence, if it can matter at all, cannot matter except inasmuch as it is intercalated with an Other. The response given to this question, too, will powerfully 'orient our practical and political lives.'

Both Gadamer's account of human solidarity and freedom and my account of men as relationally free and routed entail the irresponsibility of both politics of vision and politics of will or might. Both of these sorts of politics, as I have already shown, effectively deny, in one fashion or another, the fundamental finitude, historicality, and intersubjectivity of human existence. One central aspect of this denial is that each of them, implicitly if not explicitly, rejects the full weight of human temporality. For a politics of vision, nothing essential to the vision is presently undetermined. Nothing essential to the vision need be awaited from new agents coming into play in the future. For a politics of might or will, the past can be given an exhaustive determination, a determination which is to control all future determinations of that past. The moment of present decision owes no essential debt to either past or future persons except, perhaps, purely formal debts. Each of these sorts of politics claims exemptions for its agents from the conditions which bear upon the rest of mankind.

But apart from adherents to either politics of vision or politics of will or might, numerous people have acknowledged, more or less explicitly, the inescapability of thoroughgoing involvement with an Other which remains perpetually other. They likewise admit the ineliminably historical character of this involvement. The question at stake here is: how is this involvement to be understood and assessed?

In this chapter, I want to defend the claim that an interpretation of this involvement in terms of hope rather than in terms of any available alternative gives rise to the most responsible politics. A man can indeed acknowledge and live out his relational freedom in many ways. And he can give expression to his freedom in different ways. But if he is to engage in a politics which is fully responsible, then he must, or so I will argue, live out his freedom in hope.

More specifically, my argument runs as follows. The sort of politics which most adequately acknowledges that man, the political actor, is essentially *en route* and relationally free and which therefore is genuinely responsible is, as I have shown in Chapters 3 and 4, one which provides for as extensive active participation from as many men as is possible. Such a politics, to be responsible, must also seek to preserve itself. Those agents who act on the basis of hope, I claim, best insure the preservation of responsible politics.[7] If this is so, then it is irresponsible to engage in politics in ways incompatible with hope. And it is always responsible to foster hope. Therefore, the most responsible of politics is a politics of hope.

To make my case, I will first briefly mark off politics of hope from its competitors. Then I will set forth in some detail precisely what hope consists in and show that such a hope does fulfill the political role I claim for it. Finally, I will defend the practical possibility of a politics animated by hope.

I

Among the people who acknowledge the inescapability of a thoroughgoing, temporally complex involvement with the Other and who thus stand opposed to both politics of vision and politics of will, there are nonetheless those who either trivialize or demean this involvement. In so doing, they in effect either trivialize or demean politics in the very course of their political practice.

Man's involvement with the Other is trivialized by what can properly be called the politics of presumption. A politics of presumption assumes that present political policy and practice will either perdure unaffected into the future or will somehow naturally evolve into an equally good or even better politics. The future, for such a politics, is simply the time for extending present accomplishments or for progress. It poses no significant threat. The task for the political actor in a politics of presumption is, in the final analysis, simply to foster and not impede the unfolding of an era of well-being already, at least in its essentials, underway.

Today, in the face of threats of multiple sorts of cataclysms, any politics of presumption shows itself to be preposterous. Thus, when such a politics is occasionally proclaimed or extolled, often in celebrations of some kind, it is regularly dismissed without serious consideration. Nonetheless, such a politics is dangerous.[8] It either assumes that what political agents do is of small significance and so whatever they do will affect well-being only slightly, or it assumes that whatever one political agent does is able to be undone or overcome with comparative ease by other agents. It is the kind of politics in which one hears talk of victory in nuclear war, technological cures without untoward side effects for all ills, etc. Such a politics cannot take its own practice as in any sense decisive. It thereby trivializes all politics, including its own.

More vigorous contemporary competition for a politics of hope comes from the sort of politics which does not trivialize man's involvement with the Other but rather demeans it. Those who practice politics of this sort see this involvement primarily as something to be outmaneuvered or neutralized. Sometimes this approach to politics has taken the form of resignation. Epicurean and Stoic responses to the human condition have had a long history. And sometimes this approach has taken the form of defiance. Rebels with little or no cause are rarely in short supply. And either of these forms of sterilizing the otherness of the Other can be lived out either wakefully or sleepily.[9] Neither of these approaches to politics is easily identifiable with any systematically developed body of theoretical doctrines. But both do show up with frequency in practice and in the deliberations and explanations offered in support of either proposed or accomplished political undertakings.

Each of these approaches to politics acknowledges, in its own way, both that man is ineluctably *en route* and that he is necessarily intertwined with the Other. But each, again in its own way, takes these to be characteristics of the human condition by which men are restricted or confined rather than as characteristics by which they obtain strength and opportunity for achievements. Both of these approaches to politics, in effect, yearn for some more or less well defined *status quo*. This *status quo* is taken to be imperiled by the Other, whether the Other be construed simply as some other group of people or whether it be construed as some mix of other men and material and cultural circumstances. These approaches can well be labeled, respectively, as 'politics of resignation' and 'politics of containment.' A politics of resignation proceeds with sorrow to accept accommodations to the Other which erode its preferred *status quo*. A politics of containment resists the Other as much as possible and regards any alteration in its preferred *status quo* to be a setback which it makes sense to seek to undo. In terms of man's routedness, then, a politics of resignation regrets its inability to maintain a stable abode at some location of its own choice on the route. A politics of containment, by contrast, struggles to make a self-selected specific location as fixed as possible and, when the inevitable departures occur, to return as close as possible to this 'fixed' point.

Both of these approaches basically distrust the future, for part of the very sense of any future is that it need not be just like any past or present. This distrust amounts to a demeaning of the future by effectively denying that the future could bring anything of positive worth. Similarly, both of these approaches demean the relational character of freedom. For them, the positive worth of freedom would consist solely of the capacity to keep oneself, or one's favored group, immune from the consequences of involvement with the Other.[10]

Whether there is a conceptual incompatibility between a politics of resignation and a politics of containment is hard to say. But there is no practical impediment to a concrete politics which, while persisting in its fundamental depreciation of involvement with the Other, readily switches from one to the other. Neither of them, though, is either conceptually or practically compatible with a politics of hope.[11]

Whatever the difficulties hobbling politics of presumption on the one hand and politics of either resignation or containment on the other, hope would nonetheless seem at first glance to be an unpromising alternative candidate for inscription as an essential constituent for maximally responsible politics. Throughout the history of Western thought, sober thinkers have warned against hope on the grounds that it begets and sustains dangerous illusions. And yet, perhaps because of the urgency of the contemporary scene, my claims in favor of the political pertinence of hope are not unprecedented. Even so rationalistically inclined a thinker as Sartre came to speak of hope in connection with politics. Freedom alone, he came to see, is too underdetermined to provide the basis for a responsible politics for men who are essentially *en route*.

In three conversations with Benny Levy, published in March 1980, a month before Sartre's death, Sartre introduces elements into his ethico-political considerations which are simply dissonant with both *Being and Nothingness* and *Critique of Dialectical Reason*.[12] He is led to speak of hope as a necessary constituent of action.[13] This hope is not a temporary stage, something to be transcended. It is that in which Sartre says he will die.[14] The search for a new moral basis for the Left, he says, must be rooted in Man's hope and social desire.[15] Hope belongs to a universal brotherhood recognized as such by all. This brotherhood, according to Sartre, is diametrically opposed to violence.[16]

A more important precedent for my claims for a politics of hope is, in my view, to be found in Merleau-Ponty's work. His political doctrine, I believe, should properly be seen as a politics of hope.[17] Though he does not deal thematically with the issue of hope, it is operative throughout his political studies. He constantly urges a politics which falls prey neither to trivializing the differences among men nor to absolutizing any specific set of those differences.[18] As such, his politics stands in opposition not only to any politics of vision or politics of might or will but also to any politics which either demeans or trivializes man's involvement with the Other.

Nonetheless, however useful these precedents may be, they do not provide a well-developed account of the kind of hope which might have a crucial place in politics.[19] If hope is to be ascribed a substantial place in a theory of politics, one must first make explicit its distinguishing characteristics and then articulate its political significance. I now turn to the first of these tasks.

II

A first purchase on the concept of hope can be attained by attending to the meanings connected with the term 'hope' in traditional Western Christian usage. Precedent for these meanings can be found in both Greek and Hebrew thought. And these meanings are not radically foreign to at least some traditions of Eastern thought.

In passing, let me point out that an attempt to elucidate a concept purportedly of substantial import for political thought through a discussion of a term most obviously associated with religion is not so odd as it might initially seem. The putative radical separation of politics from religion is a relatively recent, thoroughly Western enterprise.[20] Most human experience and thought has taken place in contexts in which such a radical divorce was not even conceived of. As Johannes Metz says: 'The unity and co-ordination of religion and society, as well as religious and social existence, was acknowledged in former times as an unquestionable reality.'[21] Something of the same sort of intertwining persists today both in practice and thought. Claims such as 'women and men together must recognize that the essence of Christianity (or Judaism) is the prophetic call for liberation of the oppressed' are far from unusual.[22] Thus, there has not been in the past, and there is still not today, an unproblematic way to segregate religious vocabulary from political vocabulary.

A review of the way in which the notion of hope has been deployed in classical Greek, Hebraic, Christian, and Stoic sources shows that hope has rather consistently been understood to have the following features.[23] These features remain constant, whether hope is praised or, in the cases of Pindar and the Stoics, is damned. (1) Hope is essentially connected with the conviction that the future need not be like the present or merely the unfolding of mechanisms already presently established. In this respect, hope is linked with memory. If memory shows that, for better or worse, the present is not like the past, then, again for better or worse, the future can be different from at least one of them. (2) Hope goes hand in hand with the conviction that free agents can, through their activity, influence somehow the character of the future. The influential agent may, but need not, be the one who hopes. But he who hopes thereby allies himself with the influential agent and thus seeks to reap the benefits of that agency. An example of this 'benefit by association through hope' is the effect upon prisoners of war of even hints that their compatriots may liberate them. Thus, in at least the minimal sense of allying oneself to the efficacious agent, hope claims to be efficacious. At the very least, it furnishes the 'primary' agent with an appropriate audience. (3) The object of the act of hope is always complex and is never fully determinate. The object is never fully determinate both because hope is never certain of its own outcome and because it lays no claim to foresight into some well-defined future state of affairs.[24] The object of hope is always complex because hope is necessarily directed both toward some other person, either human or divine, and toward some future state of affairs, however ill-defined this state of affairs may be. Hope, then, is a double-rayed act.[25]

Reflection on these constant features of hope permits further important clarifications of the phenomenon of hope. Fir.᾿ hope is indeed an act in its own right. It has its own object and its own temporality. It is not merely an 'adverbial' modification of some other act. That is, hope is not merely one kind of modalization, among others, to which acts are susceptible. Thus, a person does not marry hopefully, or despairingly, or cynically. He hopes and marries. He despairs and marries. Or he is cynical and marries. The temporal duration of hope is not necessarily identical to that of some other act. The temporal duration of one act of hope can embrace the combined durations of several acts of other sorts. A person can successively talk, run a race, and build a chair during the same act of hope that his beloved will agree to marry him. Conversely, more than one act of hope may be performed during the duration of some other single act. For example, in the course of an unwavering conviction that the future will be transformed for the better, one might perform several acts of hope whose object is to ally oneself with the agent of that transformation. Within Rabbinic Judaism, for example, there was apparently abundant confidence that the Messiah would come to inaugurate his reign over a new kingdom, but there was no comparable confidence about one's own participation in the glories of that kingdom. It is easy to imagine that, during the course of his one steady conviction that the Messiah would come, a man might perform multiple acts of hope concerning his own participation in those glories. These acts of hope might well be punctuated with acts of either despair on the one hand or presumption on the other.

It is, though, characteristic for an act of hope to endure for lengthy stretches of a person's life.[26] It can be reaffirmed when threatened or taken note of when another person displays something contrary to it. Thus, for the most part, the act of hope serves as a latent background against which more patent acts are performed. In times of crisis, however, the act of hope can either be brought to focal presence or be reinforced by being repeated.

A second clarification of the phenomenon of hope comes from further consideration of its double-rayed character. Acts of hope always introduce a polyvalent tension into the flow of experience. On the one hand, hope, in its orientation toward other persons, contains some expectations about the outcome of their activities. The fundamental expectation, the expectation without which there would be no hope, is that if the other person acts as a genuine agent, then his doing so is what is of primary value both to him and to me. That is, hope involves the conviction that it is necessarily better for a man to be associated with other agents rather than with puppets, even if he were the puppeteer. Further, it includes a yearning for these others actually to exercise their agency. Hope then is constituted in part by the courageous confidence that one's own agency is not compromised by the agency of others.[27] And, at the same time, for all its expectancy, hope is patient. The other's activity is to be elicited, not compelled. And it is never sure that its expectation will be fulfilled. Hope, then, must struggle against ultimata or deadlines from any source. This appreciation of what hope requires is perhaps most expressly articulated in the traditional Christian understanding of hope. On that view, as reported by S. Harent, patience, hope, and courage are basically linked to one another.

> Just as patience helps hope to continue and to endure, so, in return, hope helps one to be patient, to resist, to struggle. There is a reciprocal influence. *Courageous in its desire, serene in its courage, hope is a principle of action.*[28]

By reason of its other ray, its orientation towards states of affairs, hope acknowledges the finite, situated character of all agency, its own and that of others. For hope, states of affairs, in their specificity, do count. They weigh upon all agency. They provide either favorable or unfavorable conditions for its efficacy. Hope, then, deals with things as well as persons. But he who hopes thereby admits that he has no certitude about the precise effect of any concrete set of circumstances upon specific human endeavors. If he

107

knew this effect, he would have the kind of incontrovertible foresight which renders hope otiose.

If a human performance lacks either the orientation to persons or the orientation to states of affairs, it cannot be hope. If it is not oriented toward other efficacious agents, then it is merely either wish or want. If it is not oriented towards concrete states of affairs, past, present, and future, then it is either presumption or fanaticism. Both of these latter ways of dealing with the Other regard the concrete circumstances in which human activity occurs as fundamentally inconsequential.

Hope's rays, however, are not of equal weight. The primary ray is that which is directed toward other agents. However important circumstances may be, so long as there is hope no present or future circumstances can be taken to cancel the agency either of the one who hopes or of him in whom one hopes. At least one agency, capable in principle of restoring agency to others regardless of circumstances, must be admitted. Thus, for example, if one takes men to be basically helpless, to have hope he must at least acknowledge some savior who can remove this helplessness. Otherwise, there is despair.[29]

The foregoing considerations provide the basis for the following characterization of essential features of hope.[30] Hope is, first, a double-rayed act whose object is both complex and never fully determinate. The complexity of its object is so ordered that some form of priority is always given to the person or persons in whose efficacy one hopes over the states of affairs for which one hopes. The necessary indeterminacy of the object of hope guarantees both that every formulation of that object is always reformable and that the object of hope is not the sort of thing which can be definitively attained thereby rendering continued hope pointless. Second, hope is inseparable from the conviction that the future is open to efficacious activity in which he who hopes, by the very act of hoping, either does or can participate. For those who have such a conviction, hope makes sense. For those who have no such conviction, hope is senseless, if not pernicious.[31] Hope, then, is essentially that act by which a self-admittedly finite agent both embraces his historical involvement with other agents in a world not fully pliant to their pleasure and comports himself with courage and confidence toward a future understood to be open to human agency.

My account of hope is in the main consistent with Gabriel

Marcel's description of it.[32] Marcel also recognizes that hope both transcends all particular determinate objects and expresses a fundamental appreciation of man's intersubjective condition. To hope is to stand ready both to receive from others and to give to them. It is to involve oneself in a unique process, to weave the multiple strands of one's experience in a special way. Hope requires both freedom and a relaxed patience. Both hope and freedom, Marcel says, presuppose that a person has the power in the exercise of his judgment to override the claims arising not only from his perception of present circumstances but even from his imaginative capacity to depict other circumstances. That is, hope presupposes the capacity to outstrip one's powers of imaginative construction and thereby to await an essentially unforeseen future. But at the same time, hope does not disdain either the past or the present. Hope, according to Marcel, says, 'as before, but differently and better than before.'[33]

On one critical point, though, Marcel's account is vague. He claims that he who hopes in effect says: 'I hope in thee for us.'[34] Is this 'thee' necessarily the Absolute Thou who is, whether one recognizes it or not, God? Marcel's description can readily lead one to think that hope always and necessarily refers somehow to God.

My account of hope does not preclude reference to God, but neither does it necessarily imply such a reference. Rather, on my account, hope can be directed either to divine or human others or both. Further, the kind of hope pertinent to the domain of politics is explicitly, though not necessarily exclusively, directed toward other human beings.[35]

If my description of it is correct, then hope is a permanent human possibility. It is a distinctive way in which man can orient and bear himself toward other persons across the circumstances in which their relationships transpire. When hope is actualized, it substantially affects man's involvement with the Other. If man is indeed essentially *en route*, and if he is so in a relationally free way, then actualized hope in such a man ascribes unequivocally positive worth both to the future possibilities arising from this routedness and to the concrete relations which constitute it. The consequences of such a hope are substantial both for understanding one's politicality and for living it out. Here I will first point out the most salient general consequences of a politics of hope and then defend the practicality of such a politics. In subsequent chapters I will show how a politics of hope distinctively shapes both the understanding of and the working with some central political phenomena. These consequences, taken together, constitute compelling reasons for adopting a politics of hope.

III

To clarify the place of hope in politics, let me turn back to the matter of the conceptual and structural connection between the domains of politics and religion. The reason for focusing on this connection in this context is primarily historical rather than theoretical. But the history is rich and illuminating.

Consider again the double-rayed character of hope. The primary ray, I have argued, is that which is directed toward other persons in whose efficacy one hopes. This ray holds priority over the ray directed toward some specific desired or sought state of affairs. If the primary ray is directed toward some divinity or some superhuman agent, then the hope in question is religious.[36] But if the primary ray is directed toward human persons, then it is possible for the hope to be political. A hope extended toward both human and superhuman agents can be political only if it is, in a nontechnical sense, 'Pelagian.' What distinguishes political hope from other hopes addressed to human agents is the following feature. Hope is political if and only if those in whom one hopes are regarded as actual or potential co-participants in the activity of establishing or maintaining a structured context, a world, in which multiple sorts of human activity can find space in which to appear.

Politics, whether hope-filled or not, is a 'totalizing' totality. That is, the political domain claims to have responsibility for providing the framework in which all other sorts of activities, e.g. educational, economic, artistic, and religious activities, can occur. Politics takes as its task the allocation of space and time for each sort of activity. Thus, on the one hand, politics makes room for each sort of activity. On the other hand, it regulates them to prevent any of them from unwarranted encroachment upon others. But in all such doings it likewise works to maintain itself as the appropriate source of such allocations.[37]

This view of politics and its totalizing function is in the main consonant with Aristotle's discussion of communities. He writes:

All communities are like parts of the political community. . . .
We think of the political community as having initially come
together and as enduring to secure the advantage of its
members. . . . Now, all other forms of community aim at some
partial advantage. . . . But all these communities seem to be
encompassed by the community that is the state; for the political
community does not aim at the advantage of the moment but at
what is advantageous for the whole of life. Thus all associations
seem to be parts of the political community.[38]

In a similar vein, Michael Oakeshott has argued that every mode
of utterance, including poetic utterance, should be construed as
being set in a society of conversationalists rather than in a society
devoted to scientific inquiry or one engaged in some practical or
productive enterprise. Politics, for Oakeshott, is a conversation
and political education involves learning how to participate in this
conversation.[39]

But as a matter of historical record, politics has not been the sole
claimant to the title of that totalizing activity in which all other
associations are parts and by which they receive allotments of space
in which to make themselves manifest. Religion, too, as I noted
briefly in Chapter 3, has also claimed this totalizing function. In
fact, throughout most of recorded history, both of East and West,
religion and politics have been closely intertwined, either in struggle or in collaboration.[40] Often, the bonds between them have been
so tight that they have been regarded as two facets of the same
fundamental order of reality. Theocracies and civic religions do not
stand as counterexamples to this generalization. They are simply
two of the many shapes which the connection between religion and
politics can and did take.[41]

If religion has historically been the principal competitor with
politics for the function of totalizer, it may well be the case that the
major competition for politics today comes from another quarter,
from a managerial technocracy for which the sole determinant of
appropriate or rational activity is measurably efficient production
of goods and services. This latter-day threat to politics, discussed
earlier in this study, would arrogate to itself the exclusive preroga-
tive of setting goals, of determining what counts as significant
human conduct. Insofar as other activities could contribute to such
conduct, they would be allowed space in which to appear. Otherwise,

they would be discouraged if not positively extirpated.[42]

Against this historical and conceptual background, I wish to argue: (1) that the political community cannot responsibly yield the function of being the totalizing community to any other community, religious or otherwise,[43] and (2) that a politics infused by hope, functioning as a totalizing community, does not threaten any other distinctive type of activity. Rather, it allows other types of activity to take place in peace. This is the case because a politics of hope precludes both the view that it is the mere handmaid of other types of activity and the view that it is itself the ultimate justification or end of all other types of activity. A politics of hope eschews all unequivocal hierarchizations and does so not by reason of weakness but by reason of strength.

Precisely put, my claim is that a politics of hope necessarily both develops and maintains the political community as a totalizing community while at the same time it forestalls all attempts to convert the activity of any community, political or otherwise, into the activity of a totalized community. None of its standard competitors, political or otherwise, necessarily embodies both of these objectives. Therefore, a politics of hope is preeminently responsible politics.

To put the case in other terms, a politics of hope is radically incompatible with both tyranny and totalitarianism and furnishes abundant resources with which to ward them off. Nonpolitical competitors of a politics of hope, e.g. religion and managerial technocracy, are not so radically incompatible with these perversions. And its political competitors, namely politics of presumption, resignation, and containment, at best supply comparatively slim resources against them.

Consider once more the contrast between hope-filled politics and its nonpolitical competitors for the function of totalizer. All large, widespread religions have, as a matter of fact, required as a qualification for full membership uniform beliefs of one sort or another concerning the overall good or goal of human life. This fact becomes most patent when representatives of two or more religions confront one another in vying for the allegiance of the same group of people.[44] Politics, to the contrary, need not require uniformity of belief in such matters. And responsible politics explicitly eschews such a requirement. When a political movement demands uniformity in such matters, it taints itself with nonpolitical characteristics. It effectively splits the community into two classes, the members of one of which are treated as distinctly inferior to or hostile to members of the other.

The difference between the hope-filled political and the religious way of dealing with diversity of belief about the existence or character of an ultimate goal of human life has been made vivid in recent years by efforts toward religious ecumenism. For all the successful efforts to reduce friction among religious communities, the problem of conversion has proved intractable. To be true to itself, a specific religious community must regard every conversion of one of its members to another religion as a defection, a repudiation. It must hold that the person in question has lost something of religious importance with no compensating gain. Each religion must insist upon its own essential superiority, at least for its own members, over any other religion.

Such exclusiveness is not an essential feature of hope-filled political communities. Migration in political terms can but need not imply repudiation of the political community one leaves behind. Sometimes the migration is prompted by political repression. In these cases, the oppressors have forfeited the allegiance of those who migrate. Sometimes the migration is prompted by the political or economic weakness of the home community. Then migration is undertaken with a regret not necessarily marked by repudiation. In fact, such migration might even be undertaken for the sake of the home community. And sometimes the migration is, at least in intention, only partial or temporary. In cases of this latter sort, the migrant can sustain filiations to more than one political community which are tantamount to multiple citizenship, whether legally recognized or not.

In sum, whereas religion tends to be a totalized, fundamentally closed community, the political community need have no such tendency.[45] And when it is infused with hope, the political community esteems its openness as a strength and not as a weakness. It esteems a relational freedom which eschews any attempt to fix its constituent relations in immobile patterns.

Much the same sort of differences distinguish hope-filled politics from managerial technocracy. Though managerial technocracy tends to consign religion to irrelevancy, it, like religion, does lay claim to being in possession of 'the one thing necessary.' As such, it claims that at least in principle it can provide a definitive totalization for the human community. It would not only allot room for whatever is to be allowed to appear. It also claims to be ultimately the sole source of legitimacy for human activity of any sort.

What yokes religion and managerial technocracy is their claim to possess knowledge not only of the existence of a goal in which man's routedness terminates but also of at least some of that goal's defining characteristics. That is, for both of these, the question about the point of man's existence is essentially closed, is definitively answered. Whatever is still undecided is taken to be essentially either minor or peripheral. It is either inconsequential and therefore optional or a detail to be filled in according to the requirements of the fully determinate end. Any politics which is radically subordinated to or regulated by either religion or managerial technocracy cannot provide security against tyranny or totalitarianism. None of its provisions could prevail against claims entailed by the definitive, determinate goal of man's existence.

Hope-filled politics, politics which is faithful to its own origin and limits in man's essential finitude, historicality, and intersubjectivity, claims no such knowledge. Knowledge of this sort would make all subsequent innovation and the freedom from which innovation springs either trivial, or impossible, or pernicious. By acknowledging that the question about the point of man's existence as one who is essentially *en route* cannot and should not be closed, a politics of hope stands radically opposed to all forms of tyranny and totalitarianism.[46]

The proximate political competitors against a politics of hope, namely politics of presumption, of resignation, and of containment, are, perhaps, just as conceptually incompatible with tyranny and totalitarianism as is politics of hope. But, unlike politics of hope, they supply rather slim resources against these threats.[47] Politics of presumption trivialize the riskiness of the future. The presumptious man tends to forget that tyranny and totalitarianism always remain possible. Presumptious politics is sleepy politics. Politics of resignation and of containment demean the future and thereby enshrine either the past or the present. The resigned man tends to forget that tyranny is not inevitable and thus tends to struggle less than confidently for bulwarks against tyranny. The man of containment tends to cling exclusively to already established bulwarks at the expense of failing to seek new ones. Both the man of resignation and the man of containment view their political activity as basically reactive. This activity, both conceptually and practically, is construed primarily in the terms of that against which it reacts. Such defensiveness inspires small confidence in one's ultimate success, for their successes are defined exclusively in terms of defeats averted or avoided. The practitioner of politics of hope, by contrast, is emboldened by that very hope not only to resist tyranny and totalitarianism but to undertake innovations and transformations of the relationships in which he lives for their own intrinsic worth, even if such activity is neither necessary nor directly pertinent to warding off impending dangers.

The strength of a politics of hope becomes more evident when one takes cognizance of the way hope affects one's participation in the several kinds of mediational relationships. In Chapter 4, I argued that respect is an essential condition for all responsible political manifestations of efficacious freedom. Through respect, each of the three basic types of relationship – the hegemonious, the egalitarian, and the subsumptive – can be seen as having its own distinctive worth, its own distinctive possibility for efficacy. When respect is fused with hope, then one has no temptation to resign himself to these various sorts of relationship as those in which, *faute de mieux*, he is compelled to participate if he would accomplish anything. In hope, one relies upon all the participants for mutual enhancement.

Thus, in hegemonious relationships, in relationships explicitly displaying distinctions between ruler and ruled, both command and obedience are substantially modified when they are lived out not only in respect but also in hope. The gap between ruler and ruled is maintained but is also bridged. Ruler and ruled seek each other's positive contribution. In egalitarian relationships, hope promotes the sort of listening or hearing which is not confined merely to having one's own discourse somehow confirmed. It promotes a quest for ever more efficacious and comprehensive discourse, even if this quest leads to radical change from the sort of discourse in which one has been participating. That is, hope insures against unwarranted claims for monological discourse. Hope similarly modifies subsumptive relationships. Here again, the gap between men and that to which they submit is not cancelled. But they rely upon that to which they submit to enhance the sense of their lives and not to detract from it.

Hope also works to preserve and expand the number of participants in these relationships. One way in which this is achieved is through the transformation of the sense of forgiveness. Transgressors are forgiven, when hope infuses respect, not because weakness has somehow rendered their transgressions not fully their own but precisely because what they have to contribute, strengths often enough manifested in the transgression itself, is appreciated as being of irreplaceable importance.

Hope, then, provides a vital specification for the interpretation of man as one who is essentially *en route* and endowed with a finite, relational freedom which, for its maximal efficacy, requires respect. The specification provided by hope does not necessarily show up in each individual performance of the man who hopes. It does however appear in his endeavors both to participate in innovative patterns of activity and to join in ventures with new participants. Whereas respect without hope would permit such endeavors, respect infused with hope explicitly elicits them.

If my account of hope is accurate, then it becomes clear that hope involves a 'preferential option' for man. That is, those who hope are committed to work to insure that, so long as it is physically possible, there will be men.[48] In terms of this hope, whatever the surrounding circumstances, the struggle with the Other must always be for man.

In political terms, one must always hope for other men and their continued varied activity. One must always seek harmony-struggle with them in a common world. In short, one must always hope that there will continue to be political practice which esteems the very existence of men.

Hope then stands as a practical political '*a priori.*' If there can be politics, then one should participate in it in hope. Only hope can sufficiently determine respect and relational freedom in such a way that the latter cannot be taken either merely as 'temporary' requirements brought on by the peculiarities of contingent circumstances or as a 'second best' condition which must be endured. Hope so modifies the actual living out of respectful relational freedom that an essential dimension of appropriate living is the effort to ensure continuing human living. This entails, of course, living freely in the context of multiple sorts of relationships. On this view, some men might be able to be sacrificed for other men.[49] But there could be no sense to sacrificing all men for an idea or 'principle' or to attempting to impose a permanent, inflexible pattern of activity upon all men. Hope thus insures that, so long as it is present, there will be politics.

No other modification of respect, namely presumption, resignation, or containment, requires so stringent a commitment to the preservation of politics. Alone among these possible modifications, hope entails that a responsible politics necessarily strives for a preservation of politics.

But hope does more than just insure the preservation of politics. It also engenders specific requirements which a thoroughly responsible politics must honor. Not only does a politics of hope, as I indicated above, stand opposed to all dogmatisms, whether it be dogmatisms based upon supposedly definitive knowledge or dogmatisms rooted in the sort of voluntarism which treats appeals to evidence as irrelevant. A politics of hope also necessarily preserves and protects struggle as essential to its harmony. That is, any concrete politics of hope esteems and keeps room for opposition to the specific policies and practices it itself has in fact adopted for its particular community. Without opposition of this sort, the interplay of men would be truncated. Such mutilations at least sterilize and at worst destroy politics. Without this opposition, there could be no sufficiently defined 'you' in whom 'I' could hope for 'us.' With opposition, however, both criticism and self-criticism flourish. And criticism is a necessary condition for avoiding the repetition of errors. Further, both because the need for criticism never ends and because no person is immune to all criticism, forgiveness must always be available to all. The critic too needs forgiveness, and this precisely for the sake of continued criticism. Forgiveness and criticism, in the context of hope, reinforce one another.

A politics of hope, though, never forgets the seriousness of the struggle which is ingredient in the human condition. It is never presumptuous about itself. It recognizes that its own policies and principles need defense. The mere enunciation of its own position is not enough to make that position prevail. Its opponents do not merely need to be enlightened. They will need encouragement, coercion, or both if they are either to accept practitioners of hope as fellow actors on the political stage or to become themselves practitioners of hope. Even a politics of hope, then, cannot eschew all resort to force. Thus a politics of hope is not without teeth. It is not a politics of mere pious sentiments. It is a serious politics.

But at the same time a politics of hope never forgets the point of the struggle. The point of the struggle is not to subdue the Other – whether other men or the world. Rather, it is to dwell effectively with them in their otherness. In its political shape, the point of the struggle is to nurture as effectively as possible the full range of human activity and achievement. In short, the point of the struggle is to bring about brotherhood.[50] Brotherhood does not presume the removal of all differentiations. Rather, it cherishes the differences among men while harmonizing them.

Since a politics of hope aims to dwell effectively with others in their otherness, it never despairs. Even if the specific context in which one is presently lodged provides no support or opportunity for initiative, the practitioner of hope patiently and expectantly awaits changes in that context which will allow him room for action. He never simply acquiesces in his situation as though the situation could definitively preclude initiative. Similarly, the practitioner of hope never consigns his opponents to the ranks of the perpetual enemy. There is always room for today's enemy to become tomorrow's ally. A politics of hope, then, on the one hand never trivializes the differences among men. On the other hand, however, it never absolutizes any specific set of those differences.[51]

In summary, then, my contention is that, in the actual living out of relational freedom and its attendant respect, this freedom must necessarily be qualified or modalized somehow. Hope alone, among the possible acts which can modalize it while still acknowledging man's essential routedness, unequivocally modalizes it so as to promote freedom's continued efficacy. When applied to the domain of politics, hope-filled freedom embraces politics as that irreplaceably valuable but essentially unfinishable kind of activity which provides room for other kinds of worthwhile human enterprises.

Though the political manifestations of other possible modalizations of freedom, namely the politics of presumption, of resignation, and of containment, do not directly cancel freedom and its efficacy, they either trivialize it or demean it. In so doing they enervate its exercise and sow the seeds of its surrender or abandonment. A politics of presumption denies the genuine otherness of other men and so robs political deeds of their urgency. Politics of resignation and of containment, on the other hand, construe this otherness as essentially hostile and thus cannot look forward to receiving positive contributions from others. For each of these three, politics itself lacks intrinsic dignity. It is either essentially innocuous, as in politics of presumption, or it is a therapy impeding the course of disease but unable to cure it, as in politics of resignation and of containment.

A politics of hope, to the contrary, expressly calls for both the interminable preservation of politics and the inclusion of as many people as possible as participants. It is therefore appropriate to rank politics of hope as the best of politics and to describe the place of hope in politics as I have done above. That is, a politics of hope necessarily both develops and maintains the political community as a totalizing community while at the same time it forestalls all attempts to convert the activity of any partial community, including the political community, into the activity of a totalized community.[52]

A politics of hope, then, is not bemused by utopianism in any form. But neither does it regret the impossibility of utopias. It unswervingly acknowledges that man, in his aims as wells as in his deeds, is always and essentially *en route* and finds in this acknowledgment the stimulus to unremitting cooperative effort. He has no 'answer,' even in thought, which can exhaustively satisfy the 'essential questions.' But he finds in this condition the opportunity for significant response on his part to these 'questions.' Responsible politics, politics taking responsibility for itself, then, requires hope. A politics of hope is quintessentially responsible politics.

For all its merits, however, a politics of hope such as that which I have presented must face some pertinent criticisms. In responding to two crucial objections, I will both show that a politics of hope is defensible and at the same time clarify further just what a politics of hope consists in.

IV

My account of politics of hope, as I have said, builds upon leading themes of Merleau-Ponty's political thought. Ironically, perhaps the most vigorous objections to such a politics can be formulated in ways also suggested by Merleau-Ponty. In the course of his discussion of politics, he set forth two tests which a political doctrine must pass if it is to count as a defensible, responsible basis for political conduct. One can then appropriately ask: Can a politics of hope pass these tests?

The first test seeks to determine whether a political doctrine possesses a sufficiently strong norm or guideline to distinguish between a politics which genuinely respects the uniqueness of concrete historical moments and a politics which is merely opportunistic. At first glance, a politics of hope may appear too permissive, to be too vague to provide a secure basis for distinctions between the genuinely opportune and the simply opportunistic. In brief, a politics of hope may appear to rule out so little possible practice that nothing would run afoul of it and hence it would be normatively vacuous.

Initial impressions notwithstanding, however, a politics of hope turns out on examination to be hardly too lax. If anything, it runs the risk of being excessively restrictive. A politics of hope, committed as it is to acknowledge the relational freedom of men who are essentially *en route*, can in principle countenance only policies and practices which are recognizable to all men as something which each person or political entity could rationally endorse being carried out by someone, even if not by oneself. If anything, such a requirement threatens to be too strict to be observable in practice. What policy or practice could win so wide an acceptance?

This threat can be removed, though, if this normative requirement is interpreted in the following way. A policy or practice is defensible in a politics of hope if it is recognizable *at least mediately* to all as something which all can rationally approve someone carrying out. Rationality, on the view I am defending, does not demand that one reject everything not directly consonant with his own specific articulation of his principles. Rather, the rational man recognizes that his articulations are always open to reform. A major stimulant to such reform in the political realm is precisely the confrontation between clashing policies or practices. Rationality, then, both guides one's pursuits and makes one aware of the limitations of one's entire enterprise.[53] Since all political performances occur in a historical context constituted by other performances both by the same agent and by others, single performances cannot be fully assessed. The apparently objectionable performance, if properly situated in context, may well prove to be endorsable precisely because it induces a reconsideration of established policy and practice.

Such an interpretation, while forestalling the danger of legitimating too little, does not lead to the legitimation of too much. No matter how contextualized, political policy or practice which is tantamount to the denial of man's routedness and the relational character of his freedom cannot win endorsement. Even if no definitive formulation of norms is achievable, widespread torture, indiscriminate killing and devastation, and systematic neglect of vital needs, are unquestionably ruled out. They are, whether verbally articulated or not, fundamentally incompatible with hope.

Hope, then, in its modification of the way one understands and lives out one's freedom, functions critically rather than dogmatically. That is, hope issues no explicit, articulable requirements, but it does serve as that against which all articulable requirements are measured and found to be perpetually reformable.[54] As such, it is by no means impotent. But neither is it excessively restrictive.

The second test which Merleau-Ponty would require a political doctrine to pass seeks to determine whether practice based on the doctrine in question can successfully compete against other types of political practice in dealing with the exigencies of the historical and material context in which it is to operate. Though Merleau-Ponty does not make success a sufficient condition for approving a politics, he does take it to be a necessary one.[55] A praxis, for Merleau-Ponty, must, if it cannot be true, at least not be false.[56] Futility is a sure symptom of political falsity.

Two sorts of considerations might well lead one to doubt that a politics of hope can satisfy this second requirement. Consider first the more 'practical' sort of consideration. Can a politics of hope be successfully practiced in a world of scarcity of material and economic resources? Will not competition for these resources pit men against one another as implacable enemies?

Unquestionably, this is a most serious issue. I must admit both that a politics of hope cannot abolish the political problems posed by the scarcity of resources and that it cannot insure its own successful coping with the problem. Its competitors, however, hardly possess prepossessing credentials of their own in this regard. Military expenditures destroy huge amounts of resources. Doctrines such as that of 'triage' can hardly be implemented unless they are imposed by might. Deployment of might exclusively in one's own competitive interest can bring no peace. Nor can it win rational acceptance. It can only provoke war and the destruction of resources that always accompanies war.

The issue of scarce resources has come fully to light as a political issue only comparatively recently. It seems to be clear that if there are to be men in the future, then population growth must be at least curbed and that each individual human being cannot expect to have his life sustained as long as possible by the use of every available technical procedure. Just what sort of policies and practices will be required to cope with these population problems is by no means evident. But a politics of hope is at no disadvantage *vis-à-vis* its competitors in these matters. To the contrary, the conceptual advantages of a politics of hope, as set forth above, commend politics of hope as the most appropriate politics to contend with this urgent, extraordinarily difficult set of issues.

The second sort of consideration which might lead one to question whether a politics of hope can successfully compete against other sorts of politics is more general. It is not without plausibility to suggest that a politics of hope simply makes too many demands on people for them to sustain it for long. More specifically, the durability of politics of hope seems to be threatened from two directions. From within, there is an ineliminable danger that practitioners of hope will 'lose their nerve' and lapse into some less demanding position, whether it be complete or attenuated political fideism, voluntarism, presumption, or despair. Bluntly put, the question here is: In the face of the evidence of history, can one prudently trust that enough people with enough power will risk adopting a politics of hope so that such a politics has a reasonable prospect of success? A politics of hope is also threatened from without. How will its practitioners fare when confronted with the practitioners of competing alternatives? Consider just one aspect of the problem. A politics of hope is unremittingly committed to entertaining seriously criticism from others. Will such criticism not so weaken practitioners of hope in the execution of their policies that they cannot withstand assaults from voluntarists, fideists, cynics, etc.?

Here again, no conclusive arguments on behalf of a politics of hope are available. But persuasive reasons for adopting a politics of hope can be drawn from history. Consider, for example, the widespread penchant for federations, leagues, alliances, negotiations, etc. To be sure, these activities have often been engaged in at the expense of those who did not participate in them. But when evidence of this penchant is coupled with the unprecedented peril of nuclear, chemical, or biological devastation and the new possibilities for communication and interaction, then it is clear that a politics of hope has not already been refuted by history. To the contrary, the security of the conceptual basis of a politics of hope in contrast to that of its competitors counts substantially in its favor. Further, recent history provides examples of practitioners of politics of hope even if it is not explicitly named as such. Consider, for example, the efforts of Dag Hammarskjold, Willy Brandt, and Kenneth Kaunda. Their efforts have not been unmitigatedly successful, but they have been markedly beneficial.[57]

These general considerations admittedly do not satisfy beyond all plausible questioning Merleau-Ponty's tests for a responsible politics. But no political proposal, as Merleau-Ponty himself so well knew, could be conclusively established. Politics cannot live on truths acquired from history, for history yields no such settled truths. The truth of and for politics, as Merleau-Ponty said, consists in nothing but 'the art of inventing what will later appear to have been required by the times.'[58] The proposal of a politics of hope, made against the widely experienced failure of its competitors, expressly and steadfastly seeks to practice such an inventive art.

Nonetheless, the case for politics of hope can still be substantially stengthened. No political proposal arises in a vacuum. Each of them arises in a context of politics already in progress. If a politics of hope such as I have described were to be adopted, then it would lead to significant new ways of understanding long-established central political phenomena and striking recommendations concerning how these phenomena should be lived through. The conceptual and practical innovations which a politics of hope would introduce into these political phenomena provide further persuasive reasons for adopting a politics of hope. They do so both by reason of their own inherent plausibility and, as I will note briefly, by reason of their satisfying deep-seated and long-standing aspirations found in the tradition of Western political thought.[59] The task of the following chapters is to make explicit how my proposal would affect the way in which crucial features of politics are to be understood and appraised. These chapters will both clarify further what a politics of hope is and provide a sufficient basis for appropriate assessment of it.

6
Institutions and power

A politics of hope, springing as it does from the interpretation of man as that sort of being who is relationally free and essentially *en route*, both leads to a distinctive understanding of central political phenomena and provides norms according to which concrete political practice can be guided and assessed. In this chapter, I want to set forth some of its principal implications for how institutions are understood and lived through.[1] The resultant view of institutions in turn casts the matter of power in a new light. A politics of hope takes a view of institutions and power which differs strikingly from the views of both Enlightenment liberalism and standard organization theory. The former take institutions and power to be basically evil, necessary perhaps, but nonetheless evil. The latter tends to take them as essentially beneficient. Though politics of presumption, resignation, and containment take more subtle views of institutions and power than do liberalism and organization theory, their several positions all turn out to be less adequate to the phenomena than that to which a politics of hope gives rise. The task of this chapter is to show just how a politics of hope yields a more appropriate account of institutions and power than its competitors do.

I

Though the term 'institution' is widely used and has a readily recognizable application, it remains rather vague. An institution has been described as a 'standardized mode of behavior' which plays a crucial role in the spatio-temporal constitution of social systems.[2] More fully, 'institution' has been defined as 'the established order by which anything is regulated; system; constitution

. . . ,' as 'an established law, custom, usage, practice, organization, or other element in the political or social life of a people. . . .'³ The term obviously has applications in contexts other than the political, but it is the latter context upon which I will primarily focus.

Whatever vagueness infects this term, two definite characteristics belong to institutions of all sorts, political and otherwise. First, an institution exists to provide both direction and limits to human activity. And second, institutions are not to be identified *simpliciter* with their agents or actions. These two characteristics both provide institutions with their strength and importance and furnish grounds for questions about their essential worth or lack thereof.

Additional clarity concerning the nature of institutions can be gained by taking notice of two of their characteristic functions. First, institutions serve to distinguish an individual within a community by identifying him with a well-defined activity. That is, institutionalized activities are always specialized. Thus one can say: 'Jones is a painter and Smith is a data processor.' This same function of institutions likewise unites all those performing the same activity with one another. Thus: 'We are academicians and they are tradesmen.'

But mere specialization is not enough to constitute institutionalization. The second function of institutions is both to organize these specialized activities and to perpetuate them. As Mikel Dufrenne has seen, the specialized activities

> group the individuals who practice them into certain organisms and, of paramount importance, they are both regulated by certain norms and illustrated by certain models which preexist the individual to which the individual must be *initiated* . . . . Institutionalization consecrates *differentiation*.⁴

Institutions, then, promote and perpetuate activities which serve to unite the individual with some people and to differentiate him from others.

Precisely because the function of institutions is to *initiate* new members into activities whose fundamental pattern is fixed in advance and because the intended outcome of this initiation is to have people organized according to preestablished differentiations, institutions have been extolled by some and excoriated by others. Among the former are exponents of behavioral control, e.g. B.F. Skinner, and systems theoreticians, e.g. Herbert Simon. Prominent among the latter are Jean-Paul Sartre and, at least on occasion, Louis Althusser. Those who esteem freedom only if it is individual and autonomous would also, if they are consistent, have to condemn institutions.

Let me consider first the approach which looks upon institutions with at least distrust and at most hostility. An extreme position of this sort argues that institutions are oppressive by their nature and therefore are essentially inimical to freedom. Althusser presents one striking version of this claim. Institutions, he has said, are the natural homes for ideology. Ideology is an imaginary representation of the people's relations to the conditions of existence. As such, it obstructs freedom and propagates illusion. Institutions embody in their rituals and practices the very forms in which ideology is made concrete. Institutions, then, not only differentiate people from one another. They are also and always instruments of domination.[5]

Sartre's assessment of institutions is both vague and shifting. Several stages of Sartre's political thought can be usefully distinguished. For present purposes I will consider only two of these stages, the first of which coincides with his alignment with the Communists in the early 1950s and the second of which appears in his *Critique de la raison dialectique*.[6]

The earlier phase, represented by the texts of *The Communists and Peace with a reply to Claude Lefort*, presents the Communist Party as itself the working class. The party makes it possible for the worker to be a proletarian. Without the party there is no proletariat. In short, the party is 'the pure and simple incarnation of *praxis*.'[7] The party 'is the *perspective* from which the proletariat can put itself back into society and in its turn take as object those who make an object of it: it is the tradition and the institution.'[8] By implication, of course, all institutions antithetical to the party alienate and indeed enslave the worker who can only remain fundamentally inert when in their grasp.

Merleau-Ponty correctly saw the radical ahistoricality which underlies, and undermines, such a view. This ahistoricality, in turn, rests upon the dualism embodied in Sartre's distinction between the for-itself and the in-itself.[9] In Merleau-Ponty's own words:

> It is precisely that the Party, like the militant, is pure action. If everything comes from freedom, if the workers are nothing, not even proletarians, before they create the Party, the Party rests

on nothing that has been established, not even on their common history.[10]

In effect, Sartre in this phase of his political thought focused so exclusively on pure intentions and bursts of separate and distinct actions that he systematically neglected the intricate connections between present action and the sedimented meanings and efficacy which the present receives from already established institutionalized practice.[11] As Merleau-Ponty put it:

Contrary to appearances, being-for-itself is all Sartre has ever accepted, with its inevitable correlate: pure being-in-itself. . . . All the so-called beings which flutter in the in-between – intentions without subjects, open and dulled meanings – are only statistical entities, 'permanent possibilities' of present thought; they do not have their own energy, they are only something constituted.[12]

On this view of Sartre's, then, history is constituted exclusively by personal, conscious agents.[13] The Communist Party is not, properly speaking, an institution. Rather, it is the agent which effects the transformations in the fundamentally inert worker enmeshed as he is within institutions. These institutions have no genuine efficacy of their own. At most they embody possibilities for action. If anything, they are dangerous, for they tempt one to treat them as though they were or could be efficacious. Thus, they are occasions for mystification.

A later Sartrean view, probably reflecting his response to Merleau-Ponty's criticisms, appears in his *Critique de la raison dialectique (precédé de Question de methode)*.[14] Here one apparently finds something 'in-between' the sheer exhaustive opposition of being-for-itself to being-in-itself. Individuals, he says, are inside a culture and a language, inside a segment of the field of instruments.[15] And, he continues:

Because we are men and because we live in the world of men, of work, and of conflicts, all the objects which surround us are signs. . . . Thus significations come from man and from his project, but they are inscribed everywhere in things and in the order of things. Everything at every instant is always signifying, and significations reveal to us men and relations among men across *the structures of our society*.[16]

Apparently, there is room for efficacious institutions. But Sartre immediately adds: 'But these significations appear to us only insofar as we ourselves are signifying.'[17]

Thus some remarks of Sartre's notwithstanding, there is good reason to claim that Sartre's *Critique* fails to avoid falling into an unhistorical, nonsocial account of social and historical phenomena.[18] But more to the present point are his reflections on these 'statements of society' across which men are revealed. Particular cultures and systems, he says, are manifestations of alienation.[19] These structures, these constructions without authors, he says, function by way of a counterfinality which imposes itself upon alienated men and against which they must struggle.[20]

Thus even when Sartre does acknowledge the efficacy of institutions, he takes their efficacy to be malignant. Man, at least as long as he is alienated, confronts institutions against which he must wrestle. Institutions by their very nature, on this view, tend to deflect his free projects into results which are either unanticipated or at least elude his full control.

Much the same conclusion follows from Sartre's analysis of groups. The only sort of group whose members can be totally self-responsible, totally autonomous, is the group in fusion. Only this sort of group avoids imposing constraints upon its members. The other sorts of groups, pledged groups and serial groupings, are degradations, conceptually if not temporally, from groups in fusion. Unlike groups in fusion which are wholly independent of institutions, these other forms of groups are essentially implicated with institutions. That is, they either devise, or maintain, or spring from institutions. But institutions, inasmuch as they organize people according to preestablished differentiations and initiate newcomers into the group's activities according to previously devised norms and models, necessarily run counter to all tendencies to fusion and thus counter to all tendencies to autonomy. If autonomy is, as Sartre takes it to be, the primary characteristic and measure of freedom, then institutions are necessarily antithetical to maximal freedom.[21] At best, an institution could be beneficial if it could undercut more oppressive institutions and so tend toward negating the efficacy of any institution.[22]

Attacks on institutions as enemies of freedom are not necessarily confined to those who, like Sartre and Althusser, have links of one sort or another with Marxism. The radical basis for such attacks rests in any version of the doctrine of autonomous freedom. Belief in standard Enlightenment values has tended to be articulated in such a way that dedication to these values is finally incompatible with the acknowledgment of the intrinsic positive worth of any institution *qua* institution.

If one recalls, for example, the doctrine of freedom set forth by P.H. Partridge and discussed above in Chapter 4, one recalls that freedom is said to rule out coercion. And coercion, on this doctrine, does not consist exclusively in prohibitions and commands enforced by sanctions. Even indirect forms of control are regarded as coercive. That is, if anyone shapes or manipulates the conditions which determine or affect the alternatives available to others, he is said to coerce them.

Institutions clearly serve to shape the alternatives available to people. Through their agents they guide and, when circumstances require, goad people into compliance with their objectives. On the view of freedom enunciated by Partridge, then, there can be no intrinsic positive worth to institutions. Whatever worth they could have could only be instrumental.

The basic criticism to which these views of institutions, whether of liberal or Marxist lineage, are vulnerable is that they are ultimately ahistorical and thus excessively formal and abstract.[23] They all presuppose a radical opposition between an agent who either is or should be radically context-independent and an inert matter which either is or ideally should be totally compliant with the intentions and motives of the agent. They all effectively deny genuine interplay between the agent and its Other. All positive efficacy is one-directional. Whatever modifies the outcome of the agent's exertions is to be accounted ultimately as loss. These views of institutions ultimately depend, in one fashion or another, upon a doctrine of autonomous freedom. But inasmuch as that doctrine has been shown in Chapter 4 to be fatally flawed, then the views of institutions resting on it have been undercut and should be replaced.

A second, no more acceptable way of construing and assessing institutions is that which holds that institutions can and should be developed which preempt and render inoperative human freedom. Dostoyevski, in *The Brothers Karamazov*, has presented one version of this alternative account. The Grand Inquisitor is the agent of an institution, the Roman Church, which explicitly – according to the story – sets out to relieve men of the burden of their freedom. By supplying them with dogmas, it releases them from the task of thinking for themselves. By promulgating and enforcing a code of conduct, it releases them from the burden of deciding how they shall act. Even if the agents, the Inquisitors, must suffer the anguish of freedom, the institution they serve spares the masses of men this suffering. On this view, freedom is a reality, but a painful, ruinous one. Institutions can and should assuage or remove this pain, at least for most people.[24]

A second version of this exaltation of institutions, a version which can be called the technocratic version, regards freedom as either an illusion or simply another name for disorganization. The behaviorism of a B.F. Skinner and the organization theory of a Herbert Simon are two conceptually compatible expressions of this version. Here I will focus upon Simon's position. His position shares a view of institutions widely held in modern social science. This science understands 'institutions as patterns of action, which shape how men behave, and either frustrate or facilitate their purposes. But it cannot look upon them in an expressive dimension, as embodying certain conceptions or a certain quality of life.'[25]

For Simon, the man who is not incorporated into organizations or institutions is hopelessly confused by the rush of events. He has neither the knowledge with which to make intelligent choices nor the foresight with which to anticipate their consequences. By contrast, organization takes human limitations and disorganization as it finds them and rearranges their constituent components (skills, desires, bodily conditions, etc.) so that rational decision and action result. The organization defines the individual's functions and duties, specifies limits to his choices, and shapes his attitudes so that he has a sense of belonging to the whole. A fundamental task of the organization or institution is to adapt individuals to its requirements.[26] The point of organization is to achieve efficiency. And efficiency consists in having its members make those decisions and undertake those actions which best serve the ends and needs of the organization.[27] As Simon puts it, in words already quoted in Chapter 3 above:

> Human rationality, then, gets its higher goals and integrations from the institutional setting in which it operates and by which it is moulded. . . . The rational individual is and must be an organized and institutionalized individual.[28]

Both versions, the Inquisitor's and the technocrat's, of the effort to promote institutions and their programs in such a way that freedom is either diminished or eliminated, are fundamentally incompatible with responsible politics. On the one hand, endeavors of this sort lead logically to an endorsement of tyranny or totalitarianism. The managers, to be maximally efficient, would have to arrogate all initiative to themselves. If the managed are to be permitted any discretion or leeway, it must always be according to the terms set by the managers regardless of the concurrence or nonconcurrence of the managed. Such an arrangement is, as many of its proponents explicitly acknowledge, essentially antipolitical. To urge a community to adopt organizational rationality as its ultimate objective is to urge it to repudiate politics. But the repudiation of politics is hardly responsible politics.

On the other hand, and at least equally pertinent, is the fact that the endeavor to replace personal discretion with institutional efficiency cannot in practice be achieved without stultification. Either the organization's engineers must remain independent of institutional control or the pattern of the organization's activities becomes essentially unalterable. Whatever alterations would take place would have to be, by hypothesis, alterations fully prescribed by previously established patterns.

So long as the organization's engineers remain independent of the institution, then their personal discretion remains, at least potentially, dysfunctional to the announced objectives of organizational efficiency. But unless they are independent, then they cannot perform any nontrivial engineering innovations. They could at best be only maintenance men.

If, however, organizational efficiency could eliminate independent engineers, then there would be no source for innovation. The sole rational justification for the elimination of innovation would be that the present condition is exhaustively appropriate to the requirements of human existence. In effect, this sort of justification would have to insist upon the actual occurrence of both complete speech and perfect action. Complete speech is speech which brings to a close all need for any speech which does not essentially say the same thing. Perfect action is action which would make pointless any action which is not essentially repetitive or derivative.

But if, as I have shown in Chapters 3 and 4 above, man is indeed one who is thoroughly historical, one who is essentially *en route*, then complete speech and perfect action are impossible. Any quest for them is necessarily vain. One is thus led to conclude that the unqualified goal of maximal organizational efficiency, understood as that which is inversely related to personal initiative, is itself irrational. Either it is doomed because it must leave room for tyrannical engineers – benevolent or otherwise – who retain their own discretion if it is to be protected against ossification. Or, in its apparent success, it would require people to live out the pretense that the essentially unachievable complete speech and perfect action had somehow been achieved. The same set of objections, *mutatis mutandis*, weigh against the doctrine of the Grand Inquisitor. His doctrine expressly aims to propagate an illusion by which the many are to be pacified. The clear recognition of their thorough mystification is the source of his own satisfaction, a satisfaction which cannot be as untroubled as theirs. The Grand Inquisitor's program must stop short of including himself. Thus it cannot be a thoroughgoing program. Its limits are irremovable.

In summary, when one takes the requirements of institutions to be essentially antithetical to those of personal freedom and initiative and then attempts to choose between their competing demands, one runs aground. Whether, like Simon, one favors institutional efficiency at the expense of personal initiative or, like Sartre, favors personal initiative, one cannot consistently apply one's position without doing damage to the sensefulness of that very same position. The Sartrean position in its antiinstitutionalism tends to undercut the enduring efficacy of free action. Simon's position tends toward organizational self-stultification.

This impasse prompts one to search for some understanding of institutions and their relations to individual free persons which does not lead to the conclusion that they are essentially inimical to one another. Merleau-Ponty, among others, provides important leads toward an appropriate alternative view. These leads can be developed in terms of the politics of hope I have articulated above in such a way that both the conceptual impasse is broken and norms are ascertained concerning how individuals and institutions can fruitfully interact.

II

Merleau-Ponty's contribution to the appropriate understanding of institutions and their efficacy most obviously consists in his critique of that 'Manichean' view of institutions which would take them to be essentially malignant. His own assessment of institutions, as was briefly noted in Chapter 2, is to be read as an outgrowth of his reflection on social and political matters in terms of the interplay between *langue*, i.e. the set of sedimented background conditions which provides the resources for discourse and action, and *parole*, i.e. the actual initiating performance bringing these resources into fresh realization. With specific reference to Sartre, though his argument could be just as readily addressed to Althusser or to the standard liberal, Merleau-Ponty emphasizes that even though social 'things' or institutions can and often do degrade people, they do not necessarily do so. Institutions do not rise over and against man from some alien source. They are all man-made. 'Man,' he says, 'is everywhere, inscribed on all the walls and in all the social apparatuses made by him. Men can see nothing about them that is not in their image. . . . Everything speaks to them of themselves.'[29] Institutions, then, like all human achievements, are intersubjectively constituted. They are thoroughly historical and so perpetually permeable to new initiatives.

On the basis of this recognition Merleau-Ponty proposes an alternative concept of institutions. He writes:

> What we understand by the concept of institution are those events in experience which endow it [experience] with durable dimensions, in relation to which a whole series of other experiences will acquire meaning, will form an intelligible series or a history – or again those events which sediment in me a meaning, not just as survivals or residues, but as the invitation to a sequel, the necessity of a future.[30]

Institutions, then, do not necessarily alienate men either from themselves or from one another. Rather, they are 'the consequences and the guarantee of our belonging to a common world.'[31]

On Merleau-Ponty's account, institutions are not merely the result, the residue of past action. They are necessary mediations which allow people to see that their efforts can be genuinely efficacious.[32] It is through institutions that power is amassed and distributed as well as that power can be circumscribed.[33] Institutions, then, are neither necessarily inert nor do they necessarily induce inertia in their members. They predelineate the future and furnish the frame of reference for present and future human performances. But further, they themselves give rise to and sustain searches which inevitably lead to their own transformation. Rather than being mere constraints, institutions can and do prod people to undertake innovations which transcend the already sedimented institutions.[34]

Merleau-Ponty manages this critique of the Manichean view of institutions without falling into the trap which ensnares those who would replace personal initiative with institutional controls. Institutions, he emphasizes, make sense only in concert with personal initiative. Just as a language without fresh speech is one which is dead and one whose possibilities are not fully exploited, so too would be institutions not invigorated by personal initiative.

This initiative, it must be stressed, is not that by which the efficacy of institutions is eluded. It is precisely that by which their efficacy is maintained and fostered. Thus, initiative is not unqualifiedly opposed to institutions. It is that by which institutions themselves may flourish precisely as institutions. Institutions which set out to eliminate all initiative cannot fully succeed except at the cost of their own ossification. But such ossification is, as was shown above, devoid of rational justification.

Merleau-Ponty's assessment of institutions resembles in striking respects the position hinted at by Alasdair MacIntyre in *After Virtue*. MacIntyre there expresses approval of 'John Anderson's insight – a Sophoclean insight – that it is through conflict and sometimes only through conflict that we learn what our ends and purposes are.'[35] The conflict in question here is precisely that between the institution and the individual agent. This conflict, for Anderson and MacIntyre, plays a vital role in educating the individual to a self-knowledge that is no mere induction into institutional practices. It is education to a genuinely liberating self-knowledge.

At the same time, MacIntyre stresses that both individual and social practices always have histories. They all belong to a tradition and it is through these traditions that particular practices are transmitted. 'A living tradition,' he writes, 'then is an historically extended, socially embodied argument precisely in part about the goods which constitute that tradition.'[36] Tradition and its institutions for transmitting practices do not, therefore, unequivocally impede personal initiative. They are necessarily required if particular personal initiatives are to make sense.

These clues toward a more appropriate understanding and assessment of institutions provided by Merleau-Ponty and MacIntyre can be profitably developed by linking them with the interpretation of man, the political actor, as one who is essentially *en route*. Such a man is always involved in institutions. He is born into them and is reared in and through them.[37] Without institutions, a man's thought, speech, and conduct cannot have meaning and direction.

But these institutions do not definitively fix men either in one place or on some fully determinate course. He is always *en route*. As such, he eludes total institutional domination. He modifies both himself and the institutions he inhabits. This two-fold modification is unavoidable so long as he lives. It may be reduced to near vanishing. But it cannot be annihilated. What a person says or does, then, gains at least part of its sense (*sens*) from the fact that it modifies the context in which subsequent sayings and doings will take place.

If man is, as I claim, essentially *en route*, then he cannot rationally aspire either to independence from institutions or to an institutional arrangement designed to eliminate his initiative. The achievement of either of these goals, if such an achievement were possible, would effectively eliminate man's routedness. It would, therefore, effectively eliminate man. It would be tantamount to homicide – suicidal or murderous or both. To be a man, then, is to be one who inhabits institutions in such a way that he preserves them even while transforming them through his own initiative.

If man's essential characteristic of being *en route* is understood in terms of relational freedom, then further clarification of the sense and possibilities of institutions can be achieved. Human freedom essentially involves the capacity to join with other men in common enterprises. Institutions both make possible this joining and can expand the scope and quality of these enterprises. In Anthony Giddens's terms, institutions embody resources as well as rules.[38]

Institutions, to borrow a distinction from Paul Ricoeur, move people from situations to a world.[39] Situations are such that a person's effective involvement with others is limited to those others with whom he can have face-to-face contact with some regularity. In and through institutions, he can be effectively involved with contemporaries whom he never directly encounters. He can, in fact, be effectively involved with both predecessors and descendants.

This involvement with others in virtue of institutions, when understood in terms of relational freedom with its corresponding emphasis on the polar character of the individual, does not amount to absorption into mere moments of institutional functioning. Institutions can be assessed and wrestled with by their own members. They can be judged not only in terms of their efficacy but also in terms of their greater or lesser contribution to the relational freedom of their participants. And their participants can act upon these assessments.[40]

Institutions, of course, continue to function according to their own rhythms across the performances of the several people who participate in it. But because institutions are permeable to the endeavors of its participants, then one can appropriately speak of both individual and collective responsibility.[41] On the one hand, whatever the institutional configuration, its members, taken singly, are not absolved from exercising individual discretion. On the other hand, the specific way in which an institution bears upon either outsiders – and all of its participants are in some respects nonetheless its outsiders – and upon new members is the responsibility of its participants who have endowed it with the determinate characteristics which it has.

When the tension constitutive of relational freedom, the tension between maintaining one's individuality and engaging in common enterprises, is interpreted in terms of hope, then one gains a still further refined view of institutions and their possibilities.

If freedom is essentially intersubjective and if institutions are inevitable, then how does one assess this two-fold necessity? If one interprets freedom in terms of hope rather than in terms of presumption, resignation, or containment, then one's application of institutions and their operations is significantly modified. Among the important consequences are the following. First, it can then make sense to be a career military man, a clergyman, or a career civil servant. But those who assume these roles, if they do so in hope, do not regard themselves as having achieved independence from others. They assume these roles in the hope that the institutions they serve remain pertinent to the entire human community. This pertinence is often indirect but it is nonetheless nontrivial. In dedicating themselves to the tasks of one institution, they still recognize that they themselves as individuals and the institutions they serve belong to and have responsibilities in a broader context. They see that their roles in their institution make full sense only in the light of the interaction between other institutions and their own.

Second, the hopeful institutional agent looks to those to whom he ministers for either confirmation or criticism both of his own efforts and of the appropriateness of the institutional arrangements. He does not renounce his own judgment. But he shapes it in constant conjunction with the judgments of others. Thus, the hopeful agent never presumes that he needs no critiques from others.

Third, recipients of institutional ministrations who live in hope attend both to the strength and fragility of the institution and accept responsibility for its maintenance and modification. They neither vainly seek to extricate themselves from all institutional ministrations nor inertly acquiesce in the ministrations brought to bear upon them.

Fourth, and most generally, those who live out their relational freedom in hope, whether as agents or recipients of institutional ministrations, regard the inevitability of institutions as fundamentally an opportunity for freedom rather than as either handicap or a mere temporary expedient. This approach eschews the twin utopian visions of totally noninstitutional life and of life perfectly structured by perfect institutions. Men of hope take institutions and their inevitability as an unending source of opportunity, regardless of the perils with which every particular involvement with institutions is necessarily linked. The man of hope, who always accepts his *routedness* as that which can have no ideal terminus – whether of all-sense or of no-sense – lives then in permanent harmony-strife with the institutions which both allow him to be and threaten to cancel his being. But this is also the way in which he lives with nature. Institutions, then, of themselves, neither damn him nor redeem him. They are, rather, 'Other-selves' with whom he wrestles so as to be a self at all.

This view of institutions thus denies that freedom and institutions are essentially antithetical to one another. Rather, at bottom they presuppose one another. Obviously, the consequences of this view for a proper understanding and assessment of politics are substantial. Whether William Blackstone's remark that England is a land 'in which political or civil liberty is the very end and scope of the constitution.'[42] were in fact true or not, it was a reasonable hope, not a utopian impossibility. Though it is not, on my interpretation, a condition which can be definitively guaranteed, it is the reasonable objective of a task which is in principle unending.

A capital consequence of this view of institutions for which I am arguing is that there cannot be any institution which is in all respects preeminent over all other institutions. A responsible politics will have to acknowledge this fact both in its discourse and in its practical arrangements. A responsible politics will sustain and defend nonpolitical institutions even when these institutions limit the scope and efficacy of political institutions themselves. It will do so precisely to preserve that permeability of its own institutions to criticism and influence from extrapolitical sources. Such permeability is necessary if the political institutions themselves are to remain capable of coping with historical changes.[43]

At the same time, however, a responsible politics will not allow its own institutions to be dominated by other sorts of institutions. For example, responsible politics will never let its institutions be dominated by institutions embodying and expressing religious doctrines or scientific theories and research programs. Whatever the merits and achievements of any institution of any other sort, a responsible politics will refuse to accord it unqualified primacy and will institutionalize that refusal.

My interpretatation of the relation of politics to other domains of human activity is closely akin to the view Hannah Arendt ascribes to Pericles. The Periclean view, she says, in effect holds that:

> it is the polis, the realm of politics, which sets limits to the love of wisdom and of beauty, and since we know that the Greeks thought it was the polis and 'politics' (and by no means superior artistic achievements) which distinguished them from the barbarians, we must conclude that this difference was a 'cultural' difference as well . . . a different attitude toward beauty and wisdom, which could be loved only within the limits set by the institution of the polis.[44]

Thus, for example, a responsible politics would resist both the claims of a purportedly scientific socialism whose governmental institutions would fully control all other institutions and those of a self-certified theocracy which would subject all other institutions to complete regulation by a religious agency supposedly fulfilling a divine mandate.[45]

A politics of hope, in summary, recognizes that man who is *en route* must fashion and live through institutions of several different sorts. These institutions are necessary to the efficacy of his initiatives. Indeed, a politics of hope esteems the existence of institutions distinct from politics. Such a politics neither seeks to abolish the fact that there are institutions of various sorts nor does it entertain the illusion of 'transparent' institutions, institutions which do not affect the efficacy of personal initiatives.

A responsible politics likewise recognizes that no institution can be perfect, that every institution is finite and conditioned by the historical circumstances – both material and cultural – in which it operates. Thus, one must acknowledge, to paraphrase the classical Lutheran dictum, that all institutions, political or otherwise, are always in need of reform.[46] A responsible politics does not presume to instigate these reforms in nonpolitical institutions. But it protects the opportunity for such reforms. And a responsible politics is perpetually attentive to the need to reform its own institutions.

Thus a politics of hope, as a responsible politics, recognizes that institutions cannot redeem men either from their freedom or from their finitude. But institutions can enhance the efficacy of finite human freedom. Therein lies their sense and justification. The necessity that there be institutions with their correlative necessary insufficiency does not, primarily, burden men with handicaps. Rather it constitutes opportunities. The opportunities are always risk-laden, but they are nonetheless opportunities. These opportunities are among the noblest available to man *en route* inasmuch as they allow him to achieve an efficacy which outlasts his own lifespan.

A politics of hope trusts both that every man, in principle, can contribute something of worth to the development and maintenance of at least some institutions and that every man can benefit from at least some opportunities sustained by institutions. These contributions can come not only from the apparent leaders. The apparent followers, too, have a contribution to make. Thus, at least in principle, one man's achievement is not necessarily won at the expense of another man's impotence. At least in principle, efficacy is not a zero-sum game. It is precisely the objective of a politics of hope to provide for institutions which foreswear zero-summing. Tendencies towards zero-summing are, on this view, far from rational. They are, in fact, perversions. Cooperation, and not competition, is the essential objective of politics, both for its rulers and for its ruled. Since this is the case, then a politics of hope introduces subtle but crucial changes in both the understanding and the practice of ruling and being ruled.

Implicit in the view of institutions embodied in a politics of hope is the claim that power and its exercise are not antithetical to freedom. If any politics, including a politics of hope, is to be genuinely efficacious, then it must amass and wield power. But here again the understanding and the assessment of power and its use which follows from a politics of hope is distinct in important respects from that connected with its competitors.

In this next section I will limit myself to some general remarks about the connection between institutions and power. These remarks will be given greater specificity in Chapters 7 and 8. In these latter chapters, power will be dealt with in the especially distinctive forms in which it appears in politics.

III

Because institutions exist in time and space, they necessarily involve power. An adequate account of institutions, then, requires both that one incorporate temporality into one's understanding of human agency and that one recognize that power is integral to the constitution of social practices.[47] And, as Kenneth Schmitz has seen, this link between power and institutions does not necessarily impinge upon freedom. Rather it makes possible an enhancement of freedom. In Schmitz's words:

> Although history and experience provide many illustrations of a tendency among institutions to encroach upon power that may not be theirs, in their better moments they do not escape their nature which is to obey the discipline of power. For although the actuality of the institution is the measure of its power, institutional power by its nature is not only or even principally the power of physical force. Institutional power is social, the power to move individuals, to defend the institution and society, and to co-operate [sic] with individuals, with other institutions, and with the larger society itself. An institution is a social means towards the discipline of power in its raw physical form, and in

that discipline it must meet the expectations of the community in general.[48]

Not all power, of course, is institutional power. But institutions devoid of power are chimeras. This is most obviously true in the case of political institutions.

The term 'power' has been used in many different senses. Here I will use D.H. Wrong's definition: 'Power is the capacity of some persons to produce intended and foreseen effects on others.'[49] Power:

> has three dimensions: it is *extensive* if the complying Bs [the power subjects] are many; it is *comprehensive* if the variety of actions to which A [the power holder] can move the Bs is considerable; finally it is *intensive* if the bidding of A can be pushed far without loss of compliance.[50]

And the exercise of power takes on numerous forms, ranging from persuasion to manipulation to force.[51] Or, to put the matter another way, power subjects comply with advice or commands of power holders for a variety of reasons. The two distinctive bases of political power are (a) legitimacy, 'in which the power holder possesses an acknowledged *right to command* and the power subject an acknowledged obligation to obey,'[52] and (b) coerciveness, i.e. the capacity and willingness of the power holder to use physical or psychological force to gain compliance from their subjects. Though these two bases are conceptually distinct, in practice they are always intermingled.[53] These two bases of political power do not preclude the existence of other sorts of power, e.g. charisma, competence, etc., either in politics or in other domains of human activity. But legitimacy and coerciveness are irreplaceable for politics.[54]

He who understands that man is essentially *en route* and seeks to practice a politics of hope does not decry the ineradicability of power from politics. He recognizes that, if all men were in all relevant respects the same, power perhaps could not be justified. But all communities, including all political communities, are composed of individuals of varying ages, states of health, records of achievement, etc. In short, all communities are finite and historical. Since this is so, then not only is the possibility of power ineliminable but power is indeed necessary if human freedom and activity is to have enduring efficacy. If men are to be able to develop their own proposals and projects within a context of other persons each of whom contributes in his own way to a common good which they share and which sustains the efficacy of individual endeavors, then there must be political institutions. There must be, as Charles Sherover says,

> a state, an organization of the whole, that presumes the reality of time and thereby is open to the unveiling of new possibilities that *cannot* be deductively forecast. Only a forward-looking temporality that is open to presently unforeseen possibility can offer us maximation of freedom accordant with changing problems, developing needs and novel opportunities. We require organized social prescription and direction precisely because we are not able to do, each for himself, what we can do together.[55]

This 'social prescription and direction' would be idle unless sufficient power were amassed and wielded to insure that conflicts would be reconciled while at the same time providing opportunities for change. In short, no society can function as a free society 'without a time-oriented set of institutionalizations which allow and encourage an openness to the future'[56] by means of the specific concrete activities whose exercise it both protects and enjoins. Power, then, is by no means without risk, but its riskiness is of a piece with that of the human condition itself.

A politics of hope does not, however, merely require that the inevitability of power be recognized. It understands the possibility of power to be a blessing, but, like all things, a risky blessing. It recognizes the need to struggle with power for proper power and accordingly furnishes recommendations and cautions concerning the amassing and wielding of power. The guidance it gives is quite distinct from that provided by its proximate competitors, namely politics of presumption, resignation, and containment.

A politics of hope distinguishes, as Schmitz does, political and social power from physical force. Political power cannot be dealt with exhaustively in quantitative terms. Political power relationships, then, cannot be properly construed in terms of a zero-sum game, a game in which every increment of power of any sort for one party necessarily involves a commensurate loss of power of some sort for another party. But even if power relationships do not constitute a zero-sum game, a politics of hope still recognizes that the power of one party can be and at times has been increased at the expense of another. What distinguishes the approach to power in a politics of hope is its insistence that, though increases in power can weaken others, they need not necessarily do so. Power always poses a threat to freedom. But it is also necessary for freedom.[57]

A politics of presumption fails to take seriously the riskiness of power. Though it recognizes political power's contribution to the efficacy of human effort, it fails to appreciate the threat posed by that power. 'The instinct of growth,' de Jouvenel points out, 'is proper to Power; it is a part of its essence and does not change with its changing forms.'[58] And this tendency to grow, in turn, tends to be at the expense of some others.[59] A politics of presumption is blind to this aspect of power. It unquestioningly adopts the view that increases of power for one party necessarily either trickle down to empower all the others or at least do not debilitate the others. Such a politics, then, is blind to the ineliminable threat of absolutism resident in every amassing and wielding of power. It can therefore provide at best only a fragile bulwark against the ever-present dangers of tyranny and totalitarianism.

Politics of resignation and politics of containment, on the other hand, are both keenly aware of the risky character of all changes in power. What they fail to see is the possibility that some growth of power for one party can enhance the efficacy, can empower, all. Both of these sorts of politics implicitly interpret power relationships in terms of a zero-game. Practitioners of politics of either of these sorts take their fellow practitioners to be fundamentally competitors for a fixed stock of power. What one gains necessarily subtracts from what another can gain. Practitioners of politics of resignation expect eventually to lose the game. Practitioners of politics of containment do not concede the game but aim at most for a stalemate. Either of these sorts of politics can be adopted by either power holders or power subjects. And they can be adopted in either domestic or international politics.

The fundamentally negative assessment of power and changes in power resident in both of these latter sorts of politics blinds their practitioners to power's place in the spread and enhancement of efficacious human freedom. This blindness tends to turn the practice of politics of these sorts into self-fulfilling prophecies. That is, nothing is attempted which could enhance the power of all because there is no hope for a success of this sort. As a consequence, only

143

those practices and policies are adopted which aim ahead of time at adjustments in the distribution of quantifiable might. Both of these sorts of politics in effect either cling to or seek some *status quo*. But the finitude and temporality of all human endeavors perpetually tends to undercut the *status quo* and therefore to destabilize such politics. Politics of both these sorts, by casting some people into the role of perpetual opponents, tend to provoke revolutions against them. Therefore they invite anarchy and the prospect of tyranny which lurks in anarchy's wake.

A politics of hope recognizes that since there must be institutions, then there must be power. But like the institutions themselves, particular configurations of power are temporal and finite. Both by reason of the vicissitudes of natural forces and through the impact of historical agencies, there will necessarily be changes in the configurations of power.[60] There is risk in these changes, but there is also opportunity. Exercises of power can and should aim to transform the relationship between power holders and power subjects from being a relationship to subordination into one of coordination, of reciprocal power sharing. Performances of the 'power holder' are legitimate only if they are compatible with the eliciting of genuine initiative from the 'power subject.' This goal of the exercise of political power, for a politics of hope, has been nicely expressed by Sherover. 'The power of the whole,' he says, 'when effectively used, pluralizes the sources of power, checks tendencies to tyranny by any group, and gives every citizen a vested interest in maintaining the dynamic of a free society.'[61] And, one should add, the power of a part, when effectively used, establishes and maintains the power of the whole.

This aim of political power has important consequences for how power is to be amassed and wielded within the political domain and for how political power is to interact with nonpolitical institutions and powers. Within the political domain, practitioners of a politics of hope must constantly seek to bring new members into the ranks of political actors. Because each person or group is always limited in insight, strength, and lifespan, there is always need to seek new recruits who are not merely subjects but are actual sharers in power. Newcomers, whether they be the young, the previously excluded, or the previously uninvolved, are to be actively solicited.[62]

In a politics of hope, however, the solicitation of newcomers does not spring exclusively or even preeminently from an awareness or fear of weakness. Rather, it springs from a two-fold confidence. On the one hand, the 'oldtimers' are confident that what they and their predecessors have already achieved politically can be and deserves to be prolonged, even if it must be modified to fit future exigencies. On the other hand, they regard the newcomers as those by whom this prolongation is to be accomplished, even if the newcomers give a distinctive cast to what they inherit. Institutions and institutional power, for a politics of hope, aim precisely for this 'preservation with a difference.' Practices and policies inconsistent with such an objective are unacceptable for a politics of hope. Such a politics does not construe the relationship between power holders or old-timers and power subjects or newcomers in terms of the Machiavellian poles of love and fear.[63] For a politics of hope, newcomers are above all to be respected. This respect is for both their newness and for the strength they can bring to the prized old.

For much the same reasons, institutionally sanctioned power holders in a politics of hope must always stand ready to acknowledge and respect the political power of charismatic leaders who arise apart from established institutional practice. These power holders realize clearly that every form of power of any significant scope or intensity tends to degenerate into the merely routine.[64] Charismatics, in a politics of hope, are appreciated for the revitalization which they can bring to stable institutions and exercises of institutional power.

But here again, there is no craven collapse in the face of the charismatic. The charismatic is not simply to be followed. He is to be accepted as an esteemed partner in the political discourse. In this respect, as in others, a politics of hope of the sort I am proposing satisfies the standard for a responsible politics set forth by Thomas Flynn in his perceptive critique of Sartre's political thought. As Flynn says:

> It is difficult to understand how the society Sartre advocates can exist solely on intrinsically evidential situations. The friendship and communion he prizes are themselves the fruit of fidelity-trust relations. . . . Rather than speak of command-obedience, therefore, we should refer to fidelity-trust. . . . Here as elsewhere, Sartre's 'angelism' demands the rational, when the reasonable is what we require.[65]

Similarly a politics of hope requires that a politics rejoice that not all institutions are political institutions and therefore that not all power is political power. Since power relationships do not necessarily constitute a zero-sum game, there is no necessary antagonism or opposition between political and nonpolitical power. In its full recognition of the finitude, historicality and intersubjectivity which are constitutive of the human condition, practitioners of responsible politics recognize that there is no one type of discourse – political, religious, artistic, scientific, etc. – which renders other types of discourse idle. A politics of hope acknowledges this fact with courage and confidence. It recognizes the possibility that each type of discourse can nourish the other types and seeks to actualize this possibility. A politics of hope, then, regards these multiple sources of power as capable of coordination and mutual support. This coordination and support is never to be taken for granted. It is always at risk. But it is always a reasonable objective.

Nonetheless, even if a politics of hope seeks to convert the opposition between power holders and power subjects into an interplay of power shares, it remains the case that there is no genuine politics devoid of command-obedience relations. There is no politics unless there are at least occasional occupants of the roles of ruler and ruled. A politics of hope acknowledges this essential feature of politics. But again, it provides a different interpretation of this phenomenon than that provided by its competitors. Resident in this distinctive interpretation are normative considerations concerning how the relationship between ruler and ruled is to be lived out. The next two chapters will spell out this interpretation.

7
Authority, sovereignty, and coercion

Bertrand de Jouvenel has aptly observed that two preoccupations obsess those who reflect seriously on politics. Such thinkers regularly seek to provide for (a) a legitimate supreme authority, a sovereign, who (b) nonetheless must not command anything which is not legitimate.[1] This search springs from the realization that exercises of power, even if they can and should aim to bring about general power sharing, often issue rather in domination-subjugation. Exercises of power, then, are always risky. But since there is no politics without power, a major task for political philosophy is to specify how this riskiness is to be managed, to specify what is to count as a responsible exercise of risky power.

Attempts to discharge this task have for obvious reasons long focused on the topics of authority, sovereignty, and coercion. These three are properly regarded as elements essential to political rulership. But there has been perennial debate concerning the origin, sense, and rational justification of these elements. In this chapter I will examine each of them and show how a politics of hope both clarifies them and provides distinctive guidance for their practical manifestations.

I

Though he himself does not seem to be particularly cognizant of just what is at stake, the opening lines of Leibniz's 'Portrait of the prince' nicely show how complex and problematic the issues of authority, sovereignty, and coercion are. He writes:

Since the order of the states is founded on the authority of those

147

who govern them, and on the dependence of peoples, nature, which destines men for civil life, causes them to be born with different qualities, some to command, others to obey, so that the power of sovereigns in monarchies and the inequality of those who command and those who obey in republics, are founded no less in nature than in law, and in virtue than in fortune; thus princes must be above their subjects by their virtue, and by their natural qualities, as they are above them by the authority which the laws give them to reign according to natural law and civil law. . . . It may happen, however, that though nature wishes that those to whom she has given many great qualities and who have the most virtue always rule over others, the laws of many states ordain, on the contrary, that children be the heirs of the goods and of the power of their fathers, because, as a result of the prudence of legislators and of human weakness, the civil law is often contrary to the natural law. . . . Indeed one cannot question the authority which virtue and merit give even those men [who are] without position and without [official] dignity in a republic. Scipio is a fine example of this. . . . No one is unaware, either, of the force of laws which have caused so many bad princes to reign, without any other support than that of the laws. One must, for all that, grant that the struggle of nature against the laws and of virtue against fortune, has often troubled the calm of their states, and caused revolutions in monarchies. . . . It is necessary, then, that the dominance of princes be equally based on the advantages of nature, on virtue, and on the laws, to bring an end to the struggle of virtue and of merit against the laws and against fortune, in order to assure the public tranquility, and to avoid being exposed to the effects of the power of virtue, which has so often triumphed over legitimate power.[2]

Let me consider first the matter of authority. Where authority comes from and just how a person comes to hold authority are questions with a long history.[3] The just cited remarks of Leibniz indicate that a number of different sources of authority, having no necessary connection with one another, have been proposed. A major task, then, is to prevent competition among persons holding authority under different titles. If there is to be no struggle among multiple claimants to authority, Leibniz says, then the dominance of princes must be based equally on laws, virtue, and nature. Leibniz himself apparently assigns preeminence to the legal source of authority. Part of Scipio's merit seems to consist in his refusal to challenge the legally established authority. But the preeminence of the legal is not, for Leibniz, an unqualified preeminence.

Leibniz, of course, has not been alone in his recognition of multiple sources of authority or in his effort to rank them. Max Weber's distinction of three types of authority, namely legal-rational, charismatic, and traditional authority, has become classic.[4] Recently, Dennis Wrong has spoken of five forms of authority, coercive authority, authority by inducement, legitimate authority, competent authority, and personal authority.[5]

Along with efforts to classify different sorts of authority, there have been persistent attempts to rank these sorts. Considerable contemporary discussion of this latter question has been conducted in terms of a distinction between what has been called *de jure* authority and *de facto* authority. Notwithstanding the merits of other classifications, for purposes of showing the implications of a politics of hope for the question of political authority, it is advantageous to focus on this latter distinction.

A helpful point of departure is the symposium on authority presented by R.S. Peters and Peter Winch.[6] Peters in his contribution draws attention to the difference between Hobbes's view of authority and that of de Jouvenel. In *Leviathan*, Hobbes says: 'By authority, is always understood a right of doing any act; and done by authority, done by commission, or license, from him whose right it is.'[7] De Jouvenel, by contrast, says:

> Society in fact exists only because man is capable of proposing and affecting by his proposals another's dispositions; it is by the acceptance of proposals that contracts are clinched, disputes settled and alliances formed between individuals. . . . What I mean by 'authority' is the ability of a man to get his proposals accepted.[8]

Hobbes thus can be said to hold a *de jure* concept of authority. That is, authority is intrinsically connected with having a right to do certain sorts of things. De Jouvenel, on the other hand, at least on Peters's reading, holds a *de facto* concept of authority.[9] For him, the proof of the pudding lies ultimately in the eating. Unless one has the ability to be effective in dealing with others, he cannot be said to be entitled to exercise authority.

In his treatment of political or civil authority, Hobbes stresses the notion of authorization. That is, he who exercises genuine authority is he who is authorized to do so as representative of those who have a right to do and say things. Ultimately, there is only one source of authority, namely the sovereign.[10] The sovereign's will is the source of all law and authority. Thus, for Hobbes, each civil society has a sovereign who has supreme power or dominion. Without a sovereign, there is no civil society. The sovereign, in turn, is authorized as sovereign by the people.[11]

De Jouvenel, however, argues that Hobbes's position is extravagant and indefensible. Whether the sovereign be taken to be the people or the king, the sovereign's will is insufficient fully to establish law. If, de Jouvenel says, one admits the principle of an unchecked, unbounded sovereignty of a human will, 'the resulting regime is the same, to whatever person, real or fictive, this sovereignty is attributed.'[12] Whether one attributes arbitrary, unlimited sovereignty to a king or to a people, the result is precisely the same. 'They confer the same despotic right on the effective wielder of power, who is seldom the king and can never, by the nature of things, be the people.'[13]

De Jouvenel himself holds that, though there is no juridical solution to prevent all-powerful sovereigns from abusive, arbitrary rule and though the rights of rulers and subjects regularly conflict, historically the duties of subjects and rulers have been seen to be on the whole in harmony with one another. Human conduct has always been regulated by a community of beliefs which complements and sustains the political order. Positive legislation, according to de Jouvenel, if it is not to be despotic, must depend upon some anterior order for its legitimacy.[14] The possibility of authority depends then upon the dual recognition that he who would lead accepts this antecedent community of beliefs and that what he proposes is consonant with these beliefs.

Thus, Peters notwithstanding, de Jouvenel's position suggests that the apparent neatness of the distinction between the *de facto* and the *de jure* concepts of authority is illusory. For one thing, in the political domain if there were nothing but *de facto* authority, there would essentially be only arbitrariness. How this would differ from Hobbesian *de jure* authority is far from evident. The adequacy of the distinction is further challenged when it is confronted with Weber's account of the three types of legitimation upon which authority can rest.[15] Authority based upon either rational or traditional legitimation is obviously *de jure* authority. Charismatic authority, or what Leibniz would call virtue-based authority, is not determined by any antecedently specified rules. But neither is it merely *de facto* authority. Somehow , as Peters himself acknowledges, charismatic authority generates its own system of entitlement, even if this system resists full articulation. In Peters's words: 'All that can be said is that there is something about him [the charismatic leader] which people recognize in virtue of which they do what he says simply because he says it.'[16]

In his rejoinder to Peters, Winch argues that the way Peters has drawn his distinctions effectively prevents him from specifying what it is that people recognize in the charismatic leader in virtue of which they obey him. According to Winch, both the notion of rational legitimation and that of charismatic legitimation presuppose the notion of a tradition which can legitimate authority.[17] On Winch's view, *de facto* authority always presupposes that the followers *recognize* the legitimacy of the exercise of authority by virtue of a tradition of activity which gives the decisions, proposals, and directives of any leader, charismatic or otherwise, their sense. However revolutionary the charismatic leader may be, he always acts out of a background which provides the context for recognizing what he does and why he does it. He is followed not merely because of his presently experienced forcefulness but also because how he proposes to lead is recognized as a way which has been sanctioned beforehand by a tradition.[18]

Alexander von Schoenborn has attempted to develop Winch's insight that *de facto* authority rests finally upon the recognition of some, at least putative, *de jure* authority. Rather than effectively assigning preeminence to traditional authority, as Winch does, von Schoenborn reworks the standard version of the distinction between *de jure* and *de facto* authority. He argues that whatever else authority might be, it is a principle of human affairs which bears upon attitudes, beliefs, or conduct. The key question is how one should understand the concept of a 'principle.' Is a principle to be construed as factual origin or beginning? Or is it to be understood as normative ground? Or both? Von Schoenborn accepts Arendt's conclusion that, in the matter of authority, these two senses of 'principle' are coeval.[19] Attempts to understand authority exclusively either as factual origin (*de facto* authority) or as normative

151

ground (*de jure* authority) are both doomed to fail. Genuine authority as a principle of human affairs always rests upon both factual and normative bases. Von Schoenborn is thus led to characterize authority as follows: 'Authority is recognized relevant competence on the basis of which the recognizing individual tends to believe or act in a consonant manner.'[20] He who exercises authority not only sustains or brings something into being but he also draws others to join in the work he does.

In effect, Winch and Von Schoenborn, and de Jouvenel as well, point away from thinking of authority, and particularly political authority, as residing in some property or characteristic possessed by the ruler. This is appropriate because attempts to identify political authority with some personal attribute threaten to lead to tyranny. If authority is that which one possesses absolutely independently of others, then there is no effective check against its exercise exclusively at the will of its possessor. Hobbes recognized this point clearly. There is, he says, no difference between the power of a king, an absolute monarch, and that of a tyrant. The only difference between them is in the way they are viewed.[21] And if perchance there are multiple claimants of the authority-constituting property and no force sufficient to terminate the dispute, then there is anarchy. It is an anarchy awaiting only sufficient force to become a tyranny.

Considerations of this sort, among others, have led thinkers as different as Hannah Arendt and Herbert Simon to see that authority consists in a relation rather than in the possession of a characteristic. This relation is essentially hierarchical. It requires a distinction between superiors and subordinates. The former command or guide and the latter obey or follow. Subordinates obey and follow not because they are persuaded of the correctness of the directive but because they recognize the superiors as superiors. Superiors, as Simon says with some exaggeration, do not seek to convince subordinates. They are satisfied with acquiescence.[22]

Even so, authority is not essentially antithetical to the freedom of the subordinates. Superiors need not deprive their subordinates of all initiative. Indeed, superiors need the active support of their subordinates. By their free acquiescence, subordinates positively contribute to the establishment and maintenance of authority and its efficacy. If exercises of power and authority are to be validated as legitimate, then there must be room for active cooperation by subordinates with superiors.[23]

A clue to the proper assessment of political authority springs from the recognition that the relationship constitutive of political authority is primarily a discursive relationship. 'The working of words upon action,' de Jouvenel notes, 'is the basic political action.'[24] The complexity of discourse, with its strengths and limitations, both determines what sort of account should be given of authority and delimits what counts as responsible exercises of authority. Failure to appreciate the complexity of discourse leads to both conceptual and practical mistakes concerning authority and its possibilities.

Since all manifestations of political authority involve discourse, they are all intrinsically historical and finite as well as intersubjective. They all involve both a speaker and a hearer. The speaker who has no audience is without efficacy. An audience is a necessary condition of his efficacy, of his authority. Though the audience listens because *for now* it has nothing to say, it has by no means forfeited all claims to be entitled, at some time or other, to speak. All manifestations of authority, then, presuppose audiences which are not unqualifiedly passive. De Jouvenel is correct when he says:

> We should not, I believe, regard the *vis politica* as a 'quality' inherent in the *dux* and therefore capable of producing more or less effect according to the responsiveness of the particular society; rather it should be thought of as a relationship in which suggestion and response are part of a global process.[25]

In politics, then, everyone is in principle both agent and patient. No speaker can be genuinely authoritative and at the same time ignore the exigencies imposed upon him by an audience destined to respond.[26]

This clue which de Jouvenel furnishes for a proper understanding and assessment of political authority finds its appropriate culmination when one first recognizes both that the discursive partners are men who are essentially *en route* and that discourse is necessarily intertwined with silence, and second interprets the sort of authority possible under these conditions in terms of a politics of hope. Such a development of de Jouvenel's clue substantially clarifies the nature of authority and permits one to specify at least partially the conditions for its responsible exercise.

If men are essentially *en route* and are endowed with a freedom which is relational rather than autonomous, then the ruler and his rulings are necessarily historical and finite. In exercises of authority, the ruler is the one who now has both the words and the capacity for action with which to address issues which his audience *both needs to have addressed and at least implicitly wants to have addressed*. The ruler's title to rule, to speak, therefore has three irreducible sources. One source is the audience's more or less explicitly experienced needs. A second source is the ruler's capacity and will to address these specific needs.[27] The third source is the already embarked upon search by the audience for the satisfaction of these needs. With such a search underway, the audience is prepared to hear the ruler's proposals and directives and to make its response. Without such a search, the ruler's proposals and directives would appear as impositions, intrusions, or irrelevancies.

Precisely because each ruler holds his authority from this complex set of sources, his authority is relatively fragile. The testimony of history shows that each of the three conditions upon which authority rests is only contingently and transiently satisfied. Thus the likelihood of simultaneous satisfaction of all three conditions in any concrete instance is comparatively low. This fact does not imply that there is *no* authority without full satisfaction of all three conditions. Rather, the vigor of authority waxes and wanes depending upon the degree of satisfaction of each condition. Indeed, because the needs are so numerous and so pressing and the search for ways of satisfying them is so persistent, the likelihood that exercised and acknowledged authority will emerge is quite high. One ruler may be replaced by another. But most likely, there will be ruling.[28]

The relationship of ruling-being ruled is constituted by silence as well as by discourse. One crucial inference to be drawn from this fact is that if there are to be responsible exercises of authority, then both the ruler and the ruled must acknowledge and accept, at least in practice, the consequences of the inevitability of silence. Principal among these consequences is the impossibility of either complete speech or perfect action. Neither the ruled nor the ruler can reasonably expect any exercise or set of exercises of authority to be definitive. None can be exhaustively adequate to the needs, none can be perfectly tailored to the search, none can truthfully claim to be the unqualified best response to needs and searches. Authority, then, can never eliminate a certain slippage between what the ruler can offer and what the audience both can and will accept.[29] It is one of the permanent tasks of a discourse intercalated with silence in manifestations of authority not only to transmit proposals and reactions to proposals but also to keep this inevitable slippage within tolerable bounds.[30]

A second, crucial consequence of the inevitability of silence in manifestations of authority is that these manifestations cannot be all of a piece. Each episode of political discourse either reinforces the already prevailing patterns of political thinking and doing or it institutes modifications in these patterns. Silence provides the perpetual possibility for shifting from one of these functions to the other.

This feature of the play of discourse and silence enters into the constitution of two distinct sorts of exercise of authority. De Jouvenel has helpfully drawn this distinction in terms of the *dux*, the leader, and the *rex*, the rectifier. The *dux* leads action which has a precise end in view, an end whose accomplishment terminates the point of the leading. Conducting a war, building a port, establishing a colony, etc. are exercises of 'ducal' authority. This sort of exercise of authority is intrinsically intermittent. The *rex*, by contrast, leads men to work and live together as neighbors. The 'regal' function is to preserve people's confidence in one another and to settle their quarrels. 'The *rex* lays down rules of conduct, enforces contracts, arbitrates disputes.'[31]

There is neither discourse nor action which can synthesize without remainder these two functions. The sorts of reasons which support these two functions are not completely harmonizable with one another. The sorts of actions to which each of these functions gives rise tend to interfere with one another. Yet neither function can be dispensed with. Neither constant innovation nor an unrelieved *status quo* can be sustained. Paradoxically, 'the social universe must be at the same time fluid, responsive to new initiatives, and a solid ground to which the individual may trust.'[32] Inasmuch as silence is that which insures the constant possibility of shifts from one sort of exercise of authority to the other, it is likewise ingredient in establishing and maintaining the requisite tension in a responsible body politic.

Because there can be no concrete exercise of authority which is exhaustively adequate to the needs which elicit the exercise, it is impossible to eliminate all title of the ruled to resist the ruler. No exercise of authority can pretend to be uniquely deduced from the established bases of authority. At best, it can be in accord with them. What is at issue here is not merely the fragility of authority mentioned above. Rather, it is the recognition that, even within a relatively stable context in which an accepted ruler reigns over basically willing subjects, it is always possible for the ruled rationally to resist specific initiatives of the ruler without necessarily repudiating his entire rule.[33] This resistance does not seek to take initiative away from the ruler. Rather it seeks to have him shift from one proposed initiative to another. Such resistance is tantamount to a practical veto rather than to an attempt to seize leadership. The perpetual possibility of the rationality of this sort of resistance arises out of the inevitable incompleteness of discourse and the imperfection of all action.

Hobbes's view of authority, then, is extravagant. Not even his sort of sovereign could exhaustively satisfy the subjects' needs. It therefore would make no sense for them to resign all possibility of shaping, through resistance, at least some of the ruler's directives. Either for the subjects or for the ruler to expect or even long for some 'perfect' exercise of authority is to chase ghosts.

When one links these considerations, namely the relational character of authority, its essentially hierarchical structure, and its preeminently discursive manifestation, with the previously established elements of responsible politics, at least two important, related conclusions can be drawn concerning what political authority can and should be. A responsible politics, I have shown, recognizes (a) that the political domain is but one of several irreducible domains of discourse and action, (b) but that the political domain is nonetheless the totalizing domain, (c) that all political discourse is essentially dialogical, (d) that all present discourse, political or otherwise, has a history and arises against the backdrop of traditions which it cannot absorb into itself exhaustively on its own terms, and (e) that by reason of silence, there can be no finished or complete discourse or action. If these things are so, then one can show that responsible politics (a) establishes an order among the multiple forms or sources of authority, and (b) requires specific sorts of restraint on the part of both rulers and ruled.

Responsible politics does not regard the multiple forms or sources of authority as all standing on equal footing. Though it does not repudiate any form or source of political authority, it insists on giving the final word to legitimate authority, to legal authority.[34]

The other bases of political authority, e.g. competence, charisma, etc.,[35] in the final analysis must yield to legitimacy. Competence is here understood to consist in the mastery of some rational technique. But such techniques are essentially abstract and, in principle, universally applicable. Politics, though, is essentially particular. It deals with spatio-temporally specific future contingencies. All determinations of the appropriate application of any sort of competency is necessarily extra-technical. Title to make these determinations must arise elsewhere.

Potential candidates for the title to make these determinations are those who hold either legitimate or charismatic (personal) authority. Charismatic authority, however, is essentially episodic. Its occurrence cannot be guaranteed. Further, it is not exclusive. Holders of charismatic authority can compete against one another. Charismatic authority, then, is inherently unstable.

Only legitimacy-based authority, therefore, can provide both stability and the specificity required for making responsible concrete determinations for handling particular future contingencies. One does not bestow legitimate authority upon oneself. It comes to one by virtue of stable historical forms established by others. Unlike both competent and charismatic authority, legitimate authority must always justify its particular exercise in terms of already accepted historical norms. Legitimate authority, more than other forms of authority, reflects the relational, dialogical character of politics.

But even if legitimate authority enjoys a certain preeminence over other forms or sources of political authority, it cannot justify stifling the emergence of these other forms. To stifle competence is to canonize ignorance. To stifle charisma is to canonize the *status quo*. Such stifling would pretend that legitimate authority is self-sufficient and self-contained. But a pretense of this sort effectively denies the historical character of all authority. It would convert legitimate authority into a dogmatic caricature of itself.

Legitimate authority, then, enjoys a preeminence which is only relative. For its own well-being it must leave room for other forms of political authority. Indeed, it must be prepared to be modified by them. Nonetheless, responsible politics does require that the preeminence of legitimate authority be acknowledged.[36]

While stressing the preeminence of legitimate authority, responsible politics also requires that all participants in the ruler-ruled relationship exercise specific sorts of restraint. In general, this restraint forbids any participant from pretending that any concrete instantiation of political authority be taken to encompass the totality of social life. Thus one cannot responsibly attempt to subsume all types of interpersonal relationships under the relationship of political authority. And equally importantly, no group of contemporaries can responsibly take themselves to constitute the whole of their society. Thus, for example, Mexico cannot properly be regarded as composed merely of the presently existing group of Mexican citizens and inhabitants. Mexico also includes both ancestors and descendants. Society, it must be admitted, is not constituted and maintained exclusively by the will of its present members. It follows, then, that the participants in relations of political authority cannot pretend exhaustively to set their own terms for the discourse which constitutes these relations. They, rather, continue a discourse which antedates them and will outlast them. As Jean Bodin saw long ago, there is a close connection between lasting authority and wisdom. This means that the participants in political authority which endures play their respective roles, rulers and ruled, in ways which are adapted both to the general exigencies of the human condition and to the distinctive material and cultural circumstances which they inhabit.[37] Part of this context is the participants' position between ancestors who cannot be totally disowned and descendants who cannot be totally owned.

The general restraint required by responsible politics of all participants in the relation of political authority entails distinctive, correlative sorts of restraint from superiors on the one hand and subjects on the other. In other contexts I have already sufficiently discussed two of the sorts of restraints required of superiors. Briefly, they are, first, that superiors undertake any particular initiative only if it is recognizably compatible either with the whole of a heritage received from ancestors and regarded by the subjects as worthy of transmission to descendants or with what is taken to be the better part of a heritage which is not thoroughly self-consistent. Thus superiors must refrain from pretending that an initiative which is totally incompatible with their subjects' heritage can be received as authoritative. Second, the political ruler must refrain, precisely for the sake of political authority, from intruding his authority into nonpolitical domains of discourse and action. Though the political ruler functioning as *rex* or regulator can prescribe bounds for the exercise of other domains, he cannot responsibly function either as *rex* or as *dux* within another domain.[38]

Though a third sort of restraint incumbent upon the ruler has also been mentioned above, it is not superfluous to return to it briefly. This sort of restraint is that which stems from the material and cultural conditions prevailing in his community. Political subjects have wants and needs, some of which they presently recognize and some of which they do not. The wants and needs relevant here are those which a person cannot satisfy either alone or by simple cooperation with one or a few consociates. Many economic wants and needs, for example, today require extremely complex, widespread activity for their satisfaction. It is the task of responsible political superiors to discern which wants and needs require their intervention to be satisfied.

The central point here is that a ruler's exercise of authority cannot be effective and so is irresponsible unless what he says and does takes into account the conditions which his subjects inhabit. Unless a man recognizes wants and needs which he cannot satisfy for himself, submission to authority would make no sense. Unless the ruler heeds the conditions in which he and his subjects live, his initiatives are pointless to his subjects and the relationship of political authority is undercut. The ruler then must restrain himself to speak and act only in accordance with what he has learned from and about the concrete conditions of his subjects' lives.

One is not, however, genuinely a ruler merely because he respects these three sorts of restraint which a ruler's discourse must honor. He might only be a philosopher. The responsible ruler not only acknowledges these restraints upon what can sensibly be proposed but also ventures to articulate and promote a positive program for responding to his subjects' wants and needs. A genuine ruler is not simply one who hears what the people explicitly and implicitly say. He also responds in his own voice with distinctive utterances and projects. These utterances and projects do not merely echo or mirror what the people report or show about their condition. What he says and does is his own. He rises or falls politically by his responses. He cannot effectively rise unless he first listens to those he would have as subjects. But simple listening and watching are insufficient for ruling. Corresponding to these three sorts of restraint which responsible politics requires of rulers are three sorts of restraint required of subjects. The first of these three sorts of restraint stems from the fact that in any concrete, ongoing political context there is a multiplicity of subjects. Though each person's set of wants and needs overlaps the others' sets, each set is, in some respects, qualitatively unique. But obviously if there is to be any vigorous, significantly efficacious politics, then similarities rather than differences must be stressed.

A major part of the political task is to establish and maintain this stress on similarities. Without such an emphasis the political community is at best weak and unstable. Thus the preservation of the emphasis on the similarity of the wants, needs, and resources among the members of the community is a concern of every responsible member of the body politic. As de Jouvenel puts it, 'the influence of man upon man, which is the elementary political process, completely depends upon there being, in the consciences of both parties, a common stock of beliefs and a similar structure of feelings.'[39] If this preservation is to be accomplished, subjects must listen to one another when they articulate their wants and needs and assign weights to them. No responsible participant in politics can responsibly assign unqualified preeminence to his own wants and needs. Each must stand ready to attend to and heed the articulations and manifestations which his fellow participants give to their own wants and needs.

The second sort of restraint required of the responsible political subject is that which consists in his readiness to quiet the expression of his own condition so that he can genuinely hear the ruler's proposals. That is, the subject must be prepared to countenance and act upon a proposal expressing the ruler's initiative. The subject must not insist upon a response which merely echoes his own expression. Authority is vacuous if the ruler is to do nothing but play back what the subject has said. Given the essential partialness of discourse, the fit between the ruler's utterances and those of the ruled is never perfect. But this fact is not a flaw in the relationship constitutive of authority. It is a condition of the possibility of authority.

The third sort of restraint which the responsible political subject must exercise is that which insures the integrity of nonpolitical domains of discourse and action. The subject, no less than the ruler, must seek to preserve the justified totalizing activity of politics from being converted into an attempted justification for reducing one or more nonpolitical domains to the political. To discharge this re-

160

sponsibility, the subject must listen and respond to voices other than that of the political ruler. Failure to do so tempts the ruler to despotism. It also overburdens the responsible ruler and so undercuts the efficacy of the entire authority relation.

To be a responsible subject, then, one must both speak and listen. The subject cannot appropriately ignore his own wants and needs because their satisfaction is inextricably bound up with whatever positive contribution he can make to the political life of the community. His articulation of his own condition links him with his fellow subjects in making clear what sort of response is appropriate for the ruler to make. And by showing the similarity between his condition and theirs, his support or opposition to a ruler's initiatives can be intelligible to and influential with his fellow subjects. Failure to move periodically from silence to speech tends to culminate not in a silence which is the basis for hearing others but in a muteness impervious to the community and its life. Failure to speak as well as to be silent is to fall into a condition much like that ascribed by Marx to the *lumpenproletariat*.

Both the preeminence which responsible politics accords to legitimacy-based authority and the requirements of restraint which it imposes upon both the ruler and the ruled follow from the discursive, historical character of human interaction. Ultimately, they spring from man's condition as one who is relationally free and essentially *en route*. When these features of responsible political authority are interpreted in terms of a politics of hope, their sense and bearing take on a distinctive cast.

A politics of presumption ignores the riskiness intrinsic to granting even relative preeminence to any particular form or source of authority. Granting preeminence to legitimacy-based authority risks canonizing the *status quo*. Granting preeminence to competency-based authority risks degeneration into some elitist technocracy. Granting preeminence to charismatic or personal authority risks constant turmoil, confusion, and demagoguery.

Politics of containment and resignation both acknowledge the requirements of restraint but depreciate their significance. For them, restraint is nothing more than a necessary concession to weakness. The reason for restraint, for them, is to make a bad situation tolerable.

Unlike a politics of presumption, a politics of hope is thoroughly awake to the riskiness of giving preeminence to any particular form or source of authority. It constantly stresses the relativity of the preeminence granted to legitimacy-based authority. And it constantly emphasizes legitimacy's need for frequent revitalization through competency and charism.[40] A politics of hope never forgets that political rulers perpetually need both to hear what their subjects say and to be moved by what they hear.

Unlike politics of containment and of resignation, a politics of hope understands the multiple sorts of restraint required by responsible politics to be necessary conditions for new human initiative. If there is to be efficacious freedom, then not only must power, as Montesquieu said, be checked by power.[41] It must also be amassed. 'The only indispensable material factor in the generation of power,' Arendt argues, 'is the living together of people.'[42] Authority, as that which binds people together, can and should contribute to their common power. For a politics of hope, 'the essential function of public authorities . . .[is] to increase the mutual trust prevailing at the heart of the social whole.'[43] The sort of obedience required for the authority which is exercised to accomplish these objectives is not only not incompatible with freedom but is actually conducive to it.[44] Further, authority as understood in terms of a politics of hope will include among the participants in its power as many men as possible. For a politics of hope, there will be as few outlaws as possible and even the eventual incorporation of these outlaws is constantly sought.

II

Just as a politics of hope embodies a distinctive interpretation of authority and its responsible exercise, so too does it embody a distinctive understanding and assessment of sovereignty. It neither exalts sovereignty to the heights nor consigns it to the pits.

Hobbes epitomizes those who exalt sovereignty without qualification. Though his doctrine of sovereignty has at present only comparatively slight philosophical support, it is often implicit in the claims advanced by political practitioners. For Hobbes, there could be no civil society without a sovereign. This sovereign must exercise supreme and absolute dominion. Since the sovereign is not under contract to his subjects, nothing he does to them can properly be called an injury or injustice. Thus the sovereign neither is nor can be subject to any civil laws.[45]

If sovereignty is construed as Hobbes construes it, then Arendt is clearly correct in maintaining that sovereignty and freedom are mutually incompatible. 'If men wish to be free,' she says, 'it is precisely sovereignty they must renounce.'[46] But both Hobbes's exaltation and Arendt's rejection of sovereignty understand it essentially to involve some version of the doctrine of autonomous freedom. If freedom is rather understood relationally, then sovereignty can find a place in responsible politics. A politics of hope yields important clarification of the nature of its place.

It is, however, true that the history of the development of the concept of sovereignty shows that it progressively came to imply that the sovereign was necessarily endowed with radical autonomy. Before Hobbes, Jean Bodin had already explicitly rejected medieval notions about the limited authority of government. For him, sovereignty is absolute and perpetual power. Sovereign power is inalienable. Only that which the sovereign commands is lawful and the sovereign is not subject to his own commands.[47] Similarly, though Machiavelli did not explicitly avow the doctrine of absolute sovereignty, he clearly took it for granted.[48]

Bodin's position obviously breaks with the doctrine that the ruler is simply a deputy either of God or of the popular sovereign, the people,[49] and is therefore ultimately bound by the instructions given to him. Nonetheless, Bodin does not deny that both the ruler and the subject are bound by some determining obligation beyond their control. He took it for granted that the legitimacy of a government depends upon its maintaining order and its acting for the good of its subjects. He presumed that if it did not do so, the people would rebel and the ruler would thereby be shown to have lost his title to rule. For Bodin, might does not *ipso facto* make right, though there is no right without might.[50] What Bodin does not make explicit, though, is the distinction between the several private goods of the subjects and the public weal.[51] It is the latter which I shall argue is both the object and the measure of both authority and sovereignty. A politics of hope can show how this is the case.

The doctrine of sovereignty I want to defend, on the basis of a politics of hope, has much in common with that of Montesquieu. What Montesquieu points to as the spirit of the laws holds the place which I would assign to the public weal, a concept to which I will return below. Further, he properly distinguishes between absolute government and arbitrary government.[52] Though I take it that Montesquieu would acknowledge that even absolute government is essentially finite, my account will make its finitude explicit.

In absolute government, this sovereign, who makes the law, is nonetheless expected to respect and obey the law. His subjects have rights and it is the sovereign's acknowledged duty to define and enforce them. As Plamenatz says:

> The sovereign is sovereign, not because he can do no wrong, but because he alone can redress the wrong he does. The prince who . . . recognizes that his own laws bind him and who is expected by his subjects to respect them, is an absolute but not an arbitrary sovereign.[53]

This view acknowledges on the one hand the irreducibility of the distinction between the ruler and the ruled.[54] On the other hand, it also recognizes that this gap does not detach the ruler from the ruled. It functionally relates them in a quite specific way. Each has his peculiar responsibilities both to himself, to the other, and to the function. The absolute character of sovereignty, then, is not a personal attribute of the ruler. It is a functional requirement if the political community is to do and say anything efficacious as a community. But for all its absoluteness, all political saying and doing is essentially finite. No political saying or doing removes either the possibility or the need for further sayings and doings. Absolute sovereignty exists, on this view, to preserve and enhance the dialogue which constitutes politics.

The principal reason for insisting upon the importance of sovereignty as well as of authority is the fact that all politics today, as Merleau-Ponty saw, has an international dimension as well as a domestic one. In a complex world composed of multiple interacting political communities efficacious authority requires sovereignty.[55] Though authority without sovereignty is not logically absurd, in the contemporary world there is an existential necessity for some sovereign to stand forth from among those exercising authority of various sorts within any particular political community if that community is to act on the international stage. For the members of a particular community to impede the development of such sovereignty is unwarranted, for it would ultimately weaken the efficacy of all their political efforts.[56] For the sovereign to fail to remember how and why he came to be sovereign is to court failure either to take advantage of the opportunities it affords or to observe the constraints within which its efficacy can be maintained. An example of the former would be neglect of alliances. An example of the latter would be international commitments which the community refuses to support.

Thus, though Hobbes is right when he says that among the several political states there is no sovereign, within each of those states there must be sovereignty if there is to be efficacious international intercourse. Sayings and doings, on the international scene as well as elsewhere, require identifiable speakers and hearers. The function of him who holds sovereignty in each particular political community is both to provide the community with a recognizable spokesman and to insure that other agents on the international scene recognize his community as a distinctive participant in international political discourse. It is only apparently paradoxical to say that efficacious international action requires the interplay of multiple absolute sovereigns.

In sum, the sort of politics I am defending endorses the existential necessity of both authority and sovereignty. It can do so precisely because of its understanding of human freedom as relational rather than autonomous. Sovereignty and authority reflect the bipolar character of relational freedom. Sovereignty tends to emphasize what might be termed the centripetal pole, the pole which precludes complete absorption into any specific relation or set of relations. Authority tends to emphasize the centrifugal pole, the pole by virtue of which people are drawn together for discourse and common action. This view, when the finitude of freedom is admitted, permits me to acknowledge that there is a justifiable sense of popular sovereignty. The responsible sovereign does not stifle his subjects. The sovereign is always for the sake of the subjects. But, likewise, if the sovereign is to be effective for his subjects, then he must be absolute. Similarly, subjects sustain and give point to the exercise of authority and sovereignty by rulers. But rulers only rule if they exercise an initiative which is clearly their own.

A politics of hope supplies significant further determination to the understanding and assessment of sovereignty. Unlike politics of presumption, containment, and resignation, all of which blur the distinction between private interests and what can be called the public weal, a politics of hope firmly insists upon the sharpness of this distinction. A politics of presumption too readily assumes the coincidence of private interest and public weal. Politics of containment and of resignation effectively either deny that there is a genuine public weal to which politics can make a distinctive contribution or assume that there is an irreconcilable opposition between all private interest and the public weal. For a politics of hope, the play between private interest and public weal is always risky. But there is no necessary opposition between them. Nonetheless, exercises of sovereignty, for a politics of hope, are justifiable only insofar as they promote the public weal.[57]

For a politics of hope, the public weal is always the weal of a body of men who are relationally free, finite, and essentially *en route*. They are thoroughly historical and have widely varying private interests. The public weal requires first that there continue to be men, and second that their historical variety be respected. This variety, for a politics of hope, makes possible the diversified discourse necessary for innovation. History suggests, with no substantial evidence to the contrary, that this second requirement can be met only if there are in fact multiple political communities, each of which is sovereign.[58] Beyond these two requirements, the meaning of the concept 'public weal' is, to borrow Gadamer's distinction again, regulative rather than dogmatic.[59] But even if the public weal cannot be fully defined, it serves for a politics of hope as that against which all political activity is to be measured.

Sovereignty, then, for a politics of hope, is justifiable only insofar as it acknowledges that the relation between superiors and subjects subsumes them all under something to which they all owe allegiance. The subsumption in question here is not that which merely subordinates particular interests to more general ones. The subsumption needed to justify sovereignty in a politics of hope supposes an objective against which all interests, particular or general, are to be measured. For a politics of hope, this objective is nothing less than the establishment and maintenance of an order in which men's essential routedness is not merely acknowledged, but is willingly embraced, an order in which the public weal is paramount.

In keeping with the relational character of the finite freedom with which man is endowed, the public weal has two dimensions. One dimension is that which recognizes the fundamental sameness of the human condition in all men. I will call this the global dimension of the public weal. And I will call efforts to respect this sameness efforts in support of a general good. The other dimension is that which recognizes the uniqueness of each sovereign body politic. I will call this the distributive dimension of the public weal. And I will call efforts to respect this dimension efforts in support of a particular good.[60] The preservation of each of these bodies politic in its distinctiveness is a fundamental requirement of the public weal, one not to be subordinated to the interests of some other body politic. Neither size nor wealth suffice to make the preservation of one state preferable to that of another.[61] One of the crucial tasks for any body politic is so to organize its action and discourse that it can perdure as a distinct political community. A substantial component of the *raison d'être* for political authority and sovereignty is that they are necessary conditions for this perdurance.

But even if one state is not to be subordinated to another, a particular state may have to refrain from some efforts to promote its own particular good if that effort threatens the survival of some other state. Thus one community may have to refrain from some technically feasible endeavor if that endeavor is (a) inessential to its own survival, and (b) incompatible with the survival of another community as a sovereign political entity. If state A, for example, were able to corner the rice market but need not do so to survive as a state, and if its doing so would make the survival of state B as a sovereign state impossible, then state A must refrain from cornering the rice market.

Further, if a political community attempts to equate its particular good with the general good on grounds that it embodies the general good, it falls into nonsense. Part of what makes a particular good a genuine good is its particularity, its fittingness for the particular group of people in question, and hence its difference from other particular goods. There are, then, no messianic political entities or entities with 'manifest destinies.' Slogans such as 'The United States should make the world safe for democracy' or 'Communism is destined to rule the world and the Soviet Union is its appointed agent' are absurd. Unless such slogans are interpreted in so vacuous a manner that they could be satisfied in any number of ways, they rest on the necessarily false notion that there can be complete political speech. That is, such slogans would assume that some particular form of democracy, communism, or some specific third alternative could be the political last word, that politics has a predetermined *terminus ad quem*. But since complete speech is impossible, the apotheosis of any component of the distributive dimension of the public weal into the global dimension of it is likewise impossible.[62]

The dialectic, then, between efforts to foster the distributive dimension of the public weal and efforts to foster its global dimension is interminable because their coincidence is precluded by the principle of incomplete speech. Indeed, this principle also prevents any effort in support of either dimension of the public weal from justifiably claiming to be complete or perfect.

For a politics of hope, then, the people of state A, both rulers and ruled, are inextricably bound up with the people of state B in a mutual conversation demanding of all participants an unending interplay of speaking and listening. What this conversation is to articulate always includes not merely the particular interests of the current participants but also the antecedent and perpetually binding commitment of its participants to the public weal in both its global and distributive dimensions. Similarly, within both A and B, the conversation among its participants must be such that international conversation can proceed.

For the international conversation to occur, authoritative spokesmen – agents for the several states – must be readily recognizable. Sovereignty is the title for these authoritative spokesmen. Sovereignty, then, is a practical necessity for international politics. The domestic politics of a state must be so arranged that it can participate in international relations. But because international politics, like all politics, is thoroughly historical, its agents and their accomplishments are necessarily open to change. There is no reason, therefore, for any state to assign sovereignty irrevocably to any person for life. Indeed, for numerous reasons already developed in this study, a state should be so ordered that, while there is always a holder of sovereignty, whoever holds the sovereignty should be regularly reviewed.

Sovereignty, then, as construed by a politics of hope, does not release its holder from his bonds to his fellow citizens. It does not cancel the dialogical character of politics. Sovereignty exists for the sake of the political conversation. Its objective is to provide for the active participation and initiative in politics of as many people as possible in as many ways as possible.

III

Nonetheless, because the intricate political conversation among men in the face of an only partially pliable world can be disturbed, threatened, or curtailed by some doings and sayings, justifiable coercion is an ineliminable possibility both within political communities and in the interchanges among them. Marx notwithstanding, there is little reason to expect or even to want the state, with its coercive power, to wither away.

To say that coercion is an ineliminable possibility is not to say that it is logically necessary. But given the impossibility of either definitive, exhaustive speech or perfect action and the gapped character of the human will, coercion is existentially a permanently possible and potentially justifiable mode of activity for any particular political community.[63]

The incompleteness of each exercise of political rule entails that it is necessarily open to challenge. No exercise has resources with which to preclude all challenges for which reasons can be proffered. To borrow de Jouvenel's terms, political problems cannot be solved. They can only be settled. To solve a problem is to *satisfy in full all the terms* of the problem. To settle it is to leave some terms either wholly or partially unsatisfied. When solutions are impossible, then settlements are appropriate.[64] But any specific settlement always leaves in its wake bases on which it can be challenged.

Political settlements are responsible precisely insofar as they are consonant with the public weal. An essential part of the public weal is the existence of identifiable rulers who fashion settlements. If a political settlement is to hold, to be efficacious, then rulers must be able to prevent attempts to press claims which would undercut it. If they can satisfy this requirement through persuading all their subjects to accept the settlement willingly, then all is well. But if willing acceptance cannot be elicited, then rulers still must be able to make settlements hold. To do so in this latter instance they may have to resort to coercion or to the threat of coercion. Failure to do so when necessary to protect the settlement would be irresponsible.

But not all proposed settlements are consonant with the public weal. This would particularly be the case when the proposed settlement would effectively hinder the subjects' participation in subsequent political discourse. Such settlements are simply repressive and tend toward tyranny. A ruler who insists upon an initiative which would effectively thwart the complex political dialogue is to be resisted. If he yields willingly, then all is well. If not, then recourse by the subjects to sufficient coercion to insure the integrity of the political discourse is justifiable and perhaps required.

The way is opened for responsible political acts of coercion not only by the essential incompleteness of speech and action but also by the gapped character of the human will. St Paul's famous remark, 'The good which I want, I do not do and the evil that I do not want, that I do,' vividly testifies to this gap. The gap is not merely a remediable weakness. Rather, it is of the very essence of the will that what I choose, what I do, and what I acknowledge need not, and perhaps cannot, be coextensive.[65] Thus, for n ⋅ther the ruler nor the ruled can there be a perfect willing of any particular initiative.

It follows from these two factors, namely the incompleteness of every manifestation of political rule and the gapped character of the human will, that neither the ruler nor the ruled can responsibly renounce the possibility of resort to coercion. They cannot responsibly preclude the use of techniques or physical instruments to impose their will upon another's conduct against the latter's will. Thus, to be in a relation of authority, whether as ruler or as ruled, is to risk having either to exert or to endure coercion. But if authority and sovereignty are relationships of discourse which are meant to enhance the efficacious freedom of all the participants, then coercion is defensible only if it is ultimately directed toward fortifying the bond among fellow members of a political community rather than bringing about or solidifying their separation from one another. Because it is not impossible to fulfill this condition, coercion is not the unqualified contrary of relational freedom.[66] Coercion for the sake of freedom, including the freedom of the coerced, is not self-contradictory. Nonetheless, because coercion can be destructive as well as constructive, it, like everything political, is essentially risky.

If a concrete act of coercion is to be justified, it must satisfy two necessary conditions, First, it must be exercised in direct response to some present danger posed to the intricate discourse required for the preservation and promotion of the public weal. There are two basic sorts of danger to this discourse. Each of them springs from a failure to observe one or more of the restraints mentioned above as requirements for responsible political discourse. The first kind of danger is constituted by attempts to subordinate the public weal, in either its distributive dimension or its global dimension, to some private or special group interest. Attempts of this sort take one of two elementary forms. One form of this kind of danger is the attempt to undercut effective rulership. This form occurs when people withhold their assent from the establishment or maintenance of a political community which would incorporate them as participants. It also occurs when people violate the laws prevailing within the body politic in which they are incorporated.[67] A second form of this kind of danger occurs when rulers shape the law and administrative practices themselves to promote private interest at the expense of the public weal. This form effectively disregards the ruled.

Coercion can, in appropriate circumstances and within proper limits, be employed to protect the public weal against both of these forms of conduct. When the subject's conduct – discursive or actional – tends to undercut the exercise of authority, the ruler has grounds for compelling either the participation or the obedience required for the public weal.[68] In the case of wrong-headed lawmaking, subjects have grounds for resisting the ruler through demonstrations, strikes, massive noncompliance, etc., the object of which is to change either the offensive laws and practices or the rulers or both.[69]

The second basic kind of danger to the intricate conversation needed for upholding the public weal is that which is constituted by attempts to subordinate without qualification the global dimension of the public weal to the distributive dimension or vice versa. If one or several political communities pursue their particular goods at the expense of the general good, then, under appropriate conditions, coercive resistance is justifiable. Thus, for example, if one political community bolstered its national defenses through weapons testing which was poisoning the seas, other communities would have grounds to try to force the cessation of these actions. Or again, if in the name of world unity or of some other supposedly ultimate ideal or of a sheer quest for domination, some state undertook to root out political diversity by forcibly subjugating another state which did not threaten its existence, then there are grounds for justifiably resisting this subjugation.

But even though each of these several circumstances constitutes a necessary condition for justifiable coercion, they alone, for a politics of hope, would be insufficient to justify it. Coercion is justifiable only if it also can serve *and be seen to serve* that dimension of the public weal on whose behalf it is exercised. By reason of the principle of incomplete speech, no definitive codification of the conditions for justifiable acts of coercion can be formulated. But a politics of hope of the sort I propose, unlike politics of presumption, containment and resignation, sheds significant light on this latter condition.

A politics of presumption trifles with the matter of coercion. Either it assumes that coercion can be abolished and so is at most a temporary expedient or it takes coercion as a matter of course which poses no substantial problem for politics. Politics both of containment and of resignation take coercion seriously. But they both assume that politics is essentially competitive and not cooperative. They further assume that politics is in effect a zero-sum game. Coercion, then, may be regrettable, but it is inevitable.

For a politics of hope, however, no one is definitively an opponent. Therefore every justifiable exercise of coercion must be visible as that which leaves room for the conversion of opponents of the public weal in its two dimensions or of those who are indifferent to the public weal into those who are its proponents. For this to be possible, an act of coercion must always be accompanied by discourse which explains it and its objective. This discourse can only fulfill its role if it makes clear that those who exercise coercion are also exercising restraint in hope of converting the coerced into fellow promoters of the public weal. Every justifiable act of coercion must be *recognizably* undertaken to seek the termination or at least the minimization of coercion.[70]

These necessary conditions for justifiable coercion in a politics of hope have two important corollaries. First, an act of coercion is justifiable only if there is some reasonable prospect that it can succeed in fostering the public weal. Without such a prospect, it would have to be regarded as vindictive, as an expression of revenge. Thus with Hobbes, though for quite different reasons, one should admit that he is 'forbidden to inflict punishment with any other designe, than for the correction of the offender, or direction of others.'[71]

It is possible that a political community discover that there are no justifiable acts of coercion available to it to preserve its existence. In such cases, the community in question is simply doomed. It cannot retaliate for its doom by recourse to unjustifiable attempts at coercion. Thus if state A cannot survive, it is not entitled to attack state B, even if B is the unjustified aggressor against A, bringing about A's destruction, unless by doing so A is and is seen to be seeking either B's conversion or the protection of some other viable political community C. It follows, then, for example, that those versions of nuclear deterrence which suppose a willingness to retaliate even without hope of survival are unjustifiable unless – and I have never encountered such a suggestion – the retaliation is to benefit some other state which can survive the conflagration. One whose removal from the discourse constitutive of the public weal cannot be prevented is not entitled further to diminish the discourse by eliminating other participants.

A second corollary of the necessary conditions for justifiable acts of coercion is that they are to be measured by the discourse they are meant to support. The possibility that coercion can be justifiable is always rooted in a weakness obstructing political discourse rather than a strength. The sole objective of justifiable acts of coercion is to compensate for that weakness. To the extent that it is effective, justifiable coercion tends to make further use of coercion pointless and unjustified. Thus the best use of coercion is that which maximally reduces the field for subsequent uses of defensible coercion.[72]

A politics of hope situates these general conditions for justifiable coercion in the context of the requirements for the protection or promotion of the conversation which both unites rulers and ruled within a particular body politic and links the network of political communities into a complex global unity. This conversation depends upon mutual respect among all participants. The principal manifestation of this respect is the acknowledgment both that others are worth speaking to and listening to. Further, what is listened for is neither prescribed nor circumscribed in advance. The only fixed condition is that what is said is in principle capable of contributing to the preservation or enhancement of this conversation. Thus, all justifiable coercion must preserve and not seek to prevent the play of speech and silence necessary for both speaking and listening.

Finally, though coercion's justifiability springs from dangers to this conversation, a politics of hope recognizes that coercion alone cannot strengthen the conversation. It must give way to forgiveness. Forgiveness works both ways. He who coerces must terminate the coercion in forgiveness. In fact, Montesquieu goes so far as to say that a conqueror in a justified war has a heavy obligation to repair the injuries he has occasioned.[73] On the other hand, he who has been coerced must be willing to terminate the antagonism by forgiving his coercer, even if the coercion in some of its parts has exceeded the bounds of justifiability.[74] As Plamenatz puts it in describing Hegel's position: 'We must have judgment between men but also forgiveness. The judge who forgives identifies himself with the wrong-doer, just as the wrong-doer who accepts punishment as his due identifies himself with his judge.'[75]

If exercises of coercion observe the measures of respect, silence, and forgiveness, then these acts cannot be of the sort which definitively exclude the coerced from participation in the public weal. Coercion is justifiable only if it is an expression of hope for the full incorporation of the coerced into the conversation which sustains and enhances the public weal.

The place of coercion within a politics of hope can thus be summed up in the following three conclusions. (1) The possibility of justifiable coercion is ineliminable from politics. For political efficacy, some person or group must be both responsible for restricting and empowered to restrict some conduct for the sake of maintaining the entire political fabric. (2) Any exercise of coercion which seeks to overcome definitively the essential finitude and fragility of the political domain is *politically* indefensible. No political activity can reasonably have as its aim the removal of man from the exigencies of his historicity, from his being *en route*. The endeavor to remove man from wayfaring is indefensible violence *par excellence*. (3) No exercise of coercion can be politically justified which excludes in advance the possibility of associating others, including those presently coerced, in the conversation of politics.[76]

This chapter has focused upon the appropriate exercise of political power. I have shown how a politics of hope understands the origin, sense, and rational justification of authority, sovereignty, and coercion. I have also shown that a politics of hope, as a responsible politics, insists that each of these essential elements of political life must be exercised with specific sorts of restraint.

No responsible politics fails to provide guidance for both the ruler and the ruled in their deliberations concerning how these elements are to be deployed in concrete instances. This guidance supplies the context within which responsible political activity of all sorts is set. Proximate guidance for political actors is provided by law. More remote guidance and preparation for political action is provided by political education. To fill out what a politics of hope involves, I will show in the next chapter how such a politics interprets the place of these two sorts of guidance in responsible politics.

8
Law and political education: exercises in guiding and goading[1]

In Chapter 7, I argued that the responsible political exercise of authority, sovereignty, and coercion is always characterized by restraint. In addition to the self-determined restraint which a responsible political agent exercises in performing some specific, concrete political deed, there is a system of historically developed, more or less institutionalized, restraints which people inhabit and in terms of which much of their conduct – social, economic, and political – finds its sense and efficacy. The most prominent, if not the most pervasive, of these institutional restraints is that which goes by the name of law. It is in law and its workings that political activity is, at least in large measure, given embodiment. Law and its workings give the several exercises of authority, sovereignty, and coercion a cohesiveness and predictability which contribute in no small measure to their efficacy.

Nonetheless, throughout recorded history there has been a deep-seated ambivalence about law and its workings. As the large body of utopian literature attests, besides the distinction between what is law and what is not, there is also a crucial distinction between good law and bad law.

Paul Ricoeur's remarks in *History and Truth* about what he describes as the paradox of politics are in substantial measure transferable to the matter of law. Law deals with power, with the division, distribution, and deployment of power. Power, as the capacity to shape the conduct of men among themselves and in their dealings with nature, is one of man's splendors. And yet, this very splendor is prone to evil, prone to destructive exercise. Law constitutes a state and the state claims a monopoly of legitimate constraint. Without law there is no state. With law, there is a state in which it is always the few who rule over the many, exacting compliance from them. Without law, man's power is negligible. With law, whatever power the subject has is always threatened with subjection or annihilation by the superior's power. Abuses of legal power are particularly pernicious. To paraphrase Ricoeur, legal evil is eminently serious because it is the evil of man's rationality, the specific evil of man's splendor.[2]

The practical paradox resident in the workings of law is perhaps more clearly brought to light by noting that nonroutine human action regularly strains against the stability of institutions and laws while at the same time it likewise seeks incorporation in stable institutions and laws.[3] And of course, the formulation and application of law are themselves accomplished in and by human action. Thus, the establishment and exercise of law involves initiative which subjects some human doings to other human doings in the name of the efficacy and importance of human doings and initiatives in general.

A politics of hope provides a distinctive way of interpreting the sense and worth of law and its workings and thus of conceptually managing law's paradoxical character. The first task of this chapter will be to show how the conceptual and practical difficulties posed by the phenomenon of law are to be addressed in a politics of hope.

The second task of this chapter is to consider the issue of political education. By reason of the mortality of its members, a body politic needs continual reinvigoration through the introduction of new members. If these new members are to be wholesome additions to the group, they must be aware of and, in general, embrace the aims and objectives of the group. The process by which these new members come to this knowledge and acceptance is political education. Thus one might well say that as there is no body politic without law, so there is no enduring, flourishing, body politic without political education.

But both historical and conceptual considerations show that political education is hardly an untroubled and untroubling enterprise. Political utopias have regularly sought to build something radically new by having the teachers exercise absolute superiority over their pupils so as to bring these pupils to the vision of political well-being already possessed by their teachers. Such an enterprise involves what amounts to a dictatorial intervention into the lives of those who are to be taught. It denies on the one hand that these 'newcomers' are in any sense equals to be engaged through persuasion.

177

On the other hand, it refuses to entertain the possibility of a flaw in the vision or of failure in its implementation.[4] The newcomers, for all practical purposes, are to be treated as children.

Considerations of this sort lead Arendt to conclude:

> Education can play no part in politics, because in politics we always have to deal with those who are already educated. Whoever wants to educate adults really wants to act as their guardian and prevent them from political activity. Since one cannot educate adults, the word 'education' has an evil sound in politics; there is a pretense of education, when the real purpose is coercion without the use of force.[5]

However attractive the goal of restricting education to the pre-political sphere of children may be, practical exigencies such as those posed by large-scale migration movements block the effective achievement of such an aim. Some political entities suffer important losses of membership, e.g. 'brain drains.' Other political entities must cope with large influxes of adult immigrants. In either case, there is apparently a need to educate substantial numbers of adults to the political possibilities and responsibilities connected with their selection of places of residence.

Arendt's concern, though, is obviously not without substantial basis. If so-called political education turns out to be nothing other than propaganda, then it cannot effectively prepare newcomers for fully adult participation in political life. But if political education does not favor the educator's homeland, how would the education he provides avoid being either seditious or useless?

A politics of hope on the one hand sheds distinctive light upon the nature and function of political education. On the other hand it provides substantial guidance for the concrete practice of educating newcomers, particularly adult newcomers, to responsible politics. For a politics of hope, both law and political education, when responsibly deployed, are companion exercises of guiding and goading which enhance the political endeavors of all participants. Because of man's routedness and the relational character of his freedom, there can be a responsible deployment of such guiding and goading.

I

Law, whether regarded historically or philosophically, is a complex, far from transparent topic. The elementary terms 'law,' 'legislation,' 'legal system,' and locutions derived from or interwoven with them do not have an unequivocal, fully determinate range of application. For example, people speak of civil law, international law, the law of the peoples (*jus gentium*), natural law, etc. Nonetheless, the term 'law' and its related terms are sufficiently determinate in their reference that general agreement about their practical application to particular instances can be achieved. Even if common linguistic usage sanctions the use of these terms in strikingly different ways, this complexity is not unintelligible. 'Laws differ radically,' as H.L.A. Hart has said, 'both in content and in the ways in which they are created, yet despite this heterogeneity they are interrelated in various complex ways so as to constitute a characteristic structure or system.'[6]

My present purpose is not to debate specific theses in the philosophy of law. Rather, it is to reflect on the system of law and its complexity as a whole and to show, in the light of a politics of hope, what can and should be expected of law.

Let me begin by drawing attention to elementary features of what is commonly called human positive law. It is a truism, but an instructive truism to say that positive law is both discursive and prescriptive. Consider first law's discursive character. There are two pertinent aspects of law's discursivity. First, positive law, like all politics and history, can usefully be analysed, as Merleau-Ponty suggests, in terms of *langue* and *parole*. Second, positive law, like all discourse, has the form: A says p about x to B.

The analysis of law in terms of *langue* and *parole* takes place on two levels. At the intrasystematic level, one can distinguish a particular legal initiative, a *parole*, from the antecedent legal context which supplies resources to the initiative. The legal initiative, whether a legislative enactment, a judicial decision, or an administrative directive, always arises within a defining context but in doing so modifies this context.[7]

More importantly for present purposes is the consideration of the distinction between law, whether as particular initiative or as system, and its proximate other. The other in question here is

179

custom or tradition. For present purposes, I take tradition to be that common stock of beliefs and practices and a related structure of feelings which undergird the concrete living together of a people or body politic.[8] Custom is that part of tradition which embodies patterns of conduct according to which people are to deal with one another which are not specified in particular positive law.[9]

Historically, positive law has sometimes been considered to be that which replaces and supersedes custom. The point of such a supercession is to replace apparently less rational conduct with more rational conduct. At other times positive law is taken to be that which completes or secures custom rather than that which cancels it.[10]

It is not without interest to notice that it is only from the thirteenth century that the idea that law is an expression of conscious will has steadily gained ground in the West at the expense of the idea that law is primarily custom.[11] The ascendency of the idea of law as expression of conscious human will temporally coincides both with the increase in the scope and intensity of the political and military power of rulers and with a progressive secularization of law, a progressive detachment of civil law from religion.[12]

But law, as initiative, cannot simply replace custom. At least part of the sense of positive law is determined by its relationship to custom, which of course always antedates any particular legal initiative. Thus legal initiative must always contend with custom. It does so in part by its appeal to reason and in part by its deployment of coercion on its own behalf against some contrary practices, customary or otherwise.

The contention between law and custom, in ways similar to that between *parole* and *langue*, is not, however, necessarily an adversarial or hostile contention. It can be, and regularly at least partially is, a contention in which the efficacy of both law and custom is strengthened.

The pattern of this contest is nicely and explicitly displayed in the *Code of Canon Law* of the Latin rite of the Roman Catholic Church, a code which melds the heritage of Roman law with that of medieval law. In the canons providing instructions on how the substantive canons are to be understood and applied, one reads:

> a custom contrary to the current canon law obtains the force of
> law only when it has been legislatively observed for thirty

continuous and complete years; only a centenary or immemorial custom can prevail over a canon which contains a clause forbidding *future* customs.[13]

One also finds: 'Custom is the best interpreter of laws.'[14] And, 'The canons of this Code insofar as they refer to the old law are to be assessed . . . in accord with canonical tradition.'[15] Further, universal laws do not revoke particular customs.[16]

But these provisions are to have 'due regard' for canon 5, which says that customs contrary to this Code's prescriptions are entirely suppressed and are not permitted to serve in the future

unless the Code expressly provides otherwise or unless they are centenary or immemorial, in which case they can be tolerated if in the judgement of the ordinary [the local presiding bishop, abbot or other prelate] they cannot be removed due to circumstances of place and persons.[17]

This interplay of custom and canon reflects in its own way, even if not intentionally, Aquinas's remarks about the inherent changeability of both laws and customs. Sometimes, he says, human laws fail to meet the issue at hand. Then it is not wrong to act in a way not explicitly covered by law. And when cases of this sort are multiplied because of changed human conditions,

the custom is an index that a law is no longer serviceable, as would be shown by the verbal promulgation of a law that superceded it. If, however, the reason still holds good which made the law advantageous in the first place, then law prevails over custom, not custom over law. One exception would be a law that is useless because not possible according to the customs of the country, which is one of the essential conditions of human law. To set aside the customs of a whole people is impracticable.[18]

Something of the same sort of contest between law and custom is recognized by both Montesquieu and Blackstone. Montesquieu argues in some detail that laws and customs both do and should influence and limit one another.[19] And he advises: 'It is not sufficient [for the restoration of peace] . . . to let the conquered nation enjoy their own laws; it is, perhaps, more necessary to leave them also their manners, because people in general have a stronger attachment to these than to their laws.'[20]

Blackstone, for his part, divides civil law into *lex scripta* and *lex non scripta*. *Lex scripta* consists of specific acts of parliament. *Lex non scripta* 'includes not only *general customs*, or the common law properly so called; but also the particular customs of certain parts of the kingdom; and likewise those particular laws, that are by custom observed only in certain courts and jurisdictions.'[21] With characteristic Enlightenment optimism, Blackstone goes on to say that *lex scripta* is itself composed of two principal parts. On the one hand there are those statutes which declare what *lex non scripta* is. On the other hand, there are those statutes which remedy defects in *lex non scripta*. *Lex non scripta* always gives way to *lex scripta* and later statutes take precedence over earlier ones.[22] Nonetheless, he admits, law does get at least some of its force from custom.[23]

Blackstone's 'optimism' about the capacity of *lex scripta* to supersede *lex non scripta* has not been universally or unqualifiedly shared. Not a few today would agree with John Plamenatz when he says:

> We cannot do what we like with laws and customs, we cannot easily change them to suit ourselves. What we can do with them is limited by what they are; for they are the context of our lives and purposes . . . . Their spirit is around us and in us, expressed in our habits and our prejudices, in our unthinking responses, in the assumptions we make without even being aware that we make them. We are creatures of law even more than creators of law.[24]

One need not opt for either Blackstone's 'optimism,' which emphasizes '*parole*,' or Plamenatz's 'pessimism,' which emphasizes '*langue*.' It is more judicious to see the practical interplay of these two elements. Neither is independent of the other and both, each in its own way, is addressed to an audience to which it appeals for consent. When custom is found wanting, it is overturned by law. When law is found wanting, it is undercut by custom. But when each acknowledges its own limitations, they can sustain one another.

Thus, every particular act of legal initiative confronts a previously established set of customs and laws which must be recognized if the initiative is to achieve its objective. It can achieve its objective only if it wins acceptance. Even if the initiative in question overturns a custom or replaces a previous law, it can find acceptance if it is practically compatible with the set of customs and laws into which it is introduced.[25] If it is accepted, then it becomes part of the set which subsequent legal initiatives must confront. Thus, as Lucas sees, 'law is not simply something the sovereign tells his subjects to do, but is rather something that the subjects themselves work out in their daily lives.'[26]

Custom and established law, as the set of prescribed practices which legal initiatives must confront, are themselves part of a larger whole. Even if law is a distinct order of human experience, it is not independent of a broader context. As Merleau-Ponty saw:

> Religion, law, and economy make up a single history because
> any fact in any one of the three orders arises, in a sense, from
> the other two. This is due to the fact that they are all embedded
> in the unitary web of human choices.[27]

The name for this larger whole into which both law and custom fit is tradition.[28] Tradition is the synthesis of a vast multiplicity of human performances, all of which have been somehow marked by judgments. By virtue of these judgments, which yield beliefs as well as practices, some sorts of performances have been conserved and others have been sloughed. But tradition is not simply the result of an explicitly executed chain of judgments performed by identifiable individuals. Rather, it appears as the inherited network of beliefs and practices which provides the background necessary for the sensefulness of any particular action of any sort.

Tradition involves 'prejudgment,' prejudice in the sense of that term spelled out by H.-G. Gadamer.[29] Tradition embodies judgments made by predecessors which have successfully withstood the test of time by showing themselves to be appropriate responses to conditions still perceived as obtaining. The present agent receives these judgments as judgments which have succeeded and brings them to bear as prejudgments, as prejudices, on the situations with which he is confronted. In Hannah Arendt's words:

> Without tradition – which selects and names, which hands down
> and preserves . . . – there seems to be no willed continuity in
> time and hence, humanly speaking, neither past nor future, only
> sempiternal change of the world and the biological cycle of
> living creatures in it.[30]

Tradition, in short, functions as a general *langue* whence any initiative of any sort, any *parole*, can spring.[31]

One central feature of the relation between law and tradition is that tradition delimits, though scarcely with precision, the domain in which legal initiative is appropriate. Though it may well be the case that some community at some time or other has dealt in legal terms with each distinguishable domain of human existence, all actual nontyrannical government has acknowledged that some domains of human existence are immune to legal initiative. The law may explicitly announce these immunities and punish their violation. But in such cases the law does not and does not claim to beget the immunities. It simply admits that the immunities exist. No doubt, as history has shown, the boundaries for law established by tradition have in fact shifted. But there is no reason to think that these boundaries can be totally eliminated without a lapse into tyranny. Conversely, there is no reason to think that the time for new legal initiatives will come to a definitive end.

Legal initiatives, in fact, like most initiatives of any sort, inherently seek incorporation in a tradition which antedates them. They seek to shift from being intrusions thrust into an already established context to being integral parts of that context. Without such absorption, any initiative, including legal initiatives, is essentially ephemeral.

The interplay described here among law, custom, and tradition is far from conceptually neat. But neither is it sheerly chaotic. It is, rather, just as fuzzy as one would expect, given the finite, historical character of the human conduct with which it deals.

Let me turn now to a second important aspect of the discursivity of human positive law. Like everything discursive, law has the form A says p about x to B. This form invites two complementary considerations, (a) that of the relationship between A and B, and (b) that of the nature of x and of the relationship between x and p.

The discursive relationship in legal matters between A and B superficially appears to be a basically monological relationship between a ruler and a subject. But reflection on the interplay among law, custom, and tradition warns one away from too ready acceptance of this superficial view. A, the ruler, is not 'pure' speaker and B, the subject, 'pure' heeder. B has a history and bears a tradition with which A must reckon if his lawgiving is to achieve its intended results. B, differently but no less surely than A, is also an actor in the legal enterprise. It is more accurate, then, to characterize legal discourse as dialogical rather than as monological. But, as I will show below, even to call it dialogical is not sufficiently subtle.

Precisely because law is dialogical there is substance to the long-standing Western tradition that law, rather than being essentially inimical to freedom, is its necessary condition. Aristotle, for example, argued that government and law are the only alternatives to tyranny and despotism. Law restrains the ruler and allows the ruled to be citizens.[32] True forms of government regard the common interest and constitute a community of free men.[33] 'Men should not', Aristotle says, 'think it slavery to live according to the rule of the constitution; for it is their salvation.'[34]

This tradition appears in one form or another in writers as diverse as Aquinas, Hobbes, Locke, and Montesquieu. Among its clearest expressions is that articulated by Blackstone, who holds that 'the first and primary end of human laws is to *maintain* and *regulate* those absolute rights of individuals.'[35] In more detail, in praise of England and its laws, Blackstone says that England is perhaps the only land

> in which political or civil liberty is the very end and scope of the constitution. This liberty, rightly understood, consists in the power of doing whatever the laws permit; which is only to be effected by a general conformity of all orders and degrees to those equitable rules of action, by which the meanest individual is protected from the insults and oppression of the greatest.[36]

Nonetheless, this tradition notwithstanding, it must be acknowledged that there is something distinctly paradoxical, both practically and conceptually, in the contention that law fosters rather than thwarts freedom. The practical paradox is that freedom is fostered through submission to law only if the scope of law is itself limited either by law or by something much like law. The conceptual paradox is constituted by the conjunction of the notions of freedom, rule, duty, etc.[37] Ernest Barker, for one, has neatly set forth the practical paradox. He says: 'The greater the liberty of the individual, the greater the interposition of government: the more rights, the more law, and therefore the more activity of the State in declaring and enforcing law.'[38] This paradox, though, drives no wedge between the citizen and the state. Rather, the citizen learns to embrace, 'a tension, which is as healthy as it is necessary.'[39] Nonetheless this paradox and its attendant tension shows that in practice the connection between law and freedom is contingent and somewhat tenuous.[40]

That law and freedom can coexist is made possible by the fact that human law, both in its making and in its enforcement, is limited. Whether these limits be thought of as extrinsic to human law or as part of its source, positive law is recognized by all except the crudest, most fundamentalist legal realist as arising and getting its sense from a source other than law itself. Just what this means can be clarified by a consideration of the relationship in legal discourse between p, what is said, and x, that which the saying is about. In general, this relationship can be discussed in terms of the relationship between the legal declaration and what is just.

Here, too, the Western tradition of legal thought is most instructive. Aristotle, in particular, is most helpful. He notes that the terms 'just' and 'unjust' are used in several senses. He says that, in one sense, the just is the lawful and the fair and the unjust is the unlawful and the unfair. 'Everything lawful is in a sense just. For "lawful" is what the art of legislation has defined as such, and we call each particular enactment "just".'[41] But Aristotle also makes it clear that this equation of the lawful and the just holds good only in those communities which aim at some version of the common good. Where this is not the case, there is no justice in this sense, but only something which somehow resembles the just.[42] Apparently, there is no justice without legal judgments which *decide* what is to be done and what is to be avoided. But the mere decision alone is insufficient to constitute justice in conduct.[43]

This gap between legal declaration and what is just leads Aristotle on the one hand to distinguish between that which is just by nature and that which is just by convention and on the other hand to introduce the concept of equity (*epikeia*) into his doctrine of justice.

Let me consider the question of equity before taking up the distinction between the just by nature and the just by convention. All positive law, as Aristotle saw, is subject to an ineliminable 'internal' constraint, namely to the constraint imposed by the language in which it is cast. For the most part, law is formulated in universal terms. But it is meant to be applied in particular cases. If positive law is to bring about justice, then its application must be tailored to the particular circumstances of the case. In short, it must be supplemented by equity.

Equity (*epikeia*), Aristotle says, is a corrective for what is just.

The law to be rectified by equity is not itself necessarily incorrect. But because actions are particular, the law by itself cannot be completely appropriate.[44] The rectification supplied by equity 'corresponds to what the lawgiver himself would have said if he were present, and what he would have enacted if he had known (of this particular case).'[45]

In commenting on this section of the *Nicomachean Ethics*, Aquinas adds that 'by equity a person is obedient in a higher way when he follows the intention of the legislator where the words of the law differ from it.'[46] Thus Aquinas is led to conclude:

> The nature of the equitable is that it be directive of the law where the law is deficient for some particular cases. . . . On account of this, after enactment of the law a decision of the judges is required by which the universal statement of the law is applied to a particular matter. Because the material of human acts is indeterminate, it follows that their norm, which is the law, must be indeterminate in the sense that it is not absolutely rigid.[47]

Whether one should see the equitable application of the law through the decisions and opinions of judges, counselors, or administrators as a rectification of a deficiency in the law or as a completion and fulfillment of the law,[48] the law, taken simply as legislation, is clearly insufficient to accomplish its own objectives. What the lawmaker produces requires further determination by other legal initiatives. The lawmaker cannot rationally prohibit this supplementation. Nor can he prescribe the precise features of the supplement. Attempts by nontyrannical legislators to forestall unforeseen supplementation are irrational and probably doomed to failure. The lawmaker can neither reasonably nor successfully insist upon having either the only word or even the last word.

The principle of equity has, on occasion, given rise to a second set of rules. Thus, within English law there was once a set of rules administered by the Courts of Equity which was distinct from the rules administered by the Courts of Common Law.[49] But the principle of equity cannot be exhaustively captured by any such second set of rules. The supplements in question, embodied in such staples of legal practice as judicial opinions, judicial discretion, out-of-court settlements, etc., necessarily resist exhaustive replacement by rules of any sort.

Thus, though equity is a supplement to law, it is no mere optional supplement. Blackstone, to be sure, is not completely without justification when he says:

> Law, without equity, though hard and disagreeable, is much more desirable for the public good, than equity without law . . . as there would then be almost as many different rules of action laid down in our courts, as there are differences of capacity and sentiment in the human mind.[50]

But law, in turn, if consistently unmodified by equity, would become oppressive and odious.[51] It would squander the respect it would otherwise enjoy. Perhaps the ineliminable importance of equity is best seen in the long-standing, general recognition that in situations of necessity, all positive law is superseded.[52] Supercession of the law in cases of necessity is itself a preeminent case of equity at play.

In addition to the 'internal' constraint of equity upon positive law, an equally long-standing, but perhaps less general, part of the Western legal tradition has maintained that there is a second, 'external' constraint to which positive law is subject. This constraint has regularly been spoken of as the law of nature or natural law.

The terms 'law of nature' and 'natural law' have, over the centuries, been understood in a variety of ways.[53] But however the term is defined, the natural law tradition uniformly claims that positive law must fit into an a priori context of requirements which human conduct is duty bound to observe. This ambient context bears heavily upon all human conduct. A typical enough example of the force of natural law, one given by Aristotle, is Antigone's insistence that she must bury Polyneices in spite of Creon's prohibition. As Aristotle explains: 'There really is, as everyone to some extent divines, a natural justice and injustice that is binding on all men, even those who have no association or covenant with each other.'[54]

For the natural law tradition, then, positive law cannot be a mere matter of human will. Nor can it reasonably pretend to establish its own scope or merit. If positive law is genuinely to promote the preservation and welfare of the people it governs, it must admit that it cannot fully justify itself. At least part of its justification must come from its admitted subordination to natural law. Every positive law and rule, then, appeals beyond itself for its justification. And however one construes that to which appeal is made, it is never merely an appeal to some other positive rule or law. Whatever validity positive law can give to itself, it cannot fully assure its own value.[55]

The natural law tradition, however, has regularly claimed that universal and necessary provisions of natural law can be articulated. But claims that its principles and their articulations are immune to historical conditions, among other reasons, has given rise to numerous arguments against the existence of natural law.[56]

A politics of hope, rooted as it is in the understanding of man as one who is essentially and thoroughly historical, cannot admit ahistorical articulations of natural law. But it can and does recognize that the value of positive law rests ultimately beyond itself. It rests on law's promotion of the public weal in both its global and its distributive dimension. What constitutes the content of the public weal is always historical and contingent. But it is always necessarily something more than the sheer concoction of human wills. For a politics of hope, what the law of nature, or natural law, requires of positive law is neither more nor less than that positive law promote the public weal in all its dimensions. Positive law, then, is never identical with the public weal. And the public weal itself, as I noted in the last chapter, is for the most part a regulative rather than a dogmatic concept.[57]

At this point, let me summarize these reflections on the discursive character of positive law. Not only is discourse of this sort basically dialogical rather than monological. The legal dialogue is itself subsumed under some requirement to which it is answerable and from which at least part of its value comes. Part of its value does rest in its very dialogical character.[58] But this dialogue always aims for a value beyond mere dialogicality, though including dialogicality. It aims to support the public weal and thereby satisfy the law of nature.

Positive law, as I mentioned earlier in this chapter, is not only discursive. It is also prescriptive. Legal discourse does not merely describe appropriate human conduct. It also prescribes it. Prescription, rather than simple description, makes sense, as Kant has indicated, whenever reason is complicated by desire. Reason is concerned with the universal and the necessary. Desire, by contrast, is always concerned with the particular and the contingent. Man's gapped character, the irreducible tension between his thought and his desire make it necessary that his reflections on how appropriate human conduct is to come about requires prescriptions and not only descriptions.[59] Since both the ruler and the ruled possess this same gapped character, then prescriptions should be addressed to both of them.

Taken together, the discursivity and prescriptivity proper to positive law substantially determine what can count as responsible law. Responsible law, it is evident, cannot claim to provide exhaustive justification for itself. A body of law resting exclusively on the will of its formulators and adherents ignores or denies the referentiality of legal discourse, like all discourses, to something other than itself. It likewise fails to take into account the gapped character of the legal actors. However much sway they give to desire, they cannot, so long as they are human, totally repress the appeals issuing from their own rationality. The kind of law implicit in a politics of sheer might, then, a politics giving full sway to desire, is fundamentally flawed and irresponsible.

Conversely, the kind of law implicit in a politics of vision is also fundamentally defective. Law, in such a politics, would have to claim either that it was already perfect and had rendered custom otiose or that it contained within itself everything required to bring it to this sort of ideal completion. This law would claim either fully to embody the requirements of natural law or to articulate rules which are unquestionably consonant with a natural law which is known and can be precisely articulated. Whether such a body of positive law is destined, upon completion, to wither away as law, that is, to have no need to retain its prescriptive character, or whether it would achieve a permanence in no need of amendment, it too flies in the face of man's gapped character. If man is, as I have argued, essentially finite, historical, and intersubjective, then who could formulate this perfect law? Pretensions to perfection on the part of positive law either deny or truncate the implications of these irremovable features of human existence.

Responsible politics, in its legal doctrine and theory, rejects both of these extreme positions. It insists upon the irreducibility of the tensions and complexities resident within both the articulation and the implementation of positive law and it resolutely rejects any claim of law to be self-justifying. Within the scope of responsible politics, a politics of hope surpasses its proximate competitors, namely politics of containment and politics of resignation, because the interpretation it can assign to the components of those complexities and tensions shows both how they spring from man's condition as one who is essentially *en route* and how they all can and should be conducive to his well-being. A politics of hope is thus able to avoid pernicious dualisms of all sorts.

Law, for a politics of hope, is not merely a deplorable, if unavoidable, intrusion into the more natural intercourse among people guided by custom or tradition. Something of this bleak view of law can be found in Pascal's *Pensées*. He says:

> Custom makes equity in its entirety, for the sole reason that it has been received. This is the mystical foundation of its authority. He who would trace it back to its source [*principe*] would destroy it. Nothing is so faulty as those laws which redress faults.[60]

Similarly, Rousseau says in *A Discourse on the Origin of Inequality:*

> I would have desired that . . . everyone . . . be convinced that it is above all the great antiquity of laws which makes them holy and venerable . . ., that in growing accustomed to neglect old usages on the pretext of making improvements, great evils are often introduced to correct lesser ones.[61]

Views of law of this sort are characteristic of politics of resignation.

But neither is law to be understood, as in politics of containment, as exclusively a bulwark against a natural tendency among men to destroy one another and the communities they inhabit. This latter view, found for example in the positions of Marsilius of Padua and Hobbes, maintains that law is basically the means by which a ruler wards off the populace's tendencies 'to fighting and separation and finally the destruction of the state.'[62]

For a politics of hope, positive law is both a rule and a resource.[63] Law not only goads, it also guides. A politics of hope does not forget that every nation with its laws is the outgrowth of what Paul Ricoeur has called an inceptive violence. This violence overthrows an old legitimacy of ruling and replaces it with a new one. The new ruling, in turn, 'always retains a note of contingency, something strictly historical which its violent birth never ceases to confer upon it.'[64] But a politics of hope, drawing inspiration from Merleau-Ponty, understands law to be more than simply an extension of this inceptive violence. It is a human achievement which can improve the quality of human existence.[65] A politics of hope does not presumptuously overlook the riskiness intrinsic to every legal initiative. But it recognizes that men cannot be efficacious in their mediations without risk. Risky though it is, the institution of law can make a unique contribution to human efficacy.

Thus, a politics of hope takes the finitude and historicality of law to be primarily an opportunity rather than a handicap. On the one hand, the tension between law and custom affords an opportunity for the present generation to make its own mark on the norms of conduct by which its community is governed. The fact that custom is not destroyed but rather is elaborated through legal initiatives allows the hope that this new legal initiative will be lastingly effective. On the other hand, the perpetual amendability of the law leaves open opportunities for future generations to undertake their own legal initiatives without having to repudiate the achievements of its predecessors.

Similarly, a politics of hope interprets the connections between positive law and both natural law and equity as benefits rather than obstacles. By reason of its recognition of the essential finitude and historicality of all human performances, a politics of hope eschews claims to either complete speech or perfect moments. Natural law, for a politics of hope, cannot be given definitive propositional formulation. It plays, in Gadamer's terms, a critical rather than a dogmatic role.[66] Similarly, there is no perfect moment when the equitable solution would eliminate the need for a body of positive law articulated in universal terms. Without law, and custom for that matter, the principles of both natural law and equity would be fruitless.[67]

Positive law is never, therefore, without point. The fact that it cannot reasonably aspire to be complete speech, that it needs supplementation by reference to the principles of equity and natural law, does not entail any depreciation of positive law. Indeed, for a politics of hope, the interplay of positive law, equity, and natural law is recognized as one in which the efficacy of each is enhanced rather than impeded.

A politics of hope also casts a distinctive light upon the gap between reason and desire which necessitates the prescriptive character of positive law. Desire, in contrast to reason, is always particular. It is historical, spatio-temporally situated. Reason, by contrast, is universal. Positive law shows traces of both reason and desire. It is couched in universal terms but, at least in part, it addresses specific spatio-temporal situations and the desires associated with these situations. But, as I have just mentioned, the way the law addresses these situations is never perfect. On the one hand, it cannot capture the several unique facets of the situation. On the other hand, wedded as it is to some historical context, no positive law can achieve universal, omnitemporal acceptability.

A politics of hope, resting on the interpretation of man as one who is essentially *en route*, understands this condition of law in terms of the necessary interplay between man's mediational and his nonmediational performances. Specifically, discursive performances mediate perceptual and appetitive performances. But, as the phenomena of terminal silence shows, this discursive mediation is itself perceived to be necessarily nonexhaustive. Perception, both before and after discourse, is never out of order. Translated to the issue of law, this means that reference to equity and natural law, each involving a kind of perception, is appropriate both to the framing and to the implementing of positive law.[68]

Because positive law has this essential link to a specific spatio-temporal context, it is capable of expressing the needs and desires of the particular community in question. Because it likewise is essentially linked to the perception of the universality of natural law which cannot be given adequate linguistic formulation, the positive law of any particular community can acknowledge the defensibility of alternate bodies of positive law for other communities. Thus positive law, when properly understood, can contribute to rather than impede the maximally extensive dialogue among all men of all times and places which a politics of hope is committed to promote.

Considerations of much the same sort show that every body of positive law, and the desires associated with it, has both a local and a global significance. Any desire for finite resources has an impact on other desires. Since the world men inhabit is now clearly seen to be finite, no body of law can have only exclusively local effects.[69] Domestic law today can be seen necessarily to have international ramifications.[70]

Positive law, then, for a politics of hope, at its best recognizes the multiple tensions at play within and among men who are essentially *en route*. This law, precisely in and through its finitude and historicality, promotes the optimal expression of the constituent components of these tensions among the largest number of people possible. In the final analysis, for a politics of hope, positive law, like all political phenomena, can and should promote the most extensive possible dialogue concerning what constitutes the public weal and how to foster that weal. It does so both by goading people to coordinate the satisfaction of their desires with others and by guiding them to effective ways to achieve this coordination.

II

A second, critically important feature of responsible political life is political education. This topic is, if anything, more complex and vexing even than that of law. Unlike law, political education has regularly been neglected. Aristotle in fact claimed that it was universally neglected.[71] And Sheldon Wolin, in his reflections on contemporary constitutionalism, makes a similar complaint.[72] Further, unlike law which has historically had quite adequately defined institutions and agents to give it a distinctive voice, the credentials of agents and institutions claiming to provide political education are by no means unassailable. But like law, political education is a matter of both guiding and goading. The guiding and goading of law has been shown not to be incompatible with the routedness of men who are endowed with a freedom which is relational rather than autonomous. Rather, law turned out to be both necessary and capable of being positively beneficial. For basically the same reasons, a politics of hope maintains that political education can and should contribute to both the efficacy and the well-being of men, whether taken singly or in community.[73] In fact, for a politics of hope, political education is a *sine qua non* for any responsible politics.

Neglect of political education would appear to be generally consistent with social contract theories of politics. These theories apparently entail that the participants in such contracts already know what they are about when they enter into contracts. Prior to their participation, logically, if not temporally, the participants would have their education, political or otherwise, already in hand. Education then would have no part to play within politics as such. Thus attempts to introduce education into politics would seem to be both conceptually confused and practically either worthless or maleficent.

More serious, perhaps, is the argument I mentioned above which Hannah Arendt advances against the introduction of education into politics. Politics, for her too, is an interaction among those whose education is already complete. Education, for her, always requires an authoritative teacher superior who instructs a student subject. It is somehow dictatorial. Politics, by contrast, involves 'joining with one's equals in assuming the effort of persuasion and running the risk of failure.'[74] Therefore genuine education neither should nor can have a place in genuine politics.

A politics of hope, however, not only allows for but indeed elicits genuine political education. Arendt herself, even if somewhat obliquely, supplies grounds for such an education. In her discussion of education, she correctly sees the connection between it and the fragility endemic in all finite historical communities. The fragile community must, on the one hand, be protected against 'being overrun and destroyed by the onslaught of the new that bursts upon it with each new generation.'[75] But on the other hand, if the community is to avoid degeneration and ossification, it must undergo constant renewal by newcomers. As she points out:

> Our *hope* always hangs on the new which every generation brings; but precisely because we base our *hope* only on this, we destroy everything if we so try to control the new that we, the old, can dictate how it will look.[76]

The task of education cannot be to guarantee the renewal of the community. That would be an impossible task. But it can provide newcomers with the wherewithal to make renewal a live possibility.

Notwithstanding Arendt's own explicit position to the contrary, a man who is essentially *en route* is always in some respects a newcomer. Today this is as clear as it ever was. The material and cultural conditions in which politics is played out can and do undergo substantial changes even within the span of a single person's adult years. So too do the political possibilities. All education, political and otherwise, is therefore always in danger of becoming outdated. The time for education of all sorts, then, has no definitive or natural *terminus ad quem*. Fully adult members of any body politic remain constantly in need of further education of all sorts, including political education. In almost every other sort of topic-centered discourse, the need for continued education is expressly admitted and addressed through meetings, journals, etc. Political discourse has many of these same sorts of means available for political education. But, whether through thoughtlessness or confusion

195

about just what political education can and should accomplish, its use of these means has in fact been for the most part haphazard.

For a politics of hope,[77] the ultimate objective of political education is the same as that of politics itself. Politics is basically a conversation and political education prepares one to participate in this conversation.[78] Education for a politics of hope inevitably will have a reflexive cast. It will emphasize both the distinctiveness of political activity and the case for a politics of hope as opposed to that of its competitors. More specifically, because political education is political, the task for its teachers is to make clear to newcomers (a) that politics is irreplaceable by any other sort of activity and is by no means optional, (b) what are the distinctive possibilities and limits of political thought and activity, what, in short, distinguishes responsible from irresponsible politics, and (c) what are the politically relevant material and cultural conditions peculiar to the era both the teacher and the student inhabit.

Likewise, because it is political, political education is practical. That is, it is oriented toward improved political practice in the future by both teachers and students. It presumes that both the teachers and the students are and will be fellow political actors in a common community.

But because political education is indeed education, the distinction between teachers and students cannot be obliterated. This distinction, of course, is basically one of roles rather than one of persons. Individual persons may well occupy one of these roles at one time and the other at another time. The teachers are to continue the initiation of newcomers into the body politic. They guide by suggesting new hypotheses, evidence, and methods of inquiry concerning political judgment and reality. They suggest solutions for contemporary problems. They goad by criticizing previously reached political activity and judgments whether of other peoples or of their own community, including those adopted by their students. Students, for their part, are to be attentive and responsive, willing to learn but still critical.

The guiding and goading intrinsic to political education cannot, however, extend to include the spheres of deliberation and decision. In these latter spheres, the spheres of debate, voting, etc., the distinction between teacher and student is no longer valid. Citizens then join one another as fellow participants. Political education, because it is education, belongs primarily to the domain of discourse rather than to that of action. But because it is also political, it cannot, as I pointed out in Chapter 1, be innocent.[79]

The interplay between political education, with its distinctions between teacher and student, and political deliberation and decision, with its requirement of basic equality, can be instructively compared to some aspects of legal trial practice. In some trials, expert witnesses supply jurors with information which laymen could not be expected to possess. They educate jurors. But jury deliberations and decisions are not supposed to be mere ratifications of the experts' testimony. Once the testimony has been received, the function of the teacher lapses and their 'students' begin deliberations as peers.

The point of expert testimony is to bring about a well-informed jury. It would be foolish for the jurors not to accept instruction from the hands of experts. But expert witnesses are not to supersede the jurors. It would pervert the system if jurors were simply to acquiesce without deliberation and decision in such testimony.

Different trials at different times call for different expert testimony. Intellectual developments in the course of time can make the expert testimony given at one time obsolete or irrelevant at a later time. New testimony and indeed new experts are needed. Similarly, because it is thoroughly historical, political conversation can never be definitely finished with political education. Changes in both material and cultural resources and in knowledge about them make the need for continuing political education permanent. Without fresh education, the political conversation stagnates.

The central content of political education is always the public weal. This education must first make clear the distinction between the global and the distributive dimensions of the public weal. It must show that this distinction is irreducible and that both dimensions are equiprimordial. That is, neither can be given unqualified preeminence over the other. Second, it must provide guidance concerning just how the constituents of the distributive dimension are to be determined. For example, what is to be said about the Scottish separatist movement? Is the same thing to be said about both it and the Welsh separatist movement? Third, political education should help students understand the nature and quantity of the resources available in the contemporary world.

Paul Ricouer has helpfully proposed a somewhat more specific list of salient features which contemporary responsible political education should encompass.[80] Political education, first, should make plain just what are the basic economic features of the contemporary world. It must take note, on the one hand, of the scarcity of resources and the details of that scarcity. No responsible politics can ignore such scarcity. On the other hand, political education must also deal with the fact that contemporary society, worldwide, is characterized by 'industries.' Industries (*outillages*) are 'collections of means and mediations which allow a human collectivity to create new goods.'[81] They are assemblages of tools, techniques, documents, and specialized experience through which disposable goods of any sort are developed, produced, and distributed. These goods may be hoes, shoes, turbines, computers, fashion styles, books or anything else which can be treated as an object of commerce. None of these things is tied essentially to any particular people or culture. Each of them is essentially a universal acquisition available to men anywhere. In Ricoeur's words:

> Every invention is by right acquired for all men. Technological history of the human race is that of humanity considered as a single man. . . . In this sense civilization is in the singular: there is *a* civilization; there is *the* civilization.[82]

Part of the task of political education is to make clear the basic nonsense involved in any effort by any body politic to acquire industries or products which it can surely preserve exclusively as its own and withhold from other peoples. The very nature of industries is such that no nation or alliance of nations can achieve permanent, unqualified superiority either in technology or in the products of technology. This consideration should be influential in discussions of economic and military power.

Political education cannot be content, though, simply to call attention to facts of scarcity and of technological universality. It must also make clear that the intersection of scarcity and industry is never without political and moral significance. Whatever economic necessities obtain, they are always affected by human choices. Men are responsible for the systematic development of industries. The exercise of responsible influence, however, cannot be efficacious if it is left to merely a series of choices by individuals. Only exercises of collective choice can effectively order economic activity toward human well-being. But collective choice does not occur automatically. Political means must be fostered which promote it. In sum, then, the first task of political education is to show (a) that scarcity and industries know no political boundaries, (b) that economic developments extend the field of human responsibility, and (c) that a crucial function of responsible political communities is to establish and maintain institutions through which this collective responsibility can be exercised.[83]

A second task for political education is that of showing that abstention from politics in the name of some supposedly higher norms, ethical or religious, is ultimately irresponsible. Whatever the attraction of a utopia devoid of ambiguity and uncertainty, a responsible politics can never lay claim to being either perfect or definitive. Nor can it responsibly yield to what Ricoeur, following Max Weber, calls an ethics of conviction. An ethics of conviction, appealing to articulable absolutes of some sort, e.g. religious re-velations, dogmatic formulations of natural law, etc., is not essen-tially hostile to responsible politics. But responsible politics cannot allow the principles of any such ethic to be either the exhaustive or the primary principles of its own activity. It can and should give such an ethic a hearing but it cannot give this ethic the final word. It cannot, for example, simply translate the principles of this ethic into its positive law. Proper political education shows why this is so. In responsible politics there is no 'final word.' Proper political educa-tion shows that man, who is essentially *en route*, deceives himself so long as he seeks salvation, political or otherwise, from his routed-ness.

Contemporary political education, third, has the task of showing how the global politico-technological civilization can be integrated with the uniqueness of each historically singular human group. It is to show how a part can belong to a whole without losing its identity as a unique part. The heritage of each group in its distinctiveness will be shown to be cherishable and worth fostering, even if it is the case that all contemporary politics necessarily has global ramifications.[84] A responsible political education will acknowledge that for several reasons, of which scarcity is not the least, it is senseless to aim for the survival of all of the particular values of the several historical groups. But it will promote those particular values which can be so reinterpreted that they continue to vivify a multi-plicity of diverse political groups.[85] And it will acknowledge that the loss of any particular values is indeed a loss and not a gain. The point of this educational enterprise is to protect the dialogue constitutive of political discourse against the 'monologic' tendencies indigenous in the global scope of technological civilization. Political education is to support the diversity required for living dialogue.

A politics of hope is mindful of the dangers inherent in the enterprise of political education to which Arendt has pointed. There is always the possibility that the teacher-pupil relationship will be made global and permanent. This would have the effect of installing the reign of an elite corps of experts who would of course be self-certifying. There is likewise always the possibility that education would be replaced by propagandizing manipulation. These dangers are irremovable. But for a politics of hope they are simply consequences of the politically more fundamental, irreducible distinction between the ruler and the ruled.

A politics of hope does not disregard such dangers. It resists the presumptuousness of regarding these dangers as either minor or remote. But it also eschews the presumptuousness of thinking either that the fruits of responsible political education are negligible or that they can be gotten without that education. A politics of hope, then, accepts the risk of allowing and promoting political education.

But for a politics of hope, political education, like everything political, is dialogical rather than monological. Not only is there the dialogue between teacher and pupil. There is also need for a dialogue among the teachers as well as among the students. It is of particular importance that the dialogue among the teachers be conducted within the hearing of the students. For a politics of hope, this dialogue, like all political dialogue, is no mere accommodation to the unavailability of complete speech. A maximally extensive dialogue is sought precisely because something of benefit is hoped for from every participant.

Within a politics of hope, it is recognized that appropriate dialogue does not occur automatically. It must be fostered. Accordingly, multiple institutions should be either established or encouraged in order to insure that this dialogue takes place. Institutions insure that there will be political teachers. The multiplicity of these institutions, each with its own structure and dynamics, insures that there is dialogue among teachers with different messages and not merely a multi-voiced monologue. Further, these institutions must leave room for people to take upon themselves the tasks of political educators without institutional sanction. Without such room, the institutional network would pretend to a completeness which it simply cannot have.

Examples of institutions which serve to identify and clarify political teachers are a press which is independent of those holding political rulership, political parties, bureaucracies charged with making information relevant to political judgments available to citizenry, and, in one respect at least, parliamentary or congressional hearings and debates. A politics of hope acknowledges that teaching is part of the function of some rulers. But it insists that the rulers not be the only teachers able to address the citizens.

A politics of hope, then, calls for rulers who promote responsible political education. And responsible political education, given the essential finitude of its teachers, requires them to both accept and promote interventions from their pupils. Correspondingly, a politics of hope calls for citizens who both demand such educational opportunities and take advantage of them. Unless citizens obtain this education they are ignorant actors and therefore dangerous both to themselves and to others.

For political education to be responsible, it must at times be subject to the judgment of the pupils. That is, just as a responsible hierarchical relationship between ruler and ruled requires, as I said above, that sometimes they act together on a common footing, so too a responsible teacher-student relationship also requires occasions on which the students can determine whether to continue their political education under the same teachers or turn to others. Obvious examples of such occasions are elections of one sort or another. For a politics of hope such moments are not necessarily times in which the choice of winners is tantamount to the repudiation of losers. Since no teacher is the perfect teacher and no student has endless time in which to attend to every available teacher, selections must be made. But no one can responsibly claim that any selection is definitive.

In sum, then, political teachers and students reciprocally both goad and guide one another. Teachers guide by calling students' attention to salient facts and clarifying proposals for course of political action. They goad by challenging the students to rethink their own political assumptions and predispositions. Students guide teachers by supporting or withholding support for their teaching in the course of evaluating the teaching they have received. They goad a teacher either by objections to or protest against or by indifference toward the teacher's message.[86] The guiding and goading which occur in political education is obviously less formal and unequivocal than that which takes place in classroom settings. But it is by no means necessarily less efficacious.

For a politics of hope, this reciprocal guiding and goading is not a regrettable or deplorable affliction from which the body politic suffers. Rather, it is a healthy condition for men who are essentially finite, historical, and intersubjective, for men who are essentially *en route*. The strife evidenced in the guiding and goading does not show a radical hostility between man and man. To the contrary, it can and should promote the reciprocal and mutual enhancement of their efficacious freedom and the concomitant mutual respect for each person's capacity to contribute to the enhancement.

When understood in terms of a politics of hope, political education and positive law, each taken as a whole, are seen to be themselves in dialectical tension with one another. They both need and support one another. Political education needs the support of positive law if it is to have stable institutions through which to work. At the same time, political education has not done its work unless it makes clear the necessarily limited validity of all claims made by all concrete expressions of positive law. Political education cannot be responsible if it is simply set in fixed opposition to the positive law of the peoples in whose midst it takes place. If it were so set, it could not contribute to the continuous induction of newcomers into a structured world. It would fail to be genuinely educational. But political education also fails to be responsible if it simply slavishly endorses whatever law happens presently to exist. Were it to do so, it would attempt to deceive the newcomers by pretending that positive law can have a completeness which is always impossible.

Positive law, for its part, would be irresponsible if it were to sanction political education dedicated to its own destruction. To do so would be to trivialize its own worth. But it would also be irresponsible if it sought to limit political education to support for the legal *status quo*. To do so would pretend to absolutize its own worth.

For a politics of hope, the dialectic between political education and positive law, when properly appreciated and participated in, fosters rather than frustrates efficacious freedom. And today, given the nature of the international dimension of all politics, which Merleau-Ponty and so many others have made clear, this dialectic is not confined exclusively to either domestic or international matters. In both law and political education, this dialectic has both domestic and international ramifications. That it does have both dimensions is, for a politics of hope, an important constituent of the positive worth of both the dialectic and its two poles.

9

Conclusion

This study, as I indicated in the first two chapters, aims to respond to two sets of stimuli. First, as I showed in Chapter 1, the domain of politics as such has been and is subject to attacks and depreciations of various sorts. The central objective of this study has been to set forth a vindication of politics. One part of the vindication is conceptual. The other part consists of a set of recommendations and cautions for political practice designed to enable that practice to show in deed its own irreplaceable worth.

The second stimulus to which this study responds is a congeries of insights and arguments concerning responsible political practice enunciated by a number of contemporary thinkers. Prominent among these thinkers are Hans-Georg Gadamer, Paul Ricoeur, Anthony Giddens, Charles Taylor, and J.R. Lucas. But above all, as Chapter 2 makes clear, the political thought of Maurice Merleau-Ponty has furnished both a point of departure and fruitful conceptual resources.[1] My effort here has been to build upon his contribution with the aid of the other thinkers just mentioned. These sources, in one fashion or another, recognize the validity of practical philosophy as a worthy enterprise in its own right and not merely as the byproduct of speculative thought. They thus prompt, explicitly or otherwise, attention to Aristotle's majestic accomplishments in the *Nicomachean Ethics*, the *Politics,* the *Rhetoric*, and the *Poetics* and to the influence of these accomplishments upon Western political thoguht. My study by no means pretends to syncretize these fertile, diverse resources. But it happily acknowledges its heavy indebtedness to them.

In fact, in addition to the analyses and evidence I have presented in support of a politics of hope, I also claim that a persuasive reason for adopting such a politics is precisely that it salvages so much of the tradition of Western political thought. My proposal is by no means cut from whole cloth. It is a *parole* clearly made possible by and vivified by a rich *langue*.

In the course of this study, I have often referred explicitly to one or another component of this tradition. I have, for example, shown several links between a politics of hope and Montesquieu's political thought. But it is not amiss to point briefly to some other important traditional insights which my study salvages and refurbishes. A politics of hope is not merely opportunistic. Success is not a sufficient condition for responsible political conduct. Accordingly, a politics of hope salvages from politics of vision of various kinds the insight that there is some principle or requirement which responsible politics does not invent but must acknowledge. This principle or requirement is, to be sure, critical and not dogmatic, as politics of vision would have it. But it is not merely the creature of some specific political community.

Conversely, success is a necessary condition for responsible politics. This admission allows a politics of hope to salvage the Hobbesian insight that human survival is an essential issue for any responsible politics. It is not, as vulgar Hobbesianism would have it, the exclusively ultimate task for a concrete politics. But it is never irrelevant.

The sort of politics I propose can also salvage and refurbish the Rousseauian distinction between the always valid general will and the often misguided will of the multitude. It does so by its recognition (a) that politics is an affair of volition and excellence in doing rather than basically a matter of speculation and excellence in seeing, and (b) that the volition to be considered in any responsible political conduct cannot be merely the will of some present moment detached from its historical setting. A politics of hope is not, obviously, simply a form of politics of will. But neither is it a politics without will.

In similar fashion, the Marxian distinction between the communists and the proletarians on the one hand and the Lockean doctrine of executive privilege, when coupled with their common insistence that rulers lead by leave of the ruled, can be seen as important, if flawed, attempts to articulate the realization that political leadership is a form of virtuosity. This virtuosity cannot be guaranteed ahead of time. Nor is the virtuoso able to insure his virtuosity. Virtuosity exists only in the deed. Only the witnesses to the deed can determine whether it embodies virtuosity. And there is necessarily something retrospective in such certification. Thus 'space' must be allowed to rulers to try their hand at virtuosity. Political rule cannot be shorn of the riskiness involved in this grant of leeway.

Precisely because my proposal sets out to and does refurbish important constituents of the tradition, it can and does aspire to find its place in that tradition. It expressly presents itself as a *parole* made possible by a *langue* which it aims both to modify and to win incorporation within.

My proposal respects, and indeed gives greater specificity to, the central abiding desiderata or principles noted in Chapter 1 as features which the tradition holds to be crucial for any responsible politics. It observes the reasonableness principle by insisting that the exercise of political rule is always set in a dialogue in which the ruled, as well as the ruler, have an active role to play. It observes the effectiveness principle by emphasizing the necessity of adapting political policies and practices to prevailing circumstances. It observes the justice principle inasmuch as it requires that all politics aim at the greatest possible participation by the greatest number of people. And it observes the freedom principle by insisting upon the relational character of all freedom, including that of the ruler.

But as I have frequently indicated, the tradition of Western political thought has often ignored or misrepresented the finite, historical, intersubjective character of political actors who are essentially *en route*. It has often given rise to exorbitant doctrines. Pertinent to the appropriate assessment of a politics of hope of the sort I defend here is the intrinsic modesty of both the proposal and the politics it recommends. This modesty, if I am correct in describing man as one who is essentially routed and whose freedom is relational, is necessary for any responsible theory or practice of politics. This modesty is not, however, a characteristic which confines. It is not one which leads to timidity. Rather, in a politics of hope, this modesty provides room for ever more extensive engagement among the political actors.

Because the modesty of my proposal is so integral to its overall sense and direction, its *sens*, let me rehearse its most salient features. My proposal is modest in the following respects. First, my proposal does not claim to have identified all the elements of responsible politics. Second, I do not claim to have exhaustively characterized any of the elements I have identified, though I do claim that those elements which I have picked out, namely man as one who is *en route*, a freedom which is relational, and a hope which is fully this-worldly and universal, are essential features of any politics which is maximally responsible. It is part and parcel of my argument that aspirations to exhaustive, definitive accounts and characterizations are fundamentally misguided.

A second aspect of the modesty of my proposal is that it makes no pretense to have invented politics of hope. Political practice has not rarely been in fact, if not in name, animated by just the sort of hope for which I argue. The aim of my proposal is to analyse such practice and promote it by giving as systematic an account of it as I can. Similarly, my proposal is modest inasmuch as it recognizes that its objective is not to cancel the tradition in which it is rooted but rather to enhance it.

There is a third important dimension to the modesty of this work. The doctrine for which I have argued does not entail that every concrete instantiation of politics of hope would have identical provisions. It does not entail that all instantiations would have the same sort of constitution, foreign policy, etc. To the contrary, by its emphasis on the historicality of all political practice, my position rather suggests a diversity of institutions, practices, etc. My proposal makes no pretense that strife is totally eliminable from the political arena. But this strife is held in the bounds of a mutually cherished dialogue. And the diversity is interpreted in terms of hope as something to be cherished rather than to be overcome or regretted.

One might object that my proposal is so modest that it has no 'sharp edges' and thus cannot provide the resources necessary to distinguish responsible politics from irresponsible politics. Such an objection, however, is misplaced. The position I defend here presents a well-developed critique of sharp-edged political doctrines. Concrete instantiations of both politics of vision and politics of might or will tend by their nature to eliminate or neutralize alternatives. They are sharp-edged. My position sharply rejects such sharp-edged political practice as ill-founded. As a politics of hope, rather than one of containment or resignation, it applauds rather than regrets the absence of the sort of bifurcation which sharp-edged politics tend to produce. In keeping with the spirit of Merleau-Ponty's philosophy of ambiguity,[2] the sort of politics endorsed in this study is a politics of ambiguity, of rich, fertile ambiguity.

Sharp-edged political doctrines tend to treat too many concrete issues as matters of principle rather than as matters of prudence or, better, of practical wisdom (*phronesis*) in Aristotle's sense.[3] Practitioners of such doctrines regularly exaggerate the number and kinds of political questions which can be determined by drawing deductive or inductive conclusions from fundamental premises or unambiguous evidence. They regularly foreshorten the field which properly belongs to practical wisdom. Thus, for example, concrete questions about responsible coercion or responsible political education are often treated as though they can be definitively and unequivocally solved.

The field of practical wisdom, however, is one in which grounds for well-founded disagreement are always available. To foreshorten this field is to exaggerate the force of available evidence and thereby to tend toward the substitution of ideology for critical political thought and practice. A far from trivial virtue of the position I have enunciated is the protection it provides against tendencies to the partiality ingredient in ideology.

Thus the ambiguity and modesty of this study which I acknowledge contribute to its strength rather than show forth its weakness. They show how politics can foster and maintain the sort of open dialectic among men necessary to acknowledge man's essential routedness. But there are other admissions which I must make which have nothing to do with becoming modesty and appropriate ambiguity. These other admissions are confessions of weaknesses of this study. Two of these weaknesses are especially obvious. First, this study clearly needs to be augmented by detailed analyses of the impact of economic factors on responsible politics. I have argued, persuasively I believe, both for the irreducibility of the political domain to that of economics and at the same time for the inextricability of these two domains from one another. Part of the Other with which political agents must always deal is the economic context of their action. But I have not presented a sufficiently detailed account of just how economic factors, e.g. food supply, affect either domestic or international politics. There is every reason to think that a detailed study of the place of economics in politics would modify in nontrivial ways the practical implications of my position.

Second, the logic of my study requires that all nations have a voice on the international scene. Small, economically and militarily weak nations deserve to be heard no less than do large, powerful nations. But my study provides scant help to show how this requirement of responsible politics is to be implemented. Nor have I dealt sufficiently with the difficult matter of how long a nation should survive. Can a nation be or become so weak – it has been suggested that Chad, for example, verges on this extreme weakness – that it should cease to exist as a nation so that its people can be absorbed into another, more viable body politic in which its people can find political voice?

I must confess that I have no clear recommendations to offer to offset either of these weaknesses. Nonetheless, these weaknesses, and others, notwithstanding, this study does provide a serious alternative to currently prevailing patterns of political thought and practice. It therefore contributes something of substance to the contemporary dialogue of politics. Merleau-Ponty, in all of his work, political and otherwise, sought a 'third way' between empiricism and rationalism. My study, taking its point of departure from him, likewise spells out a third way for politics. As Merleau-Ponty saw, this third way was not to be the 'last word,' for there is no last word. But that in no way detracts from its being a serious word, a word which supports rather than seeks to terminate political dialogue in all of its essentially risky richness.

Notes

Chapter 1   Initial demarcations

1   See in this connection Sheldon S. Wolin, *Politics and Vision* (Boston: Little Brown & Co., 1960) pp. 1–68. Hereafter *PV*.

2   Though my work is not, at bottom, Hegelian, I recognize that Hegel has good reasons both for saying that 'the truth about Right, Ethics, and the state is as old as its public recognition and formulation in the law of the land' and that the thinking mind is not content until it grounds these commonplace verities upon solid rational foundations. See his *Philosophy of Right*, tr. by T.M. Knox (Oxford: Clarendon Press, 1942) esp. pp. 3–4.

3   This formulation is an amended version of a description provided by Wolin. For his own version, see *PV*, pp. 10–11.

4   These four principles are not all logically independent of one another but nothing would be gained by reducing some to others. Indeed, such a reduction might lead one to fail to notice one or another of these principles.

5   Philosophical literature is replete with studies of the flaws of both rationalist and voluntarist politics. On the weaknesses of rationalist politics, see for example Hannah Arendt, *Between Past and Future* (New York: Viking Press, 1968) and Alexandre Kojeve, 'Tyranny and wisdom', in Leo Strauss, *On Tyranny* (New York: The Free Press of Glencoe, 1963). Hereafter TW. On the weaknesses of voluntarist politics, see for example Charles Taylor, *Hegel and Modern Society* (Cambridge: Cambridge University Press, 1982) and Michael J. Sandel, *Liberalism and the Limits of Justice* (Cambridge: Cambridge University Press, 1982). Hereafter *LLJ*. Other pertinent works include J.R. Lucas, *On Justice* (Oxford: Clarendon Press, 1980) and Alasdair MacIntyre, *After Virtue* (Notre Dame: Notre Dame University Press, 1981). Hereafter *AV*, and Patrick Riley, *Will and Political Legitimacy* (Cambridge, Mass.: Harvard University Press, 1982). Hereafter *WPL*.

6   See John Plamenatz, *Man and Society* (New York: McGraw-Hill, 1963), vol. I, p. xx.

7   See Alasdair MacIntyre, *After Virtue* (Notre Dame: Notre Dame

University Press, 1981) p. 58, and TW, pp. 172–3. Thomas Langan has accurately observed: 'Failure to think things through to principle and to achieve consistency among principles is not just dilettantism, it is the recipe for unreliability in action. Even the man who knows well what he stands for can suffer a failure of nerve. But the person who does not even try to think things out . . . will show his confusion in every crisis situation.' See his 'A strategy for the pursuit of truth,' *The Review of Metaphysics*, vol. XXXVI, no. 2, December 1982, p. 299. What Langan says here has a special pertinence to the realm of politics.

8   *PV*, p. 13.
9   For an important example of self-styled positivism in political philosophy, see Thomas D. Weldon, *Vocabulary of Politics* (Baltimore: Penguin Books, 1953). For another kind of criticism of 'Weldonism' see Alexander Passerin D'Entreves, *The Notion of the State* (Oxford: Clarendon Press, 1967), p. vii.
10 *PV*, p. 8.
11 See *PV*, pp. 17–21.
12 Lucien Goldmann, *Lukács and Heidegger*, tr. by William Q. Boelhower, (London: Routledge & Kegan Paul, 1977) p. 93. Hereafter *LH*.
13 It is a fool's game for an author to try to render his starting point fully transparent. But both for his own sake and for that of his readers he has to make explicit his point of entry into the ongoing discussion.
14 Aristotle, *Politics*, 1253a 7–34. Whether my interpretation of man and politics is in the final analysis genuinely Aristotelian (whatever that means) is not of decisive importance. As I will shortly point out, I draw upon other important sources as well. But it is the case that I have found Aristotle to be immensely instructive.
15 See Hannah Arendt, *The Human Condition* (Garden City: Doubleday & Co.,9) pp. 25–7. I do not endorse her remarks on 'the social.' See also in this context Bhikhu Parekh, *Hannah Arendt and the Search for a New Political Philosophy* (Atlantic Highlands: Humanities Press, 1981) esp. pp. 141–9, and Lucien Goldmann, *Lukács and Heidegger*, tr. by William Boelhower (London: Routledge & Kegan Paul, 1977) p. 37.
16 See my *Silence: The Phenomenon and Its Ontological Significance*, (Bloomington: Indiana University Press, 1980). Hereafter *SPOS*.
17 Whether some other, different, nuclear arsenal with different consequences could be developed is outside the scope of the present exigencies with which political actors must cope.
18 Aristotle already noted the international dimension of politics. See *Politics* 1265a 19–24 and 1267a 18–19.
19 See in this connection Michael Oakeshott, *On Human Conduct* (Oxford: Clarendon Press, 1975) esp. pp. 270–4.
20 Albania seems to be something of an exception. What this distinctive position bodes either for Albania or for other nations is not clear.
21 *PV*, p. 429.
22 *PV*, pp. 430–2. See also in this connection Alasdair MacIntyre's

incisive critique of bureaucratic managerialism in his *After Virtue*, pp. 76–102. This critique would apply both to communist and non-communist Western nations.

23 Aristotle, *Politics*, 1266a 1–5, 1279a 17–21, 1293b 29.
24 Aristotle, *Politics*, 1261a 10–30.
25 Parekh, *op. cit.*, pp. 32–6.
26 The essentially inbuilt autonomy of contemporary individualism differs from the Aristotelian sense of autarchy inasmuch as autarchy always depends in part on favorable circumstances, chief among which is residence in an appropriate community. Admittedly, Aristotle does not thematize the intersubjective dimension of autarchy as well as one might wish. But the man without friends (*Nicomachean Ethics*), who makes no active contribution to the life of the *polis* (*Politics*) and is ill-prepared to speak in public (*Rhetoric*) would hardly qualify as autarchic.
27 Michael Sandel, writing from a somewhat different perspective, calls the view I am pointing to here 'deontological liberalism.' Its core thesis, Sandel says, is: 'Society, being composed of a plurality of persons, each with his own aims, interests, and conceptions of the good, is best arranged when it is governed by principles that do not *themselves* presuppose any particular conception of the good; what justifies these regulative principles above all is not that they maximize the social welfare or otherwise promote the good, but rather that they conform to the concept of *right*, a moral category given prior to the good and independent of it.' (*LLJ*, p. 1).
28 Descartes announces this sort of equality at the very beginning of the *Discourse on Method*. He needs this postulate for his enterprise to hold together. See Descartes, *Discourse on Method*, tr. by Paul J. Olscamp (Indianapolis: Bobbs-Merrill Co., 1965) p. 4.
29 It should be noted that there are both 'conservative' and 'liberal' versions of this view. For the 'conservative,' since all are already basically free and equal, each can take care of himself if he so chooses. For the 'liberal,' help is needed to bring each into the condition of equality and freedom which is his natural inheritance. Once arrived, he can then be left to his own discretion. For both the 'conservative' and the 'liberal' the goal is the same and it is attainable.
30 Aristotle, *Politics*, 1268a, 20, 1332b 12–1333a 3.
31 See for example Albert Camus, *The Rebel*, tr. by Anthony Bower (New York: Vintage Books, 1960). Though Camus speaks in terms of liberty and justice, the problem is the same as that between autonomous freedom and radical equality.
32 This is true even of religious acts if one wishes to speak of their specifiable efficacy in human history.
33 See Aristotle, *Rhetoric*, 1360b 4–38 and 1361a 22–4.
34 Charles Taylor, *Hegel and Modern Society* (Cambridge: Cambridge University Press, 1979) p. 131. Hereafter *HMS*.
35 *HMS*, p. 116.
36 *HMS*, p. 118.

37   John Rawls, *A Theory of Justice* (Cambridge, Mass.: Harvard University Press, 1971). Hereafter *TJ*.
38   *TJ*, p. 560.
39   *TJ*, p. 127–129.
40   *TJ*, p. 563.
41   *TJ*, p. 575.
42   *LLJ*, p. 62. My first criticism of Rawls is heavily indebted to Sandel's excellent analysis.
43   *TJ*, p. 561 and *LLJ*, pp. 58–9.
44   *TJ*, p. 269.
45   *LLJ*, p. 80. For further evidence that Rawls's theory implicitly employs an intersubjective conception of the self, see *LLJ*, pp. 80–2 and 102–3 and 150–9.
46   *LLJ*, p. 179. Sandel, further, is correct when he says that Rawls and Robert Nozick have much in common from a philosophical point of view. See *LLJ*, pp. 66–7 and Nozick, *Anarchy, State, and Utopia* (New York: Basic Books, 1974).
47   *TJ*, p. 8.
48   *TJ*, p. 378.
49   To be sure, some of what Rawls says about institutions runs counter to such a doctrine. But Rawls's treatment of institutions is not without its own problems. And his doctrine of institutions could hardly be said to be the linchpin of his theory. See *TJ*, pp. 54–5 and *WPL*, pp. 206–7.
50   See Jürgen Habermas, 'Moral development and ego identity,' in his *Communication and the Evolution of Society*, tr. by Thomas McCarthy (Boston: Beacon Press, 1979) pp. 70–1 and 90–4. Hereafter MDEI.
51   See Jürgen Habermas, 'What is univeral pragmatics,' in his *Communication and the Evolution of Society*, tr. by Thomas McCarthy (Boston: Beacon Press, 1976) pp. 1–68, Habermas, *Theory and Practice*, tr. by John Viertel (Boston: Beacon Press, 1974), esp. pp. 16–24, hereafter *TP*, and Thomas Meisenhelder, 'Hope: A phenomenological prelude to critical society theory,' *Human Studies*, vol. 5, 1982, pp. 209–10. Hereafter HPST.
52   Thomas McCarthy, *The Critical Theory of Jürgen Habermas* (Cambridge, Mass.: MIT Press, 1978) p. 193. Hereafter *CTJH*.
53   *CTJH*, pp. 306–10.
54   HPST, p. 209.
55   See *CTJH*, pp. 317–25 and all of MDEI.
56   See in this connection Jürgen Habermas, *Theory and Practice*, tr. by John Viertel (Boston: Beacon Press, 1973) pp. 27ff.
57   See in this connection Fred R. Dallmayr, *Twilight of Subjectivity* (Amherst: University of Massachusetts Press, 1981) p. 292. Hereafter *TS*.
58   See David Held, 'Crisis tendencies, legitimation and the state,' in *Habermas: Critical Debates*, ed. by John B. Thompson and David Held (Cambridge, Mass: MIT Press, 1982) p. 195. Hereafter *HCD*.
59   MDEI, p. 90. See also Habermas, *Legitimation Crisis*, tr. by Thomas

McCarthy (Boston: Beacon Press, 1975) pp. 110–11 and 158–9 fn. 16. See also *TS*, pp. 343–4 fns 49 and 50.

60 John McCumber, 'Reflections and emancipation in Habermas,' *The Southern Journal of Philosophy*, vol. XXII, no. 1, Spring 1984, p. 75.

61 Henning Altmann, 'Cognitive interests and self-reflection,' in *HCD*, p. 74. For Habermas's response see his 'A reply to my critics,' in *HCD*, esp. pp. 291 and 247–53.

62 Habermas himself is not unmindful of this point. But he cannot effectively handle it. See Dieter Misgeld, 'Critical theory and hermeneutics: The debate between Habermas and Gadamer,' in *On Critical Theory*, ed. by John O'Neill (New York: Seabury Press, 1976) esp. pp. 182–3.

63 Paul Ricoeur, 'Ethics and culture: Habermas and Gadamer in dialogue,' *Philosophy Today*, vol. 17, 1973, pp. 163–4.

64 *TS*, pp. 200–4.

65 See Rudiger Bubner, *Modern German Philosophy*, tr. by Eric Matthews (Cambridge: Cambridge University Press, 1981) pp. 187–90. See also in this connection Agnes Heller, 'Habermas and Marxism', in *HCD*, esp. pp. 22–3 and Steven Lukes, 'Of gods and demons: Habermas and practical reason' in *HCD*, esp. pp. 138–45. Lukes's essay has the added interest of relating Habermas's work to that of Rawls.

66 Aristotle, *Politics*, 1301b 11–28.

67 See in this connection *SPOS*, pp. 61–82 and 146–8.

68 In this way, I acknowledge Aristotle's admonition not to expect more precision in an investigation than the subject-matter permits. See his *Nicomachean Ethics*, 1094b 12–27.

69 Similarly, I do not claim to present a strictly Aristotelian, Heideggerian, or Marcelian doctrine. If, as Gadamer says, to understand is always to understand otherwise, then all the more so it is the case that to appropriate is to appropriate otherwise. See his *Philosophical Hermeneutics*, tr. by David E. Linge (Berkeley: University of California Press, 1976) pp. 28, 67 and *passim*.

Chapter 2 Merleau-Ponty's legacy to political thought

1 Merleau-Ponty, *Adventures of the Dialectic*, tr. by Joseph Bien (Evanston: Northwestern University Press, 1973) p. 266. Hereafter *AD*. Some have argued that Merleau-Ponty fell into an apolitical pessimism or indifference to politics in his later years. Though I do not think that this is the case, the question does not bear directly upon my present concerns. For two versions of this contention, see Sonia Kruks, *The Political Philosophy of Merleau-Ponty* (Atlantic Highlands: Humanities Press, 1981) pp. 125–8, hereafter *PPMP*, and William Hamrick, 'Interests, justice and respect for law in Merleau-Ponty's phenomenology', in *Phenomenology in a Pluralistic Context*, ed. by William L. McBridge and Calvin Schrag (Albany: SUNY Press, 1983) p. 48. Hereafter *PPC*.

2 In this respect, among others, Merleau-Ponty's thought resembles Heidegger's. In the course of this chapter I will have occasion to point out other points of contact between them.

3 Though I think that *PPMP* is seriously defective in several respects, Sonia Kruks does give a useful account there of the shift in Merleau-Ponty's assessment of Marxism as well as of a number of other important aspects of his political reflections.

4 Merleau-Ponty, *Humanism and Terror*, tr. by John O'Neill (Boston: Beacon Press, 1969) p. 153. Hereafter *HT*. On the crucial distinction which Merleau-Ponty made at this time between Soviet communism and Marxism, see O'Neill's 'Translator's note,' pp. vii–xi.

5 *HT*, p. 153.

6 Merleau-Ponty, *Phenomenology of Perception*, tr. by Colin Smith (London: Routledge & Kegan Paul, 1962) p. 442. Hereafter *PhP*. See also *PPMP*, pp. 18–20.

7 *HT*, p. 64.

8 *HT*, p. 59.

9 *HT*, pp. xxxvi and 62–4.

10 *HT*, pp. 166–7.

11 *HT*, p. 167. See also p. xxxviii.

12 *HT*, p. xliii–xlv.

13 *HT*, p. xxi. See also pp. xiv and xviii.

14 *HT*, p. 187.

15 *HT*, p. 188. It is of interest to note that Merleau-Ponty rejects thinking of the task of human coexistence as being comparable to a geometry problem (*HT*, p. 186). His position is akin to that of Gabriel Marcel who distinguishes between primary reflection which deals with objective problems and secondary reflection which recognizes that the thinker participates in the topic under consideration and is part of its 'data.' See Marcel, *The Mystery of Being*, tr. by G.S. Fraser (Chicago: Gateway Books, 1964) vol. 1, pp. 95–126. Whether Merleau-Ponty was drawing on Marcel here is not known but he was familiar with Marcel's distinction.

16 *PPMP*, pp. 101–7.

17 *HT*, p. 149. My emphasis added to 'bearers of truth.' For an excellent discussion of Marx and Merleau-Ponty on the question of violence, see Joseph L. Walsh, *Revolutionary Violence in Merleau-Ponty, Marx and Engels*, unpublished dissertation, Brandeis University, 1976.

18 See *PPMP*, pp. 107–18 for a strong criticism of Merleau-Ponty's 1950s' interpretation of Marx.

19 See Merleau-Ponty, *The Structure of Behaviour*, tr. by A. Fisher (London: Methuen, 1965) and *PhP*.

20 Merleau-Ponty, *Signs*, tr. by Richard C. McClearly (Evanston: Northwestern University Press, 1964) p. 20. My modification of McCleary's translation. Hereafter *S*.

21 Among the other special cases of history are specific arts, religions, and educational enterprises.

22　To my knowledge, Merleau-Ponty does not expressly make this point. But it is readily inferred from what he does say.

23　Ferdinand de Saussure, *Course in General Linguistics*, tr. by Wade Baskin (New York: McGraw-Hill, 1966) pp. 7–10, 71–8, and 90–100. Hereafter *CGL*. For instructive remarks on Merleau-Ponty's use of Saussure, see James M. Edie, 'Foreword,' in Merleau-Ponty, *Consciousness and the Acquisition of Language,* tr. by Hugh J. Silverman (Evanston: Northwestern University Press, 1973) pp. xi–xxxii, and James M. Edie, 'The meaning and development of Merleau-Ponty's concept of structure,' in *Merleau-Ponty: Perception, Structure, Language,* ed. by John Sallis (Atlantic Highlands: Humanities Press, 1981) pp. 39–57.

24　*AD*, p. 103.

25　*S*, pp. 218–19. For another version of this relation, with a notably different emphasis, see Bertrand de Jouvenel, *Sovereignty*, tr. by J.F. Huntington (Chicago: University of Chicago Press, 1957) pp. 137–8. Hereafter *Sov*.

26　*S*, pp. 274–5. See also *HT*, pp. xxxii–xxxiii. It is no surprise that Themistocles, Aristides, Pericles, and Thucydides could not teach their sons to be statesmen. See Plato, *Meno*, tr. by G.M.A. Grube (Indianapolis: Hackett Publishing Co., 1976), pp. 26–7.

27　*S*, p. 276.

28　M. Merleau-Ponty, *Sense and Non-sense*, tr. by Hubert L. Dreyfus and Patricia Allen Dreyfus (Evanston: Northwestern University Press, 1964) p. 143. Hereafter *SNS*.

29　*S*, pp. 302–3. As Saussure says, 'in language there are only differences.' *CGL*, p. 120.

30　According to Saussure, the synchronic laws of language report states of affairs, but are not imperative. Thus the state of affairs is precarious. *CGL*, p. 92.

31　*S*, p. 336. See also *S* p. 35, where Merleau-Ponty says: 'History never confesses, not even her lost illusions, but neither does she dream of them again.'

32　*S*, pp. 323–4.

33　*AD*, p. 23. See the useful, related remarks by de Jouvenel, *Sov.,* pp. 105–7.

34　*S*, p. 35.

35　See for example in this connection *PhP*, pp. x, 183–4, 392. Also, Merleau-Ponty, *The Prose of the World*, ed. by Claude Lefort, tr. by John O'Neill (Evanston: Northwestern University Press, 1973) p. 36. Hereafter *PW*. Also, Merleau-Ponty, *The Primacy of Perception*, ed. by James Edie (Evanston: Northwestern University Press, 1964) p. 134. Hereafter *PoP*. And *S*, p. 19.

36　*S*, p. 43.

37　*PW*, p. 112.

38　*S*, pp. 109–10.

39　*S*, pp. 328, 335. See also Merleau-Ponty, 'Pour la vérité,' *Les Temps Modernes*, 1945, p. 600.

40 *AD*, p. 124. See also James Miller, *History and Human Existence (Berkeley: University of California Press, 1979) pp. 209—12.*

41 *AD*, p. 143. Sartre later modified his views about institutions. See, for example, his *Search for a Method*, tr. by Hazel Barnes (New York: Vintage Books, 1968) pp. 100ff.

42 M. Merleau-Ponty, *Themes from the Lectures at College de France 1952–1960*, tr. by John O'Neill (Evanston: Northwestern University Press, 1970) pp. 40–1.

43 *S*, p. 349. See also *SNS*, p. 152, for an earlier version of this insight of Merleau-Ponty's. In another, related context, Merleau-Ponty has said: 'The presence of the individual in the institution and of the institution in the individual is evident in the case of linguistic change. It is often the wearing down of a form which suggests to us a new way of using the means of discrimination which are present in the language at a given time. . . . The contingent fact, taken over by the will to expression, becomes a new means of expression which takes its place, and has a lasting sense in the history of this language.' M. Merleau-Ponty, *In Praise of Philosophy*, tr. by John Wild and James Edie (Evanston: Northwestern University Press, 1963) p. 55. Hereafter *IPP*.

44 Merleau-Ponty's distinction between originative speech (*parole parlante*) and sedimented speech (*parole parlée*) in *PhP*, pp. 193, 389, does seem to give preeminence to the new over the old, to the different over the same. Such a preeminence appears inconsistent with his views on the importance of institutions and of language (*langue*). I understand his remarks in *PhP* to betray what Jacques Taminiaux has called a positivist strand in Merleau-Ponty's earlier thought which Merleau-Ponty largely overcomes in his post-1950 work. See Taminiaux, 'Experience et expression' in his *Le Regard et l'excédent* (The Hague: Martinus Nijhoff, 1977) pp. 90–115. Hereafter *EE*.

45 See Merleau-Ponty, 'Eye and mind,' in *PoP*, p. 269. Hereafter EM.

46 Albert Rabil, Jr, *Merleau-Ponty: Existentialist of the Social World* (New York and London: Columbia University Press, 1967) p. 135. In this connection see also *PhP*, 391, *PW*, p. 36, and *IPP*, p. 32.

47 There are, it is true, passages in Merleau-Ponty's works where a preeminent status is apparently allotted to philosophical discourse. I take these passages to be inconsistent with the principal thrust of his thought. For details, see my 'One central link between Merleau-Ponty's philosophy of language and his political thought,' *Tulane Studies in Philosophy*, Vol. xxix, 1980, pp. 57–80. Hereafter OCL.

48 *CGL*, pp. 77–8.

49 *PhP*, pp. 183–4, and *PoP*, p. 134.

50 *SNS*, p. 143 and *AD*, pp. 120 and 150–51.

51 *AD*, pp. 53 and 206.

52 *AD*, p. 22.

53 *AD*, pp. 56–7 and 204ff.

54 *HT*, p. 150.

55 *AD*, pp. 203–33.

56 *AD*, pp. 196–7.
57 *AD*, pp. 225ff. It may be noteworthy that some of the politics of present-day Western Europe is attempting to act as a third force between the United States and the Soviet Union. But regrettably, from Merleau-Ponty's standpoint, much of it is hardly a 'left' force. See William Pfaff, 'Reflections: Finlandization,' *The New Yorker*, September 1, 1980, pp. 30–4.
58 *HT*, pp. xxiv–xxv.
59 *AD*, p. 198.
60 *AD*, p. 207.
61 *AD*, p. 226.
62 *SNS*, p. 148 and *S*, pp. 348–9.
63 *HT*, pp. xxiv–xxxv. See also Bertrand de Jouvenel, *Sov.*, pp. 18–25 and 31–3.
64 *S*, p. 336.
65 See Willy Brandt *et al.*, *North-South: A Programme for Survival* (Cambridge: MIT Press, 1980). 'It is now widely recognized that development involves a profound transformation of the entire economic and social structure. This embraces changes in production and demand as well as improvements in income distribution and employment. It means creating a more diversified economy, whose main sectors become more interdependent for supplying inputs and for expanding markets for output.

The actual patterns of structural transformation will tend to vary from one country to another depending on a number of factors – including resources, geography, and the skills of the population. There are therefore no golden rules capable of universal application for economic development. Each country has to exploit the opportunities open to it for strengthening its economy. Structural transformation need not imply autarky. Some countries might find it feasible to pursue inward-looking strategies that rely, at least in the early stages, on using their domestic markets. Others may diversify and expand their exports. Exports can become more fully integrated with the rest of the economy, as the domestic market comes to provide a larger base, or as export industries secure more of their inputs from local sources. Yet others will concentrate initially on distributing income more evenly in order to widen the domestic market for locally produced goods and to lay the foundations for a better balance between the rural and urban sectors. But all countries need an international environment that will be responsive to their development efforts. Herein lies part of the rationale for a new international economic order.' (pp. 48–9) (See also pp. 127–8.)
66 *S*, p. 4.
67 *S*, p. 35. My modification of McCleary's translation. See also *HT*, pp. xxix–xxx.
68 *S*, pp. 324 and 328.
69 Machiavelli's weakness, for Merleau-Ponty, was that he did not have such a guideline. See *S*, pp. 221–3.

70 See *PPMP*, pp. 18–20.
71 *S*, p. 307.
72 *PW*, p. 36. My emphasis.
73 Recall here Sartre's notion of groups in fusion. See his *Critique of Dialectical Reason*.
74 *AD*, pp. 90–1. Thus, apparently, John Rawls's notion of an 'original position' is not merely counterfactual. It is also countersensical.
75 *AD*, pp. 88–91 and 206–7. 'Permanent revolution' is also a Marxist notion.
76 *AD*, p. 207.
77 *AD*, p. 205.
78 *AD*, p. 197.
79 See OCL, pp. 57–61.
80 See, for example, *PPMP*, *passim*, and my 'Merleau-Ponty's political thought: Its nature and its challenge,' in *PPC*, esp. pp. 23–5.
81 See in this regard Hannah Arendt, *Between Past and Future* (New York: Viking Press, 1968) pp. 153–4.
82 *S*, p. 222. My insertion.
83 See my 'Merleau-Ponty's political thought: Its nature and its challenge,' in *PPC*, esp. pp. 22–5.

Chapter 3   Speech, silence, and being human

1 See in this connection Hannah Arendt, *The Human Condition* (Garden City: Doubleday Anchor Books, 1959) esp. pp. 155ff. Arendt, however, slights the place of fabrication in politics. See pp. 167–9. Hereafter *HC*.
2 Reiner Schürmann, 'Principles precarious: on the origin of the political in Heidegger,' in *Heidegger: The Man and the Thinker*, ed. by Thomas Sheehan (Chicago: Precedent Publishing Co., 1981) p. 250.
3 See M. Merleau-Ponty, *The Phenomenology of Perception*, tr. by Colin Smith (London: Routledge & Kegan Paul, 1962) esp. pp. 174–99, M. Merleau-Ponty, *The Prose of the World*, tr. by John O'Neill (Evanston: Northwestern University Press, 1973) and Merleau-Ponty, *The Visible and the Invisible*, tr. by Alphonso Lingis (Evanston: Northwestern University Press, 1968).
4 For the distinction among demonstrative, dialectical, and enthymematic arguments, see Aristotle, *Prior Analytics*, 24a21–24b15, and *Rhetoric*, 1356b3–1357a18 and 1402b21–23.
5 Paul Ricoeur, *The Rule of Metaphor*, tr. by Robert Czerny *et al.* (Toronto: University of Toronto Press, 1977) p. 11.
6 Bernard Dauenhauer, *Silence: The Phenomenon and Its Ontological Significance* (Bloomington: Indiana University Press, 1980). Hereafter *SPOS*.
7 Actional performances do not primarily aim at objects lying outside the action itself. But silence interrupts streams of these performances just as it interrupts other sorts of streams of performances.

8   *SPOS*, pp. 26–7. Aristotle recognized something of the same double-rayed character of discourse. Speech, he says, should be appropriate both in its expression of emotion and character and to its topic. This is a general theme of his *Rhetoric*. See, for example, 1408a10–20.

9   For a more detailed account of forms of topic-centered discourse, see *SPOS*, pp. 33–49.

10   For fuller discussion on the levels of interpersonal involvement in discourse, see *SPOS*, pp. 65–74.

11   I do not claim that the realm of discourse is in all respects discrete from other realms. But I do claim that the several realms of human experience, e.g. perception, discourse, fabrication, are irreducible to one another and therefore it is proper to distinguish them from one another.

12   See Robert Sokolowski, 'Picturing,' *The Review of Metaphysics*, vol. xxxi, no. 1 (September, 1977) pp. 3–28.

13   Appetition or desire, of course, can occur either as attraction or as repulsion or as some mix of the two. As such, it includes both emotion and interest.

14   I am adapting to my own purposes here Paul Ricoeur's distinction between 'situation' and 'world.' He draws this distinction in the course of his discussion of the differences between speech and writing. See his *Interpretation Theory: Discourse and the Surplus of Meaning* (Fort Worth: Texas Christian University Press, 1976) esp. pp. 25–44. Another way to get at the movement between the mediated and the unmediated is through the analysis of the play of presence and absence. I do not, of course, want to map this latter distinction directly on to the former. See, concerning presence and absence, Robert Sokolowski, *Presence and Absence* (Bloomington: Indiana University Press, 1978). Hereafter *PA*. He shows there that the play of presence and absence is involved in all of our experience, perceptual, pictorial and signitive. Because this is so, I would add, mediation is possible.

15   Merleau-Ponty, *The Phenomenology of Perception*, op. cit., p. xiv.

16   See in this connection *SPOS*, pp. 155–8.

17   There would of course be no terminal silence without inaugural silence. But terminal silence, or so it seems to me, brings to light especially forcefully the conditions for responsible politics.

18   For a dramatic portrayal of the felt inadequation between the signitive and the nonsignitive, consider Tennessee Williams's play *A Streetcar Named Desire*.

19   This consideration will be of special importance to the discussion of law I will present in Chapter 8.

20   For a fuller account of terminal silence, see *SPOS* pp. 16–24 and 75–7.

21   To be 'in the middle' does not entail that one is a mid-point. The American idiomatic expression 'to be caught in the middle' is closer to the mark so long as 'caught' is not taken to mean 'trapped.' But Montaigne, Descartes, and Pascal were not totally awry in taking man to be a mid-point. The contrast among their respective positions,

though, shows that to say that man is at the mid-point or even that he is 'in the middle' only opens, rather than closes, an issue.

22 For a concrete case of mediation and modification, see my 'Authors, audiences, and texts,' *Human Studies*. vol. 5, no. 2, 1982, pp. 137–46.

23 The stream of mediations can of course stop. If all mediators were to die, there would be no more mediation.

24 The term 'forces' is intended to be maximally neutral here. These forces are not necessarily confined to physical forces.

25 H.G. Gadamer, *Truth and Method*, tr. by Garrett Barden and John Cumming (New York: Seabury Press, 1975) p. 93. Hereafter *TM*.

26 *TM*, p. 94.

27 *TM*, pp. 92–5.

28 Thus a genetic engineering program either aimed at or recognized as bringing about the elimination of all men, including the human engineers, is simply countersensical.

29 Aristotle, from his own vantage point, recognized this fact. The *Nicomachean Ethics* shows clearly that the virtuous man and the happy man better exemplify what it is to be human than does the ordinary man.

30 Helmut Plessner and Arnold Gehlen have emphasized this human 'eccentricity.' See Fred R. Dallamyr, 'Plessner's philosophical anthropology,' *Inquiry* vol. 17, 1974, pp. 49–77. See also H.-G. Gadamer, 'The scope and function of hermeneutic reflection,' in his *Philosophical Hermeneutics*, tr. by David Linge (Berkeley: University of California Press, 1976) esp. pp. 55–7.

31 When a future redemption is announced, that future is always qualitatively discontinuous with the present. It is hard to say that this sort of future would belong to the same time as man's present life.

32 The *West Bank Shopper's Guide* was a local weekly published in the author's hometown during the years of his youth.

33 For the former claim, see Aristotle, *Nicomachean Ethics*, 1094al–5 and 1097al5ff. and for the latter, see his *Rhetoric*, 1355a20ff.

34 See in this connection *PA*, p. 12 and Gilbert Ryle, *Dilemmas* (Cambridge: Cambridge University Press, 1964) pp. 94–5. As Ryle points out it cannot be the case that all coins are counterfeit.

35 Heidegger, before Merleau-Ponty, saw this clearly. See, for example, Heidegger, *The Basic Problems of Phemonemology*, tr. by Albert Hofstadter (Bloomington: Indiana University Press, 1982) pp. 274–302. Hereafter *BPP*.

36 See in this connection my 'Heidegger: Spokesman for the dweller,' *The Southern Journal of Philosophy*, vol. 15, no. 2, Summer 1977, pp. 189–99. One should notice the tension here between my position and that of those religious doctrines which speak of man's destiny to an afterlife. Though I do not think that my position necessarily conflicts with those doctrines, it does conflict with versions of those doctrines which would countenance the slighting of this life for the sake of an afterlife.

37 See in this connection *BPP* p. 271 and Heidegger, 'The origin of the

work of art,' tr. by Albert Hofstadter in Heidegger, *Poetry, Language, Thought* (New York: Harper & Row, 1971) pp. 49–50 and 57ff.

38 Neither innovation nor renewal is necessarily progressive. The metaphor of linear movement is alien to the interpretation of man as one who is *en route.*

39 Something of this same notion is to be found in Sartre's notion of the way the practico-inert overtakes individual praxis. See his *Critique de la raison dialectique* (Paris: Gallimard, 1960) pp. 165–377.

40 See in this connection *BPP*, p. 19.

41 This conclusion corroborates the position of Charles Taylor cited in Chapter 1.

42 I borrow the notion of exclamatory interrogation from Gabriel Marcel. See his *The Mystery of Being*, tr. by G.S. Fraser (Chicago: Gateway Books, 1960) vol. 1, p. 137 and his *Man Against Mass Society*, tr. by G.S. Fraser (Chicago: Gateway Books, 1962) p. 172. In the final analysis, though, there are substantial differences between Marcel's position and mine.

43 On the link between temporarily and responsibility, see Roman Ingarden, *Man and Value*, tr. by Arthur Szylewicz (Washington, DC: Catholic University of America Press, 1983) pp. 105–17.

44 Religion, too, has claimed the title to allot space to mediations to appear. On the differences between politics and religion and their allotting discourses, see *SPOS*, pp. 38–40 and 43–5.

45 *HC*, p. 177.

46 *HC*, pp. 175–6. According to Arendt, however, the *polis* was conceived as structured 'space' set over against a chaotic surrounding world. Nothing in the understanding of politics which I propose would permit the definitive restriction of political space to only a portion of the globe or a segment of the world's population. Also, contrary to Arendt's own position, I find no intrinsic connection between the concept of rule and endeavors to escape from politics altogether. See *HC*, pp. 198–206.

47 Jean-Paul Sartre, *Search for a Method*, tr. by Hazel E. Barnes (New York: Vintage Books, 1968) p. 164. Hereafter *SM*. There is no need to distinguish here between the 'social world' and the 'political world.' However they are to be distinguished, the basis for a distinction will not be the presence or absence of this intertwining of man and world.

48 *SM*, p. 156.

49 This nonhuman Other includes not only other material things but science, religion, art, etc.

50 Nontrivial support for construing politics as anthropic can be found in contemporary discussions of both Marxism and liberalism as humanisms. If a doctrine were to be shown not to be a humanism, that would count against its being a responsible political doctrine. Today, one hears from several quarters denunciations of all humanisms as arrogant. Some versions of humanism may indeed be arrogant. But arrogance is not of the essence of humanism. Indeed some of the attacks on humanism depreciate the significance of man. I find these

depreciations unconvincing and even at times countersensical. See in this connection, Hans Jonas, *The Imperative of Responsibility* (Chicago: University of Chicago Press, 1984) pp. 201–4.

51   See Aristotle, *Politics*, 1278b15–30.

52   See in this connection Bertrand de Jouvenel, *Sovereignty*, tr. by J. F. Huntington (Chicago: University of Chicago Press, 1957) esp. pp. 129–30.

53   Alexandre Kojéve, 'Tyranny and wisdom', in Leo Strauss, *On Tyranny* (Ithaca: Cornell University Press, 1963) p. 153. Hereafter *OT*. In his *Spheres of Justice* (New York: Basic Books, 1983) Michael Walzer cites approvingly a similar characterization of tyranny proffered by Pascal. See p. 18.

54   Aristotle, it will be remembered, pointed out how oligarchy tended toward tyranny. See *Politics*, 1311a8–28.

55   Herbert Simon, *Administrative Behavior* (New York: Macmillan, 1947) pp. 101–2.

56   Hiero, in Xenophon's 'Hiero or Tyrannicus', explicitly points out the hollowness of praise or support extracted from people by tyrants. See Xenophon, 'Hiero or Tyrannicus', in *OT*, esp. pp. 13–14. There is, of course, the empty, merely logical, possibility that a tyrant would seek no help. History, though, furnishes no such examples which did not rapidly collapse. In this connection, recall Hegel's discussion of the master-servant dialectic. See his *Phenomenology of Spirit*, tr. by A.V. Miller (Oxford: Clarendon Press, 1977) pp. 111–19.

57   Plato says that the tyrant's soul has seen the least truth. See the *Phaedrus*, 248. The tyrannized, the man who accepts the tyrant's claim, has seen equally little truth.

58   For another objection to 'benevolent' tyranny, see Strauss, 'On tyranny', in *OT*, pp. 70–9.

59   Maoism's 'permanent revolution' exemplifies an attempt at anarchy. But obviously it is an incoherent position.

60   See in this connection Hannah Arendt, *Between Past and Future* (New York: Viking Press, 1968), p. 149.

61   For another interesting argument showing the inherent instability of totalitarianism, see Alasdair MacIntyre, *After Virtue* (Notre Dame: Notre Dame University Press, 1980) pp. 100–1 Hereafter *AV*.

62   Let me leave aside for present purposes MacIntyre's interesting claim that talk about rights is talk about witches and unicorns. See *AV*, p. 67.

63   To say that politics is 'anthropic' is not to say that it is anthropocentric. Politics need not claim that man is the greatest thing. But there is no politics which does not insist upon the indispensability of man and which does not work for his preservation.

64   See in this connection Montesquieu, *The Spirit of the Laws*, tr. by Thomas Nugent (New York: Hafner Press, 1975) vol. II, pp. 72–6.

65   Present day Iran exemplifies this sort of proposal. For an enlightening account of the complexity of the question about the relation between religion and politics in Europe from the sixteenth to the eighteenth centuries, see Quentin Skinner, *The Foundations of Modern Political*

Thought (Cambridge: Cambridge University Press, 1978) vol. 2.

66 Let me reemphasize that I do not claim here to have ferreted out *all* of the elements of a responsible politics. I do not know how so large a claim could be made even plausible.

Chapter 4   Freedom, being *en route*, and respect

1 For a splendid study of the question of freedom in Marx, see Carol C. Gould, *Marx's Social Ontology* (Cambridge, Mass: MIT Press, 1978) esp. pp. 101–28. Hereafter *MSO*.
2 Psychological handicaps of whatever sort are also part of a man's Other.
3 See Isaiah Berlin, 'Two concepts of liberty,' in his *Four Essays on Liberty* (Oxford: Oxford University Press, 1969) pp. 118–72. Berlin's own position does not get developed only in terms of this distinction. His position is much more subtle and has important similarities to the position I will defend. For another example of taking for granted the notion of freedom as autonomy, see William K. Frankena, *Ethics*, 2nd edn (Englewood Cliffs: Prentice-Hall, 1973) pp. 7–8. Hereafter *Eth*. (Englewood Cliffs: Prentice-Hall, 1973) pp. 7–8. Hereafter *Eth*.
4 See P.H. Partridge, 'Freedom,' in *Encyclopedia of Philosophy*, ed. by Paul Edwards (New York: Macmillan and The Free Press, 1967) vol. 3, pp. 222–3. Though Partridge mentions Mortimer Adler's *The Idea of Freedom*, 2 vols (Westport: Greenwood Press, 1958) he takes no discernible notice of the subtle, crucial distinctions drawn by Adler. Hereafter *IF*.
5 This basic conception of man has become a staple of the post-Renaissance Western intellectual heritage. It is articulated in various ways in the works of Descartes, Hobbes, Locke, Rousseau, Kant, Marx, and Nietzsche. A more complicated, though hardly untroubled, doctrine of human autonomy is found in the early Hegel. See, in this latter connection, Jean Hyppolite, *Studies on Marx and Hegel*, tr. by John O'Neill (New York: Basic Books, 1969) pp. 38–9 and 44–5. Hegel's own analysis of the connection between improperly construed freedom and terror should not be overlooked. See his *Phenomenology of Spirit*, tr. by A.V. Miller (Oxford: Clarendon Press, 1977) pp. 355–63.
6 See in this connection Descartes, *Discourse de la Methode*, in his *Oeuvres Philosophiques*, ed. by Ferdinand Alquié (Paris: Garnier Frères, 1963) vol. 1, p. 634. Hereafter *DM*. Descartes himself apparently held a more modest position than that which I have sketched here. He says only that we are to be *as it were* lords and possessors of nature. Marx, too, at times shows an affinity with a doctrine of autonomy strikingly similar to the one in question here. In Charles Taylor's words: 'The young Marx is heir of the radical Enlightenment . . . in his notion that man comes to shape nature and eventually society to his purposes.' *Hegel and Modern Society* (Cambridge: Cambridge University Press, 1979) p. 141. Hereafter *HMS*.

7 See Alexander P. D'Entéves, *The Notion of the State* (Oxford: Clarendon Press, 1967) pp. 78 and 212–30.

8 *HMS*, p. 74.

9 *DM*, p. 594. Again, Descartes's own views are less simple than this quotation would tend to indicate. He makes it clear that his insistence upon radical autonomy holds only for the realm of thought. He does not explicitly require autonomy for the realm of action. His epigones, both the witting and the unwitting, have not shown comparable restraint.

10 See Sartre, *Critique of Dialectical Reason* tr. by Alan Sheridan-Smith (London: New Left Books, 1976) pp. 345–478.

11 I will take up the issue of political coercion in more detail in Chapter 7.

12 See Sartre, *Being and Nothingness*, tr. by Hazel E. Barnes (New York: Washington Square Press, 1968) esp. pp. 86–112 and 559–619. Hereafter *BN*.

13 The view of freedom as autonomy is prevalent not only among those who assert that men are free. It is also widespread among those who deny that men are or can be free. Many of the arguments against freedom are, in effect, directed against the claim that men are or can be autonomous. For example, both behaviorist and structuralist objections to admitting human freedom regularly rest upon evidence which purports to show that all men are inextricably dependent upon other men and upon their surroundings. Thus, it is asserted, the sort of autonomy which is supposed to be constitutive of freedom is in principle unattainable.

14 *HMS*, pp. 6–7.

15 These three phenomena are obviously neither logically nor factually independent from one another.

16 Anthony Kenny, *Will, Freedom and Power* (New York: Harper & Row, 1976) p. 134.

17 Husserl, *The Crisis of European Sciences and Transcendental Phenomenology*, tr. with an introduction by David Carr (Evanston: Northwestern University Press, 1970) appendix 3, pp. 327–34.

18 See Merleau-Ponty, *The Prose of the World*, ed. by Claude Lefort, tr. by John O'Neill (Evanston: Northwestern University Press, 1973) pp. 143–4. Hereafter *PW*.

19 *PW*, p. 14.

20 See Merleau-Ponty, *The Visible and the Invisible*, ed. by Claude Lefort, tr. by Alphoso Lingis (Evanston: Northwestern University Press, 1968) pp. 143–55. Hereafter *VI*.

21 *VI*, p. 129. See also *PW*, p. 144.

22 See my *Silence: The Phenomenon and Its Ontological Significance* (Bloomington: Indiana University Press, 1980) Chapter 3, esp. pp. 65–74. Hereafter *SPOS*.

23 An obvious example of co-discourse is choral singing.

24 This claim, of course, is hardly original. But given the wide acceptance of the doctrine of freedom as autonomy, it is far from trivial.

25 See *BN*, p. 567.

26 See Bertrand de Jouvenel, *Sovereignty*, tr. by J.F. Huntington (Chicago: University of Chicago Press, 1957) p. 192.
27 Hannah Arendt, *Between Past and Future* (New York: Viking Press, 1968) p. 148. Hereafter *BPF*.
28 *BPF*, pp. 170–1.
29 Montesquieu, *The Spirit of the Laws*, tr. by Thomas Nugent (New York: Hafner Press, 1975) p. 150.
30 Thomas Hobbes, *De Cive or The Citizen*, ed. by Sterling P. Lamprecht (New York: Appleton-Century-Crofts, 1949) p. 114. My emphasis.
31 *MSO*, pp. 115–16. Gould also nicely extricates Marx's doctrine of freedom from changes of circularity. See pp. 112–15. For an excellent detailed account of Marx's doctrine of freedom, see also George G. Brenkert, *Marx's Ethics of Freedom* (London: Routledge & Kegan Paul, 1983) pp. 85–130.
32 *MSO*, p. 109.
33 *HMS*, p. 51. The cited passage continues: 'But the state is the collective mode of life which is backed by the full power of the community; and thus freedom must be embodied in the state.' As there are no unequivocally privileged type of discourse, so there need be no such privileged 'form of life.' See also *HMS*, pp. 6, 25, and 96 for further evidence against the doctrine of freedom as autonomy.
34 These considerations mesh nicely with the commonsensical view that dilettantism of any sort is an impoverished condition, not an ennobling one.
35 It will be recalled that Descartes, to the contrary, argued in the *Mediations* that the human will was infinite. See *Descartes: Philosophical Writings*, tr. and ed. by Elizabeth Anscombe and Peter Geach (Indianapolis: Library of Liberal Arts, 1971) pp. 93–4.
36 Anthony Kenny's formulation which describes will as the capacity to act for reasons represents some advance over the freedom as autonomy doctrine. But his view of how one is to understand reasons leaves something to be desired. See Kenny, *Will, Freedom and Power*, p. 107.
37 Aristotle, *Politics*, 1318b 39–42.
38 Aristotle, *Politics*, 1310a 32–36.
39 *HMS*, p. 168.
40 Merleau-Ponty, *Phenomenology of Perception*, tr. by Colin Smith (London: Routledge & Kegan Paul, 1962) p. 442. Hereafter *PhP*.
41 *PhP*, p. 452.
42 *PhP*, p. 453. Merleau-Ponty's position here is consonant with that of Heidegger in the latter's *Being and Time* and 'On the essence of truth.' In *Being and Time* Heidegger emphasizes that freedom is distinctive of man's kind of being, but his kind of being is always to be in the world among things and with other men. See Heidegger, *Being and Time*, tr. by John Macquirrie and Edward Robinson (New York: Harper & Row, 1962) pp. 294–331 and 417. Hereafter *BT*. In 'On the essence of truth,' Heidegger shows that freedom, which is a participation in the revelation of what is-as-such, requires both restraint and involvement with the Other. See Heidegger, 'On the essence of truth,' in *Existence and*

Being, ed. by Werner Brock (Chicago: Henry Regnery, 1949) pp. 307–19. Heidegger recognizes, even if only elliptically, that his doctrine of what he comes to see as freedom which involves no vengeance upon the Other has political consequences. He says: 'The space of that freedom which is won over vengeance is equally foreign to pacifism, to the politics of might, and to a calculating neutrality.' See Heidegger, 'Wer ist Nietzsches Zarathustra?' in *Vorträge und Aufsätze* (Pfullingen: Neske, 1967) vol. 1, p. 102. See also my 'Heidegger: Spokesman for the dweller,' *The Southern Journal of Philosophy*, vol. XV, 1977, pp. 189–99.

43 My account of freedom here is a revised version of a position I defended in my 'Relational freedom,' *Review of Metaphysics*, vol. XXXVI, no. 1, 1982, pp. 77–101. Charles Sherover, who also links freedom to finitude, temporality and historicity, reaches strikingly similar conclusions in his 'The temporality of the common good: Futurity and freedom,' *Review of Metaphysics*, vol. XXXVII, no. 3, 1984, pp. 475–97.

44 My account of freedom is structurally similar to Aristotle's account of happiness in the *Nicomachean Ethics* 1095b29–1096a2 and 1101a13–21. As happiness is an activity and not simply a capacity, so too is freedom an activity and not simply a capacity. In speaking of freedom as a process, I understand processes in much the same way as Gould does in her description of Marx's view of freedom as a process. 'A process.' she says, 'as distinct from an entity or a relation, is an activity that has continuity. The process described here also is marked by emergence, that is, by real novelty as the character of this continuity itself. It is a process of constant change. But it is not sheer flux. Rather, it is the preservation of a past state by transforming it into new forms.' *MSO*, pp. 127–8. Whether Gould has accurately captured Marx's view is, of course, irrelevant here. For other sorts of anticipations, see Alasdair MacIntyre, *After Virtue* (Notre Dame: Notre Dame University Press, 1981) p. 149, and Martin Buber, 'What is Man?' in his *Between Man and Man*, tr. by Ronald Gregor Smith (New York: Macmillan, 1978) pp. 177–81. My proposal, I think, is in the main consonant with the position of Mortimer Adler, though I give a different cast to the tension between self and other. See *IF*, vol. I, pp. 608–20. Though our vocabularies differ, my proposal is also consonant with Sheldon Wolin's argument in his 'The idea of the state in America,' in *Humanities in Society*, vol. 3, no. 2, 1980, pp. 151–68. For another sort of anticipation, see Heidegger's discussion of heritage and destiny in *BT*, pp. 434–39.

45 Thus it is plausible for Kierkegaard, in *Fear and Trembling*, to regard Shakespeare's Richard III as a man who, through his crimes, stifles his own freedom. See also Hazel Barnes, 'Introduction,' to her translation of Jean-Paul Sartre's *Search for a Method* (New York: Vintage Books, 1968) pp. xxi–xxxviii.

46 See, in this connection, William Richardson, 'The mirror inside: The problem of the self,' in *Review of Existential Psychology and Psychiat-*

ry, vol. XVI, 1978–79, esp. p. 108.

47   That my position here strongly resembles aspects of Mill's talk about qualified judges is no source of disquiet. But, clearly, our overall positions differ from one another in crucial ways. See his *Utilitarianism* (New York: Liberal Arts Press, 1957) pp. 12–16.

48   This condition is not violated by the fact that my performance of some activity *x* at time *T* precludes my performing any other activity *y* at this same time *T*. Since this fact holds for all activity, it cannot be cited in criticism of any particular activity.

49   The distinction among these three kinds of relationships is categorical, not classificatory. Concrete human relationships may involve aspects of all three kinds of relationships. Citizenship relationships, for example, apparently involve all three of these kinds of relationships.

50   The term 'reflection' designates first the minimal condition that only what are called human acts as opposed to mere acts of humans can be free. It points secondly to the fact that there can be degrees of awareness in human acts. The greater the awareness of what can be accomplished, the greater the field of freedom. Finally, 'reflection' refers to the unity of the three stages in the development of voluntary action distinguished by Paul Ricoeur, namely, decision (including choice and motivation), setting the body into voluntary motion, and consent. See his *Philosophie de la volonté: Le Volontaire et l'Involontaire* (Paris: Aubier, 1950).

51   When the patient is cured, of course, the physician-patient relationship dissolves, perhaps to be replaced by another relationship.

52   Aristotle, *Politics*, 1332b 25–26. See also 1261a 31–1261b 6.

53   Aristotle, *Politics*, 1268a 24.

54   Indeed, respect is an essential condition for any manifestation of efficacious freedom, e.g. artistic or religious manifestations, but this is not the context in which to argue for this general thesis.

55   See Rom Harré, *Social Being* (Totowa: Rowman & Littlefield, 1979) pp. 24–5. Hereafter *SB*.

56   See Michael Walzer, *Spheres of Justice* (New York: Basic Books, 1983) pp. 274–5. Walzer is discussing 'self-respect' here. But nothing stands in the way of applying his remarks to all respect. In general, I would argue that this study of mine supplies a solid conceptual underpinning for the sorts of claims and conclusions Walzer articulates in *Spheres of Justice*. Hereafter *SJ*.

57   *SJ*, p. 274.

58   *SJ*, p. 277. My emphasis. Though I fully endorse the words cited, Walzer uses them in a slightly different context. Unlike Walzer, I do not wish to link them exclusively to the notion of 'democratic citizenship.' I trust that I am not here abusing Walzer's text.

59   *SJ*, p. 278.

60   *SJ*, p. 278.

61   *SB*, p. 24.

62   See Hannah Arendt, *The Human Condition* (Garden City: Doubleday Anchor Books, 1959) pp. 215–19.

63 Heidegger's remarks on heritage and destiny support my claim. See *BT*, pp. 434–9.

64 When I take respect rather than justice to be the cardinal virtue of politics and morality, I am taking justice as that which can be a property of deeds. Respect, by contrast, is understood as that which can be a characteristic of a habitual attitude. If one understands justice as that which can belong to attitudes, then justice and respect are identical. My position in effect gives what has been called an ethics of virtue primacy over the ethics of duty. For this distinction, see *Eth.*, pp. 63–8. For other arguments in favor of the cardinality of respect in the moral domain, see Alan Donagan, *The Theory of Morality* (Chicago: University of Chicago Press, 1977) pp. 64–6. For important remarks on respect in connection with Kant's thought, see Heidegger, *The Basic Problems of Phenomenology,* tr. by Albert Hofstadter (Bloomington: Indiana University Press, 1982) pp. 133–7.

65 *SJ*, p. 278.

66 See Herbert Spiegelberg, 'Ethics for fellows in the fate of existence,' in *Mid-Twentieth Century Philosophy*, ed. by Peter A. Bertocci (New York: Humanities Press, 1974) pp. 193–219.

67 My position also meshes well with what Richard Bernstein has called, with approval, 'a latent radical strain implicit in Gadamer's understanding of hermeneutics as practical philosophy.' Bernstein refers here to Gadamer's recent emphasis on the solidarity and freedom which embrace all humanity. See in this connection Bernstein, *Beyond Objectivism and Relativism* (Philadelphia: University of Pennsylvania Press, 1983) pp. 162–5.

68 See Aristotle, *Politics*, 1253a 8–38.

69 See, for example, B.F. Skinner, *Beyond Freedom and Dignity* (New York: Knopf, 1971), Herbert A. Simon, *Models of Man: Social and Rational* (New York: Wiley, 1957), and Herbert A. Simon, *Models of Bounded Rationality* (Cambridge: MIT Press, 1982).

70 See Marx and Engles, *The Communist Manifesto*, tr. by Samuel Moore (New York: Washington Square Press, 1974) and Sartre, *Search for a Method*, tr. by Hazel Barnes (New York: Vintage Books, 1968) esp. p. 34.

Chapter 5 Hope and Responsible Politics

1 H.-G. Gadamer, 'What is practice?' in his *Reason in the Age of Science*, tr. by Frederick G. Lawrence (Cambridge: MIT Press, 1981) p. 87. Hereafter *RAS*.

2 *RAS*, p. 80.

3 Gadamer, 'On the philosophic element in the sciences and the scientific character of philosophy,' in *RAS*, p. 9.

4 Gadamer, 'Hegel's philosophy and its aftereffects until today,' in *RAS*, p. 37.

5   My analysis of discourse into monologue, dialogue, and we-discourse is, I think, both more accurate and more fruitful than Gadamer's, which gives apparently unqualified preeminence to dialogue. But to pursue these differences here would be more distracting than illuminating.

6   Richard J. Bernstein, *Beyond Objectivism and Relativism* (Philadelphia: University of Pennsylvania Press, 1983) pp. 162–3. Bernstein's work has served as my main guide to the foregoing remarks on Gadamer.

7   However well hope may insure the preservation of responsible politics, it cannot absolutely guarantee it. Nothing can. On the propriety of hope in politics, see Hans Jonas, *The Imperative of Responsibility* (Chicago: University of Chicago Press, 1984), pp. 210–4.

8   It is not irrelevant to recall that 'progressivism' was thriving in the West as recently as the 1960s. Even then, though, it made little conceptual sense. For a fine analysis, see in this connection Hannah Arendt, 'The concept of history' in her *Between Past and Future* (New York: Viking Press, 1968) pp. 41–90. Hereafter *BPF*.

9   Kierkegaard has masterfully worked out these varieties of what he calls despair. See his 'Sickness unto death' in *Fear and Trembling* and *Sickness Unto Death*, tr. by Walter Lowrie (Princeton: Princeton University Press, 1974). One might imitate Kierkegaard and label these two approaches to politics as 'politics of despair.' I refrain from doing so only in order to avoid being encumbered with all the connotations readily associable with such a phrase.

10 Arendt sees a comparable distrust of the future lurking in both liberalism and conservatism. See her 'What is authority?' in *BPF*, esp. pp. 100–1.

11 I find rather clear evidence of a switching between a politics of resignation and a politics of containment in such theoreticians as Machiavelli and Burke and, perhaps, Bodin. Even if evidence of such a switching is less obvious elsewhere, I think it occurs not infrequently in the tradition. For present purposes, though, I want only to draw attention to tendencies. I do not pretend to make a contribution to the scholarly debates concerning the doctrine of any specific political thinker.

12 For these conversations, see *Nouvel Observateur*, 3 installments, no. 802. A translation of them by Adrienne Foulke appears in *Dissent*, n.v., Fall 1980. Hereafter *D*.

13 *D*, p. 397.

14 *D*, p. 442.

15 *D*, p. 401.

16 *D*, pp. 414–15. See in this connection Thomas R. Flynn, 'From "Socialisme et liberté" to "Pouvoir et liberté": The case of Jean-Paul Sartre' in *Phenomenology in a Pluralistic Context*, ed. by William L. McBride and Calvin O. Schrag (Albany: State University of New York Press, 1983) esp. p. 38. Hereafter *PPC*. See also Ronald Aronson, *The Dialectic of Despair* (London: New Left Books, 1984).

17 I have argued for this claim in my 'Merleau-Ponty's political thought: Its nature and its challenge,' in *PPC*, pp. 14–25.

18 See for example Merleau-Ponty, *Humanism and Terror*, tr. by John O'Neill (Boston: Beacon Press, 1969) p. xxxv. Hereafter HT.

19 See in this regard Herbert Spiegelberg's extremely helpful 'Sartre's last words on ethics,' in *Research in Phenomenology*, vol. XI, 1981, esp. pp. 103–4. Hereafter *SLWE*.

20 See in this connection *BPF*, pp. 127 and 138.

21 See his 'Religion and society in light of a political theology,' in *The Future of Hope*, ed. by Walter H. Capps (Philadelphia: Fortress Press, 1970) p. 137. Hereafter *SLPT*.

22 See Mary Ann Tolbert, 'Defining the problem: The Bible and feminist hermeneutics,' *Semeia*, vol. 28, 1983, pp. 113–26, quoted in *National Catholic Reporter*, vol. 20, no. 25, April 13, 1984, p. 9. Obviously I do not want to comment here on the substance of Tolbert's claim. Other examples of the contemporary interplay between politics and religion abound. Consider the political activity associated with the 1983 American Catholic Bishops' Letter on Nuclear War.

23 For a somewhat fuller description of the history of the notion of hope, see my 'Hope and its ramifications for politics,' *Man and World*, vol. 17, 1984, pp. 453–76.

24 See *SLPT*, pp. 153–4.

25 The double-rayed character of hope is comparable to that of discourse. But unlike discourse, hope, as will be mentioned below, has a fixed primary ray. The primary ray is that which is directed toward some 'agent' apart from oneself.

26 Lengthy duration is not a distinguishing feature of acts of hope. It is also a feature of acts of love, despair, hate, etc. But it is an important feature.

27 Though Ernst Bloch dissociates confidence from hope, he gives no compelling reason for doing so. See his 'Man as possibility,' in *The Future of Hope*, ed. Walter H. Capps (Philadelphia: Fortress Press, 1970), p. 67. For the most part, what I say about hope is consonant with the basic features of Bloch's account, provided that his Marxism and atheism are not to be counted as essential features of that account. See his *Das Prinzip Hoffnung* (Frankfurt am Main: Suhrkamp, 1959). For criticism of Bloch's Marxism and atheism, see Alois Edmaier, *Horizonte der Hoffnung* (Regensberg: Verlag Friedrich Pustet, 1968) esp. pp. 232–9.

28 S. Harent, 'Espérance,' in *Dictionnaire de Théologie Catholique*, ed. by A. Vacant and E. Mangenot (Paris: Librairie Letouzey, 1939) vol. 5, part 1, p. 611. My emphasis.

29 The agency in question is, of course, always an agency which is efficacious only within and upon circumstances.

30 I do not pretend to present an exhaustive account of hope.

31 Disagreements over the character and extent of the openness of the future can lead to distinctions within hope between those acts of hope which are warranted and those which are foolish or vain.

32 See Gabriel Marcel, *Homo Viator*, tr. by Emma Craufurd (London: Victor Gollancz, 1951) pp. 29–67. Hereafter *HV*.

33 *HV*, p. 67.

34 *HV*, p. 60.

35 For documentation, see *HRP*.

36 The superhuman is, of course, not always construed as personal. But it is always construed as that which it is supposed to be both sensible and beneficial to be linked. The superhuman is never merely impersonal, if the term 'impersonal' is understood to refer only to the correlative opposite of the personal.

37 For a somewhat more detailed description of the differences between political discourse and religious discourse, see my *Silence: The Phenomenon and Its Ontological Significance* (Bloomington: Indiana University Press, 1980) pp. 38–40.

38 Aristotle, *Nicomachean Ethics*, tr. by Martin Ostwald (Indianapolis: Bobbs-Merrill, 1962) 1160a 9–29. See also his *Politics*, 1318b 38–42 and 1324a 7–14.

39 See Michael Oakeshott, 'The voices of poetry in the conversation of mankind,' in his *Rationalism in Politics and Other Essays* (New York: Basic Books, 1962) pp. 243–7.

40 Western history is surely replete with evidence of the complex intertwining of Christianity and politics. From Constantine onward, the connection between temporal authority and spiritual authority, the 'two swords,' has been an issue. Nontrivial evidence of the persistence of this confused, confusing intertwining can be found in the apparent paradox of the involvement of Roman Catholic churchmen in contemporary Polish politics on the one hand, and Pope John Paul II's demand that Catholic churchmen give up roles of political leadership in Nicaragua and the United States. The discussions which have been engendered by these factors display the complexity of the bonds between politics and religion and of thought about them. Similar issues surround Islamic states and the status of Judaism as a religion in Israel.

41 Whether art, too, vies with politics and religion for primacy in a community or whether art is an equiprimordially fundamental facet, along with religion and politics, of one and the same totalizing community is an intriguing, important issue which cannot be developed here. For hints about such matters, see Heidegger, 'The origin of the work of art,' in *Poetry, Language, Thought,* tr. by Albert Hofstadter (New York: Harper Colophon Books, 1978) and Mikel Dufrenne, *Art et politique* (Paris: Union Générale d'Editions, 1974).

42 See, in this connection, Alasdair MacIntyre, *After Virtue* (Notre Dame: Notre Dame University Press, 1981) pp. 22–3, and Sheldon S. Wolin, *Politics and Vision* (Boston: Little, Brown & Co., 1960) pp. 410–29, hereafter *PV*.

43 Individual people obviously belong to many communities and associations. In emphasizing the political community, I am giving stress to a type of activity. I am not dividing people into groups.

44 That some religions have at times relaxed some doctrinal demands shows a tendency to engage in politics. Such occurrences count in favor of my thesis rather than against it.

45 Whether religion is essentially totalized or whether it too can be totalizing without attempting to effect complete totalization is not clear. What I say here is descriptive of the way religion has been in fact and for the most part taken. My hunch is that religion does not require totalization. But this is only a hunch based upon the emphasis upon hope within religion itself.

46 I do not see any conceptual impossibility for there to be other competitors besides religion and managerial technocracy against politics for the function of totalizer. Art, as I mentioned, might perhaps be such a candidate. But in the absence of substantial historical support for any third competitor, I feel no compulsion here to discuss merely conceivable candidacies.

47 The argument against politics of hope's political competitors is admittedly enthymematic rather than demonstrative. These competitors do not demonstrably suffer from conceptual flaws. Rather, my claim is that, when they are lived out, they fail to contribute to responsible political conduct as effectively as does a politics of hope. Since the issue here is finally not whether one is to grant politics the role of totalizer but how one is to practice a totalizing politics which does not seek to terminate in a totalized politics, the argument necessarily takes the form of a recommendation and this is, in Aristotelian terms, a form of enthymematic argumentation.

48 This commitment does not, of course, imply any commitment to longevity for any particular men.

49 A politics of hope is not essentially a pacifist politics. Sending men into some battles knowing that there will be fatal casualties is not absolutely ruled out by politics of hope. I will return to this matter in my discussion of coercion in Chapter 7.

50 See *SLWE*, pp. 96–9, Gabriel Marcel, *Man Against Mass Society,* tr. by G.S. Fraser (Chicago: Henry Regnery, 1962) pp. 206–9, and, in a different vein, John Rawls, *A Theory of Justice* (Cambridge, Mass.: Belknap Press, 1971) pp. 105–7.

51 See *HV*, p. xxxv.

52 My claims about the importance of the political are compatible with but go further than those of Wolin. See *PV*, p. 434.

53 For this conception of rationality, see Nicholas Maxwell, 'Science, reason, knowledge, and wisdom: A critique of specialism,' *Inquiry*, vol. 23, 1980, pp. 19–81. I appeal only to the view of rationality advanced by Maxwell. I make no claims concerning his critique of contemporary scientific practice.

54 Gadamer distinguishes a critical function from a dogmatic function in his discussion of Natural Law. See his *Truth and Method*, tr. by Garrett Barden and John Cumming (New York: Seabury Press, 1975) pp. 285–6.

55 See Merleau-Ponty, *Sense and Non-Sense*, tr. by Hubert L. Dreyfus

and Patricia A. Dreyfus (Evanston: Northwestern University Press, 1964) p. 152, and *HT*, pp. xxxiv–xxxv.

56 Merleau-Ponty, *Adventures of the Dialectic*, tr. by Joseph Bien (Evanston: Northwestern University Press, 1973) p. 196. Hereafter *AD*.

57 The benefits brought about by the work of these people, and others, are of course not timeless. They, like every human accomplishment, must be taken up by others and elaborated anew in other circumstances. Nonetheless, one should not underestimate the power of their example and its attractiveness to serious people throughout the human community.

58 *AD*, p. 29.

59 I take it for granted that discovering that a political proposal is fundamentally at odds with the entire tradition of political thought constitutes a devastating critique of that proposal. This assumption rests on the hermeneutic principle that the major figures in the tradition had nontrivial reasons for what they said and thus there is point to their analyses and proposals. Their work, then, is to be salvaged and not destroyed.

Chapter 6   Institutions and power

1 Once again, I make no claim to give an exhaustive account of what a politics of hope would amount to because I do not believe that there is any such thing as an exhaustive account of anything nonformal.

2 A.R. Radcliffe-Brown, 'On social structure,' *Journal of the Royal Anthropological Institute*, vol. 70, 1940, p. 9, cited in Anthony Giddens, *Central Problems in Social Theory* (Berkeley: University of California Press, 1979) p. 96. Hereafter *CPST*.

3 See 'Institution', in *Oxford English Dictionary*, ed. by James A.H. Murray (Oxford: Oxford University Press, 1933) vol. 5, p. 354.

4 Mikel Dufrenne, *Art et politique* (Paris: Union Générale d'Editions, 1974) p. 19. My emphasis.

5 See Louis Althusser, 'Idéologies et appareils idéologiques d'État,' in *La Pensée*, no. 151, juin 1970, esp. pp. 23–5. Althusser's doctrine is far more complex than is represented here. For a valuable critique of his position, see Simon Clarke, Victor Seidler, Kevin McDonnell, Kevin Robins and Terry Lovell, *One-Dimensional Marxism* (London and New York: Allison & Busby, 1980) and Althusser's own *Éléments d'autocritique* (Paris: Hachette Littérature, 1974). I cite this particular essay of Althusser's primarily to illustrate what sorts of theses about institutions have been proposed.

6 For an illuminating study of the several stages of Sartre's political thought, see Ronald Aronson, *Jean-Paul Sartre – Philosophy in the World* (London: Verso, 1980) esp. pp. 216–42. Aronson's summary conclusion of Sartre's political thought is judicious. See p. 292. Hereafter *JPS*.

7   Jean-Paul Sartre, *The Communists and Peace, with a Reply to Claude Lefort*, tr. by Martha H. Fletcher and Philip R. Berk (New York: Brazillier, 1968) p. 128.
8   *JPS*, p. 220.
9   *JPS*, pp. 224–6.
10 Merleau-Ponty, *The Adventures of the Dialectic*, tr. by Joseph Bien (Evanston: Northwestern University Press, 1973) pp. 107–8. Hereafter *AD*.
11 *JPS*, p. 225.
12 *AD*, p. 142.
13 *AD*, pp. 144–47.
14 Sartre, *Critique of Dialectical Reason*, tr. by Alan Sheridan-Smith (London: New Left Books, 1976). Hereafter *CDR*.
15 Sartre, *Search for a Method*, tr. by Hazel Barnes (New York: Vintage Books, 1968) p. 113. Hereafter *SM*.
16 *SM*, pp. 155–6. My emphasis. See also p. 163.
17 *SM*, p. 156.
18 For a good analysis of CDR, see *JPS* pp. 264–86.
19 *SM*, p. 113.
20 *SM*, p. 164.
21 See *CDR*, pp. 345–478.
22 For a subtle critique of Sartre's position suggesting other ways in which his position could be developed, see Thomas R. Flynn, *Sartre and Marxist Existentialism* (Chicago: University of Chicago Press, 1984) esp. pp. 196–204. Hereafter *SME*.
23 See in this connection *AD, passim,* and Sonia Kruks, *The Political Philosophy of Merleau-Ponty* (Atlantic Highlands: Humanities Press, 1981) pp. 63–75.
24 Fyodor Dostoyevski, *The Brothers Karamazov*, tr. by Constance Garnett, revised by Ralph E. Matlaw (New York: W.W. Norton, 1976) pp. 227–45.
25 Charles Taylor, *Hegel and Modern Society* (Cambridge: Cambridge University Press, 1979) p. 126.
26 See Herbert Simon, *Administrative Behavior* (New York: Macmillan, 1947) p. 79. Hereafter *AB*. See also Herbert Simon, *Models of Man, Social and Rational* (New York: Wiley, 1957) pp. 196–200. My description of Simon's position is heavily indebted to Shelden Wolin's account of it in his *Politics and Vision* (Boston: Little, Brown & Co., 1960) pp. 380–414.
27 *AB*, pp. 38–9 and 109–19.
28 *AB*, pp. 101–2.
29 *AD*, p. 143. See also Merleau-Ponty, *In Praise of Philosophy*, tr. by John Wild and James Edie (Evanston: Northwestern University Press, 1963) p. 55.
30 Merleau-Ponty, *Themes from the Lectures at College de France, 1952–60*, tr. by John O'Neill (Evanston: Northwestern University Press, 1970) pp. 40–1. Hereafter *TL*.
31 *TL*, p. 40.

32 See Merleau-Ponty, *Signs*, tr. by Richard C. McCleary, (Evanston: Northwestern University Press, 1964) p. 289. Hereafter *S*.

33 *S*, pp. 348–9.

34 See also in this connection, Ernest Barker, *Principles of Social and Political Theory* (Oxford: Clarendon Press, 1951) pp. 277–8.

35 Alasdair MacIntyre, *After Virtue* (Notre Dame: Notre Dame University Press, 1981) p. 153. Hereafter *AV*.

36 *AV*, p. 207.

37 Recall here Socrates's explanation to Crito in Plato's *Crito* why he, Socrates, must not flee execution.

38 See *CPST*, pp. 63–9.

39 Paul Ricoeur, *International Theory* (Fort Worth: Texas Christian University Press, 1976) pp. 34–7.

40 This view of institutions allows one to distinguish between 'progressive' and 'retrogressive' institutions, a distinction which Michel Foucault, for example, struggles without apparent success to make. See, for example, his 'Politics and the study of discourse,' *Ideology and Consciousness*, Spring 1978, no. 3 (no volume) pp. 8–26.

41 See SME, pp. 173–86.

42 Sir William Blackstone, *The Commentaries on the Laws of England* (Philadelphia: Robert Bell, 1821) vol. I, p. 6.

43 It is, of course, always possible for political institutions, under the guise of other sorts, to coopt them. Perhaps state-supported religion or art tends to be a coopted religion or art. But in principle nothing makes cooption inevitable, even if an institution of one sort lends material support to institutions of other sorts.

44 Hannah Arendt, 'The crisis in culture', in her *Between Past and Future* (New York: Viking Press, 1968) p. 214. Hereafter *BPF*. In my opinion, though, Arendt's location of the political heavily in the realm of 'disinterested' judgment and taste is mistaken. See pp. 219–25 of this same work for a concise statement of her position.

45 It may be that there are no actual historical examples of attempts to implement such exorbitant claims. They may well be simply unlivable. But there are clear cases of people having attempted to make good such claims. Iran since 1979 is one example. But these efforts, on my position, are always illegitimate precisely on political grounds.

46 The Lutheran dictum is 'Ecclesia semper reformanda est.' Or, 'The Church is always in need of reform.'

47 *CPST*, p. 54.

48 Kenneth L. Schmitz, 'Community: The elusive unity,' *The Review of Metaphysics*, vol. XXXVII, no. 2, December 1983, p. 256. Hereafter CEU.

49 D.H. Wrong, *Power* (New York: Harper & Row, 1979) p. 2. For an indication of the diversity of the senses of the term 'power' see also pp. 21 and 267–8 fn. 1. Hereafter *Power*.

50 Bertrand de Jouvenel, 'Authority: The efficient imperative' in Carl J. Friedrich, ed., *Authority*, Nomos I (Cambridge, Mass.: Harvard University Press, 1958) p. 160, quoted in *Power*, p. 14.

51 See *Power*, pp. 21–34.
52 *Power*, p. 49.
53 *Power*, pp. 121–3.
54 I will discuss these different sorts of power more fully in Chapter 7.
55 Charles Sherover, 'The temporality of the common good: Futurity and freedom,' *The Review of Metaphysics*, vol. xxxvii, no. 3, March 1984, p. 492. Hereafter TCG.
56 *TCG*, p. 493.
57 See in this connection Bertrand de Jouvenel, *On Power*, tr. by J.F. Huntington (New York: Viking Press, 1949) pp. 283–5. Hereafter *OP*. Though de Jouvenel provides good insights, I do not share his basic distrust of power.
58 *OP*, p. 137.
59 *OP*, pp. 177–9.
60 See CEU, p. 257.
61 TCG, p. 496.
62 Though Arendt tends to draw excessively neat distinctions, her remarks about the induction of newcomers are of considerable use. See *BPF*, pp. 192–3.
63 Machiavelli, *The Prince*, ch. 17.
64 See *Power*, p. 75.
65 *SME*, p. 199.

Chapter 7 Authority, sovereignty, and coercion

1 Bertrand de Jouvenel, *Sovereignty*, tr. by J.F. Huntington (Chicago: University of Chicago Press, 1957) pp. 200–1. Hereafter *Sov*.
2 Leibniz, 'Portrait of the prince,' in *The Political Writings of Leibniz*, tr. and ed. by Patrick Riley (Cambridge: Cambridge University Press, 1972) pp. 85–6.
3 See in this connection the essays on 'Authority' in *Political Philosophy*, ed. by Anthony Quinton (Oxford: Oxford University Press, 1967) hereafter *PP*, and Hannah Arendt, 'What is authority?', in her *Between Past and Future* (New York: Viking Press, 1968). Hereafter *BPF*.
4 See Max Weber, *Theory of Economic and Social Organization*, ed. by Talcott Parsons, tr. by A.M. Henderson and Talcot Parsons (New York: Oxford University Press, 1947) pp. 328–29. It is useful to note the correlation between Weber's legal-rational and Leibniz's legal authority and Weber's charismatic and Leibniz's virtue-based authority. Though the link between Weber's traditional and Leibniz's natural is not immediate, they are perhaps not irreconcilable.
5 Dennis H. Wrong, *Power* (New York: Harper & Row, 1979) pp. 41–64.
6 This symposium appears in *PP*, pp. 83–111.
7 Quoted by Peters, *PP*, p. 83.
8 *Sov*., quoted by Peters, *PP*, pp. 83–4.

9 Peters's reading of de Jouvenel, as will become evident shortly, is simplistic. But it does provide a useful schematic point of departure.

10 Because of the history of these concepts, it is near impossible to discuss authority without mentioning sovereignty. But I will explicitly treat sovereignty later in this chapter.

11 See Hobbes, *De Cive*, ed. by Sterling Lamprecht (New York: Appleton-Century-Crofts, 1949) part II, ch. 5, pp. 66–9. Hereafter *DC*. Also see his *Leviathan*, part II, chs 42 and 44 (Chicago: Great Books of the Western World, 1952) vol. 23, pp. 227 and 248, and E.D. Watt, *Authority* (New York: St Martin's Press, 1982) pp. 95–6.

12 *Sov.*, p. 199.

13 *Sov.*, p. 199. Spinoza, too, holds a position much like that of Hobbes. See in this connection de Jouvenel, *On Power*, tr. by J.F. Huntington (New York: Viking Press, 1949) pp. 33–6. Hereafter *OP*.

14 *Sov.*, pp. 200–2 and *OP*, pp. 195–212.

15 A similar inadequacy would show up if one considered Wrong's classification in place of Weber's.

16 *PP*, p. 91. My insertion.

17 *PP*, pp. 107–8.

18 Winch recognizes that he has only named a problem and has not solved it. See *PP*, p. 111.

19 See Hannah Arendt, *On Revolution* (New York: Viking Press, 1963) p. 214.

20 Alexander von Schoenborn, 'Political authority: Some preliminary remarks,' unpublished manuscript.

21 *DC*, part II, ch. 7, pp. 89–90.

22 See Herbert Simon, *Administrative Behavior* (New York: Macmillan, 1947) p. 151. Hereafter *AB*. See also *BPF*, pp. 92–3.

23 See in this connection J.R. Lucas, *On Justice* (Oxford: Clarendon Press, 1980) p. 59, hereafter *OJ*, and A.P. d'Entreves, *The Notion of the State* (Oxford: Clarendon Press, 1967) p. 197. Hereafter *NS*. D'Entreves's approach to the matter of authority is, on the whole, markedly different from mine.

24 Bertrand de Jouvenel, *The Pure Theory of Politics* (Cambridge: Cambridge University Press, 1963) p. 99. Hereafter *PTP*. Though my discussion of authority owes much to de Jouvenel, I do not accept several of his conclusions. But again, this is not the place to spell out these points of conflict.

25 *Sov.*, p. 299.

26 See Hannah Arendt, *The Human Condition* (Garden City: Doubleday Anchor Books, 1959) pp. 167–9. Hereafter *HC*.

27 The ruler may address one set of needs obliquely by drawing attention to some other needs. If he diverts his people from their genuine needs to believe in illusory needs, he does not lead. He dupes. It is not pertinent to my present purposes to propose detailed criteria for distinguishing genuine from illusory needs. But obviously this is an issue of capital importance.

28 See in this connection *PTP*, pp. 104–7.

29   Sartre's play 'Dirty Hands' splendidly illustrates this inevitable slippage. See Sartre, *No Exit and Three Other Plays* (New York: Vintage Books, 1976).
30   It is impossible, I believe, to spell out a priori what are to count as 'tolerable bounds.'
31   *Sov.*, p. 34.
32   *Sov.*, p. 300. One should not fail to notice the similarity between de Jouvenel's conclusion and Merleau-Ponty's endeavor to think politics and history in terms of the distinction between *langue* and *parole*.
33   Locke, for one, clearly allows for this possibility. See his *Second Treatise of Government* (Indianapolis: Bobbs-Merrill, 1952) pp. 125–7.
34   Note that I make no such claims for legitimate authority in nonpolitical domains. Though I am inclined to hold such a position for all domains, it would be out of place to pursue that argument here.
35   I will discuss coercive authority in more detail later in this chapter.
36   De Jouvenel, in his own way, reaches much the same conclusion. He says: 'It is the sovereign's business to see that the *reges* operate to repair the insecurity caused by initiatives, not to prelude them; and it is his duty to intervene to the extent necessary for the adequate fulfillment of the function of *rex*.' *Sov.*, p. 300.
37   See in this connection John Plamenatz, *Man and Society* (New York: McGraw-Hill, 1963) I, p. 99. Hereafter *MS*.
38   It is of course possible for one and the same person to function as superior both in the political domain and in some nonpolitical domain. But the sources of his titles to do so are distinct. Thus a political ruler may also justifiably claim the right to conduct a symphony orchestra. But he will do so by reason of his musical competence and not by reason of his political position.
39   *Sov.*, p. 304.
40   Here again one sees the pertinence of Merleau-Ponty's injunction to think history, and politics, in terms of the relation between *langue* and *parole*.
41   See Charles de Montesquieu, *The Spirit of the Laws*, tr. by Thomas Nugent (New York: Hafner, 1975), p.150. Hereafter *SL*.
42   *HC*, pp. 179–80. Though I do not accept all of Arendt's position concerning strength, force, power, and authority, here I think she is correct.
43   *Sov*, p. 123.
44   See in this connection Hans-Georg Gadamer, 'On the scope and function of hermeneutical reflection,' in his *Philosophical Hermeneutics*, tr. and ed. by David E. Linge (Berkeley: University of California Press, 1976) esp. p. 42.
45   See *DC*, part II, ch. 5, p.68, ch. 7, p. 94, and ch.12, p. 131.
46   *BPF*, p. 165. See also Sheldon S. Wolin, 'The idea of the state in America,' *Humanities in Society*, vol. 3, 1980, pp. 151–68, esp. p. 152.
47   *MS*, I, p. 101.
48   *MS*, I, p. 19.

49 On the medieval doctrine of popular sovereignty, see Otto Gierke, *Political Theories of the Middle Ages*, tr. by F.M. Maitland (Cambridge: Cambridge University Press, 1900) pp. 37ff.

50 *MS*, I pp. 98ff. See also *NS*, pp. 89–103.

51 Blackstone, later, employs this distinction even if he does not expressly articulate it. See his *The Commentaries on the Laws of England* (Philadelphia: Robert Bell, 1821) vol. I pp. 46, 154–8, 233–45, and 250–1.

52 *SL*, pp. 19–28.

53 *MS*, I p. 193.

54 On the irreducibility of this distinction, see my 'Renovating the problem of politics,' *The Review of Metaphysics*, vol. XXIX, 1976, pp. 626–41.

55 See *NS*, p. 98.

56 The rhetoric of isolation often embodies a repudiation of the sovereignty needed for effective international action. But such rhetoric is also prone to slide into a justification of xhenophobic despotism.

57 De Jouvenel handles the issue at stake here in terms of 'social interest' and 'common good.' I disagree with the sharp distinction he makes between what he calls the 'collective social interest' and the 'common good' because the distinction makes the common good too abstract. The sharper distinction is that between individual interest and 'collective social interest.' For de Jouvenel's position see *Sov.*, pp. 128–30.

58 I know of no theoretical argument which would show that the diversity of peoples is essentially incompatible with the incorporation of the entire human race into a single political community. Strikingly different people do live at peace within one and the same community. But it is hard to see how this could be made universal. History gives little help and utopian literature is no more helpful.

59 See Gadamer, *Truth and Method*, tr. by Garrett Barden and John Cumming (New York: Seabury Press, 1975) p. 385. See also *Sov.*, p. 129.

60 Today, sovereign bodies politic are the national states. Obviously, this is a contingent, historical phenomenon. There were, at other times, sovereign tribes and sovereign city-states. It is hard to determine a priori either necessary or sufficient conditions for a group of people to achieve the status of a sovereign body politic. When one attends to the various separatist movements about today, one sees that not all sovereign states are stable. Further, recent history has shown that some nations have had their borders drawn for them more to insure their weakness and dependence than to acknowledge their sovereignty. But even so, once established, it is their task to promote and enhance their sovereignty. Finally, it is often the case today that within a particular sovereign state there are one or more smaller groups, each with its own customs, beliefs, etc. The distinction I make between the global dimension and the distributive dimension of the public weal in order to discuss proper international relations is, *mutatis mutandis*, likewise pertinent to the discussion of proper intranational relations. Of

course, the *mutandi*, the things to be changed, are by no means trivial.

61 Though the state is not equivalent to society, they are not opposed to one another. See in this connection Ernest Barker, *Principles of Social and Political Theory* (Oxford: Clarendon Press, 1951) pp. 275–6.

62 An urgent practical problem for which I have no detailed solution is how one can know, and respond to, conditions which demand that one's own state's weal be sacrificed to the global public weal. For example, is it ever permissible to cooperate in making one's own state completely a client state of another? Or conversely, is the 'Masada approach' always acceptable for a state? This tangled issue of client states clearly plays a crucial part in the contemporary assessment of the politics of both the Soviet Union and the United States. The one definite conclusion which can be drawn from a politics of hope is that if the only way one can prevent the absorption of one state by another is global nuclear war, one may not resort to such a war. Such a war is incompatible with 'preferential option' for man as one who is essentially *en route*.

63 See in this connection my 'Politics and coercion,' *Philosophy Today*, vol. XXI, 1977, pp. 103–14.

64 *PTP*, p. 207.

65 See in this connection Paul Ricoeur, *Freedom and Necessity*, tr. by Erazim V. Kohak (Evanston: Northwestern University Press, 1966) esp. pp. 482–6, and Alexander Pfander, *Phenomenology of Willing and Motivation*, tr. by Herbert Spiegelberg (Evanston: Northwestern University Press, 1967) esp. pp. 14–40.

66 D'Entreves, to the contrary, holds that there is no possible dialectic whereby the opposition between coercion and freedom can be overcome. See *NS*, p. 220. This position must presuppose some version of the doctrine of autonomous freedom.

67 Again it is useful to remember that people can be simultaneously incorporated into more than one political community. For example, physical inhabitance and legal citizenship need not coincide.

68 Hobbes exaggerates, but not preposterously, when he says that if anyone withholds consent from the city and its sovereign, he is to be attacked as an enemy. *DC*, p. 72.

69 For an example of such resistance, consider the events in Poland in 1980 and since.

70 Much so-called leniency in the enforcement of civil and criminal law is explicable in terms of this anticipation of a conversion. Though it is unlikely that the coerced, at the outset of the justifiable coercive act, will in fact recognize its aim to reduce coercion, it is in principle recognizable.

71 Hobbes, *Leviathian* (London: J.M. Dent, 1973) p. 79.

72 The two conditions and their corollaries for justifiable coercion approximate the classical doctrine concerning conditions for a just war. But the bases upon which these two sets of conditions respectively rest is markedly different.

73 *SL*, Book X, pp. 62–3. See also *OJ*, pp. 82–7.
74 Respect is enough to ground forgiveness. To call further for actual love as the basis for forgiveness and ultimately for the political conversation is a mistake. See in this connection *HC*, p. 218.
75 *MS*, II, p. 172.
76 This last point does not preclude the death penalty. But it does preclude terroristic summary execution, i.e. a killing unaccompanied by any genuine discourse which thus gives the condemned person no chance to understand and perhaps ratify his own death sentence.

Chapter 8 Law and political education: exercises in guiding and gooding

1 W.D. Falk's well-known essay 'Goading and guiding,' *Mind*, vol. 62, 1953, suggested this chapter title. I have not, though, drawn much upon the contents of this work.
2 See Paul Ricoeur, 'The political paradox', in *History and Truth*, tr. by Charles A. Kelbley (Evanston: Northwestern University Press, 1965) pp. 249–70, esp. p. 261. Hereafter *Pol. P.* I do not endorse Ricoeur's remarks here about the birth of the body politic from a virtual act of consent.
3 See Hannah Arendt, *The Human Condition* (Garden City: Doubleday Books, 1959) p. 170. Hereafter *HC*.
4 See in this connection Hannah Arendt. 'The crisis in education,' in her *Between Past and Future* (New York: Viking Books, 1968) pp. 175–7. Hereafter *BPF*.
5 *BPF*, p. 177.
6 H.L.A. Hart, 'Problems of philosophy of law,' in *Encyclopedia of Philosophy*, ed. by Paul Edwards (New York: Macmillan, 1967) vol. 6, p. 265.
7 This reflection will of course have ramifications for specific issues in the philosophy of law, but this is not the proper context in which to spell out these ramifications.
8 See in this connection Bertrand de Jouvenel, *Sovereignty*, tr. by J.F. Huntington (Chicago: University of Chicago Press, 1957) p. 304. Hereafter *Sov*.
9 Tradition and custom need not be internally consistent to be either efficacious or normative.
10 See Alexander Passerin d'Entreves, *The Notion of the State* (Oxford: Clarendon Press, 1967) pp. 82–91. Hereafter *NS*.
11 See John Plamenatz, *Man and Society* (New York: McGraw-Hill, 1963) vol. I, pp. 158–9. Hereafter *MS*. See also Thomas Gilby's footnote to I–II, Q. 95, art. 3 of St Thomas Aquinas, *Summa Theologica*, vol. 28, tr. by Thomas Gilby (New York: McGraw-Hill, 1966) p. 109. Hereafter *ST*.

12 See Bertrand de Jouvenel, *On Power* tr. by J.F. Huntington (New York: Viking Press, 1949) pp. 3–11, hereafter *OP*, and *MS*, I, p. 111 and II, pp. 344–5.

13 *Code of Canon Law,* Latin-English Edition, tr. by members of the Canon Law Society of America (Washington: Canon Law Society of America, 1983) Can. 26, p. 9. My emphasis. Hereafter *CCL.* The canons I cite here do not substantially differ from those in the 1917 version of the Code of Canon Law which the 1983 Code supersedes.

14 *CCL,* Can. 27, p. 9.

15 *CCL,* Can. 6, p. 5.

16 *CCL,* Can. 28, p.11.

17 *CCL,* Can.5, p. 3. My insertion.

18 *ST*, I–II, Q. 97, art. 3. Aquinas cites Isidore of Seville, *Etymologies V*, here in support of his position. It should be noted that laws, in the medieval view, were regarded as promotions of liberty, not as restrictions of it. See J.R. Lucas, *On Justice* (Oxford: Oxford University Press, 1980) pp. 110–11. Hereafter *OJ.*

19 Montesquieu, *The Spirit of the Laws*, tr. by Thomas Nugent (New York: Hafner, 1975) pp. 304–15. Hereafter *SL.*

20 *SL*, p. 141.

21 Sir William Blackstone. *The Commentaries on the Law of England* (Philadelphia: Robert Bell, 1821), I, p. 63. See also pp. 64–5. Hereafter *CLE*, I. It is important to notice that even *lex non scripta* is considered to be promulgated. Appeals to it do not amount to appeals to *ex post facto* law.

22 *CLE*, I, pp. 85–9.

23 *CLE*, I, pp. 14–15.

24 *MS*, I, pp. 264–5.

25 Where 'practical compatibility' ends and 'incompatibility' begins cannot be fully spelled out in advance. Often enough, incompatibility shows up only after some time has passed. Thus it is impossible to forestall all mistakes.

26 *OJ*, p. 101. See in this same vein *SL*, p. 6 and *CLE*, I, p. 73.

27 Merleau-Ponty, *Adventures of the Dialectic*, tr. by Joseph Bien (Evanston: Northwestern University Press, 1973) p. 19. Hereafter *AD*. It is clear that Merleau-Ponty's list of three orders makes no claim to being an exhaustive list.

28 Law, like everything political, also belongs to one realm among many realms, as I have shown above. The sense of specific laws then is also conditioned by discourse belonging to other realms. A contemporary example is found in the matter of human artificial insemination. But nothing of the present argument requires that I take up this connection between law and other realms in any detail.

29 See H.-G. Gadamer, *Truth and Method*, tr. by Garrett Barden and John Cumming (New York: Seabury Press, 1975) pp. 245 ff. Hereafter *TM*. See also MS, I, pp. 343–5.

30 *BPF*, p. 5. I do not share Arendt's view of the contemporary obsolesc-

ence of the Western tradition, a view she spells out in an essay in this book entitled 'Tradition and the modern age.' For a view of tradition today which is closer to my own, see Paul Ricoeur, 'The task of the political educator,' tr. by David Stewart, *Philosophy Today*, vol. 17, 1973, esp. pp. 146–9. Hereafter TPE.

31 For a detailed account of tradition as *langue*, see my 'Discourse, silence, and tradition,' *The Review of Metaphysics*, vol. XXXII, 1979, 437–51.

32 See Aristotle, *Politics*, 1275a 23, 1275b 18–20, and 1293b 29.

33 Aristotle, *Politics*, 1279a 17–21 and 1333a 4–5.

34 Aristotle, *Politics*, 1310a 34–35.

35 *CLE*, I, p. 124. My emphasis.

36 *CLE*, I, p. 6.

37 Within the tradition there have been several notable efforts to dissolve this paradox. Among the most important of these are the efforts of Spinoza, Kant and Hegel, each of whom proposed a solution based on some version of the doctrine of the rational will. Their efforts, however, have had the effect more of showing the intractability of the paradox than of solving it. For a clear presentation of these efforts, one which is more optimistic than I am about the prospects for future efforts along these lines, see Patrick Riley, *Will and Political Legitimacy* (Cambridge, Mass.: Harvard University Press, 1982).

38 Ernest Barker, *Principles of Social and Political Theory* (Oxford: Clarendon Press, 1952) p. 270. Hereafter *PSPT*. See also *NS*, pp. 204–5.

39 *PSPT*, p. 278.

40 Speaking of the relation between justice and freedom, Lucas says: 'It is supposed not simply that we cannot guarantee them both, which is true, but that we cannot have them both, which is false.' *OJ*, p. 198. The same is true of the relation between law and freedom.

41 Aristotle, *Nichomachean Ethics*, 1129b 13–14. Translated by Martin Oswald (Indianapolis: Bobbs-Merrill, 1962) Hereafter *NE*. Throughout this discussion I will draw only on what Aristotle says about the just in the political sense. It is not to the point of this study to deal with what he says about complete justice.

42 *NE*, 1134a 24–29.

43 *NE*, 1134a 31–36.

44 *NE*, 1137b 16–19.

45 *NE*, 1137b 22–23.

46 St. Thomas Aquinas, *Commentary on the Nichomachean Ethics*, tr. by C.I. Litzinger (Chicago: Henry Regnery, 1964) vol. I, p. 466. Hereafter *CNE*.

47 *CNE*, p. 468.

48 Ernest Barker notes that Roman law, even apart from custom, has at least a two-fold source. It involves both a legislative declaration and a legal formulation by the courts and the jurisconsults, those private persons who were skilled in the law and gave their opinion to the judges when consulted. The latter can rightly be said to complete what

the legislators had begun. Something of this same sort of supplementation is to be found in the development of English Law. See *PSPT*, pp. 92–7.

49 See in this connection F.W. Maitland, *Equity, also the Forms of Action at Common Law* (Cambridge: Cambridge University Press, 1920) esp. pp. 1–19 and 156. Hereafter *ECL*. The Courts of Common Law in Great Britain absorbed the Courts of Equity in 1875 in consequence of the Judicature Acts of that year.

50 *CLE*, I, p. 62.

51 See in this connection *OJ*, pp. 78–9 and 106–7.

52 See for example *CLE*, I, p. 151.

53 See for example Aristotle's *Nichomachean Ethics*, his *Rhetoric*, tr. by W. Rhys Roberts in Great Books of the Western World (Chicago: Encyclopedia Britannica, 1945) 1373b 6–8; *ST*, I–III, Q.91, art. 2; Thomas Hobbes, *Leviathan*, in *Great Books of the Western World*, vol. 23, pp. 86–96; Immanuel Kant, *The Metaphysical Elements of Justice (Rechtslehre)* tr. by John Ladd (Indianapolis: Library of Liberal Arts, 1965) p. 26; and *CLE*, I, p. 39.

54 Aristotle, *Rhetoric*, 1373b 6–8.

55 I have borrowed the distinction between validity and value from Ernest Barker and have tailored it to my own purposes. See *PSPT*, p. 98.

56 See in this connection Tom Rockmore, William J. Gavin, James G. Colbert, and Thomas Blakeley, *Marxism and Alternatives* (Dordrecht: D. Reidel, 1981) pp. 73–81. Aquinas, it is worth noting, distinguishes between first principles and secondary precepts of natural law. The former are fully ahistorical while the latter are subject to change 'on rare occasions.' *ST*, I–II, Q. 94, art. 5.

57 The relation between the public weal and positive law is in important respects, but not totally, like that between the natural law in the meaning that term had in Roman jurisprudence and positive law. For the Roman jurists, natural law is not, strictly speaking, law. It is, rather, a spirit of humane interpretation which affects how judges and jurists administer and enforce positive law. In this sense, natural law strikingly resembles equity as well. I will return to this consideration shortly. See *PSPT*, pp. 98–9.

58 Positive law has also been said to be constrained by the 'law of the peoples' (*jus gentium*). This vague but important concept indicates that the body of positive law governing any particular body politic is somehow answerable to the judgments about appropriate government everywhere. The point to a concept such as *jus gentium* is more evident today than ever. Apartheid is not merely a South African matter. Currency and trade regulations established in one nation have worldwide ramifications. All law, like all politics, is today willy-nilly international in its bearings. The concept of *jus gentium* has both regulative and historical dimensions. It is akin to the Roman view of natural law. The public weal as I construe it is that which both *jus gentium* and natural law point to as that which positive law should aim

to support. For another discussion on the connection between *just gentium* and other dimensions of law see my 'On strengthening the duty to obey the law,' *Georgia Law Review*, vol. 18, Summer 1984, no. 4, pp. 821–44.

59 See Kant, *Fundamental Principles of the Metaphysics of Morals*, tr. by Thomas K. Abbott (Chicago: Great Books of the Western World, 1952) vol. 42, pp. 264–6. See also his *Critique of Practical Reason*, tr. by Thomas K. Abbott (Chicago: Great Books of the Western World, 1952) vol. 42, pp. 298–301. Also see H.J. Paton, *The Categorical Imperative* (New York: Harper Torchbooks, 1965) p. 114 and Lewis White Beck, *A Commentary on Kant's Critique of Practical Reason* (Chicago: University of Chicago Press, 1960) pp. 49–51.

60 See Pascal, *Pensées*, ed. by Philippe Selbier (Paris: Mercure de France, 1976) no. 94, p. 63. See also no. 158, p. 85.

61 Rousseau, *Discourse on the Origin and Foundation of Inequality among Men*, in Jean-Jacques Rousseau, *The First and Second Discourses*, tr. by Roger D. and Judith R. Masters (New York: St Martin's Press, 1964) p. 82. I obviously do not pretend that either this citation or the one from Pascal in the previous footnote does justice to the complexities and subtleties of Rousseau's and Pascal's respective positions.

62 See Alan Gewirth, 'Introduction' to Marsilus of Padua, *Defensor Pacis*, tr. by Alan Gewirth (Toronto: University of Toronto Press, 1980) p. xxxvi.

63 See Anthony Giddens, *Critical Problems in Social Theory* (Berkeley: University of California Press, 1978) pp. 65–9.

64 *Pol. P.,* p. 258.

65 Merleau-Ponty says: 'We do not gain from the working operations of history that comprehensive understanding which would reveal the true solution. At best we rectify errors which occur along the way, but the new scheme is not immune to errors which will have to be rectified anew. . . . Since . . . in the density of social reality each decision brings unexpected consequences, and since, moreover, man responds to these surprises by inventions which transform the problem, there is no situation without hope; but there is no choice which terminates these deviations or which can exhaust man's inventive power and put an end to his history.' *AD*, pp. 22–3. He then adds: 'Perhaps history will eliminate, together with false solutions to the human problem, certain valid acquisitions as well. It does not locate its errors precisely in a total system.' *AD*, p. 23. See also *AD*, pp. 56–7 and Merleau-Ponty, *Humanism and Terror*, tr. by John O'Neill (Boston: Beacon Press, 1967) p. 188.

66 *TM*, p. 285. See also *NS*, pp. 225–8 and *OJ*, p. 78. My interpretation of natural law, then, is much like that found in Roman law as reported in *PSPT*, pp. 98–9. Note also Lon Fuller's remark: 'If I were asked . . . to discern one central indisputable principle of what may be called substantive natural law . . . I would find it in the injunction: Open up, maintain and preserve the integrity of the channels of communication

by which men convey to one another what they perceive, feel, and desire.' Fuller, *The Morality of Law* (New Haven: Yale University Press, 1964) p. 186.

67 See *TM*, pp. 285–99.
68 My position has happy analogies with that of Aristotle. For Aristotle, legal discourse like all scientific discourse was bounded on the one hand by insight into first principles and by the perception of ultimate particular facts as particular. The capacity to recognize both bounds is called *voûs*. Neither the bounds not the discourse depreciate the other. Together they constitute wisdom. See *NE* 1140b 31–1141a 9 and 1142a 25–31.
69 A particular statute or decision, e.g. parking fines, may have only local effects. But no body of law governing any community of any size or economic potential has only local effects.
70 This conclusion meshes well with Merleau-Ponty's recognition, noted in Chapter 2 above, that today all politics has international bearings and yet there are only local politics, rather than a single universal politics. See his *Signs*, tr. by Richard C. McCleary (Evanston: North-western University Press, 1964) esp. pp. 4 and 35.
71 See Aristotle, *Politics*, 1310a 12–14, 1337a 11–14, and 1337a 35–1337b 3.
72 See Sheldon S. Wolin, *Politics and Vision* (Boston: Little Brown & Co., 1960), pp. 390–2.
73 Except for the utopian writings, Western political thought furnishes comparatively little help for any attempt to give an account of responsible political education. My proposal is admittedly only a very modest contribution to that fragmentary heritage. It is hard to see, given so limited a tradition, how any proposal on this matter could aspire to grandeur.
74 *BPF*, p. 176.
75 *BPF*, p. 186.
76 *BPF*, p. 192. My emphasis.
77 The comparative poverty of Western political thought concerning political education makes it rather pointless to contrast the approach of politics of hope to this matter with those of its competitors. I will therefore confine myself to a simple straightforward description of how a politics of hope understands what political education can and should accomplish.
78 Michael Oakeshott, as I noted in Chapter 5, has emphasized this task of political education. See 'The voices of poetry in the conversation of mankind,' in his *Rationalism in Politics and Other Essays* (New York: Basic Books, 1962) pp. 243–7.
79 With a peculiar sort of reflexivity, this study of mine is itself a possible exercise in political education. Insofar as this book is addressed to other scholars knowledgeable about the matters I discuss, this book is not part of education. It is rather a contribution to a discussion among peers. If, however, it is read by 'amateurs' seeking to learn about matters with which they are relatively unfamiliar, then the book would

be for them, regardless of my intentions, a part of their political education. I will say a bit more below about how one comes to be a teacher in political education.

80 See TPE, pp. 142–52. In what follows I borrow selectively from this essay and develop these borrowings in the light of the general characteristics of the politics of hope thus far articulated. Though Ricoeur's essay as a whole is splendid, I disagree with several parts of it. But this is not the place to sort through these disagreements.

81 TPE, p. 143.

82 TPE, p. 143.

83 See TPE, pp. 148–9.

84 I must admit that there may be exceptions to this concern for the heritage of each group. If Colin Turnbull is correct in his description of the Ik, it is hard to argue that their heritage should be fostered. See his *The Mountain People* (New York: Simon & Schuster, 1972).

85 See in this connection TPE, pp. 151–2.

86 Ordinarily, a student or teacher can either guide or goad his counterpart but cannot do both at the same time in the same respect. If there are exceptions, I cannot think of any.

Chapter 9 Conclusion

1 I should reiterate here my debt to Heidegger. That debt is made evident in my 'Heidegger's contribution to modern political thought,' *Southern Journal of Philosophy*, vol. XXII, no.4, pp. 481–95.

2 See Alphonse de Waelhens, *Une Philosophie de l'ambiguité: L'Existentialisme de Maurice Merleau-Ponty* (Louvain: Nauwelaerts, 1970), and Bernard Halda, *Merleau-Ponty ou la Philosophie de l'ambiguité* (Paris: Les Lettres Modernes, 1966).

3 Aristotle, *Nicomachean Ethics*, 1140a 24–1140b 30.

Bibliography

Adler, M. (1958) *The Idea of Freedom*, 2 vols, Westport, Greenwood Press.

Althusser, L. (1970), 'Idéologies et appareils idéologiques d'Etat', *La Pensée*, no. 151.

Althusser, L. (1974) *Eléments d'autocritique*, Paris, Hachette Littérature.

Altmann, H. (1982), 'Cognitive interests and self-reflection', in J. Thompson and D. Held (eds), *Habermas: Critical Debates*, Cambridge, Mass., MIT Press.

Aquinas, St T. (1964), *Commentary on the Nicomachean Ethics*, tr. by C. Litzinger, Chicago, Henry Regnery.

Arendt, H. (1959), *The Human Condition,* Garden City, Doubleday/Anchor Books.

Arendt, H. (1963), *On Revolution*, New York, Viking Press.

Arendt, H. (1968), *Between Past and Future*, New York, Viking Press.

Aristotle (1941), *The Basic Works of Aristotle,* ed. by R. McKeon, New York, Random House.

Aronson, R. (1980), *Jean-Paul Sartre – Philosophy in the World*, London, Verso Editions.

Aronson, R. (1984), *The Dialectic of Despair*, London, New Left Books.

Barker, E. (1952), *Principles of Social and Political Theory*, Oxford, Clarendon Press.

Barnes, H. (1968), 'Introduction' to J.-P. Sartre, *Search for a Method*, tr. by H. Barnes, New York, Vintage Books.

Beck, L. (1960), *A Commentary on Kant's Critique of Practical Reason*, Chicago, University of Chicago Press.

Berlin, I. (1969), *Four Essays on Liberty*, Oxford, Oxford University Press.

Bernstein, R. (1983), *Beyond Objectivism and Relativism*, Philadelphia, University of Pennsylvania Press.

Blackstone, W. (1821), *The Commentaries on the Laws of England*, Philadelphia, Robert Bell.

Bloch, E. (1959), *Das Prinzip Hoffnung*, Frankfurt, Suhrkamp.

Brandt, W. (1980), *North-South: A Programme for Survival*, Cambridge, Mass., MIT Press.

Brenkert, G. (1983), *Marx's Ethics of Freedom*, London, Routledge & Kegan Paul.

Bibliography

Buber, M. (1978), *Between Man and Man*, tr. by R. Smith, New York, Macmillan.

Bubner, R. (1981), *Modern German Philosophy*, tr. by E. Matthews, Cambridge, Cambridge University Press.

Camus, A. (1960), *The Rebel*, tr. by A. Bower, New York, Vintage Books.

Clarke, S., Seidler, V., McDonnell, K., Robins, K., and Lovell, T. (1980), *One-Dimensional Marxism*, London and New York, Allison & Busby.

Code of Canon Law (no author) (1983), Latin-English edition, tr. by members of the Canon Law Society of America, Washington, DC, Canon Law Society of America.

Dallmayr, F. (1974), 'Plessner's philosophical anthropology', *Inquiry*, vol. 17, pp. 49–77.

Dallmayr, F. (1981), *Twilight of Subjectivity*, Amherst, University of Massachusetts Press.

Dauenhauer, B. (1976), 'Renovating the problem of politics', *The Review of Metaphysics*, vol. XXIX, pp. 626–41.

Dauenhauer, B. (1977a), 'Heidegger: spokesman for the dweller', *The Southern Journal of Philosophy*, vol. XV, pp. 189–99.

Dauenhauer, B. (1977b), 'Politics and coercion', *Philosophy Today*, vol. XXI, pp. 103–14.

Dauenhauer, B. (1979), 'Discourse, silence, and tradition', *The Review of Metaphysics*, vol. XXXII, pp. 437–51.

Dauenhauer, B. (1980a), 'One central link between Merleau-Ponty's philosophy of language and his political thought', *Tulane Studies in Philosophy*, vol. XXIX, pp. 57–80.

Dauenhauer, B. (1980b), *Silence: The Phenomenon and Its Ontological Significance*, Bloomington, Indiana University Press.

Dauenhauer, B. (1982a), 'Authors, audiences, and texts', *Human Studies*, vol. 5, no. 2, pp. 137–46.

Dauenhauer, B. (1982b), 'Relational freedom', *The Review of Metaphysics*, vol. XXXVI, no. 1, pp. 77–101.

Dauenhauer, B. (1983), 'Merleau-Ponty's political thought: its nature and its challenge', in W. McBride and C. Schrag (eds), *Phenomenology in a Pluralistic Context*, Albany, State University of New York Press.

Dauenhauer, B. (1984a), 'Heidegger's contribution to modern political thought', *The Southern Journal of Philosophy*, vol. XXIV, no. 4, pp. 481–95.

Dauenhauer, B. (1984b), 'On strengthening the duty to obey the law', *Georgia Law Review*, vol. 18, no. 4, pp. 821–44.

Dauenhauer, B. (1985), 'Hope and its ramifications for politics', in J.N. Moharty (ed.), *Phenomenology and the Human Sciences* (The Hague: Martinus Nijhoff, 1985), pp. 213–36; first published in *Man and World*, vol. 17, no. 3/4, 1984, pp. 453–76.

D'Entreves, A. (1967), *The Notion of the State*, Oxford, Clarendon Press.

Descartes, R. (1963), *Oeuvres Philosophiques*, ed. by F. Alquié, Paris, Garnier Frères.

Descartes, R. (1971) *Philosophical Writings*, tr. by E. Anscombe and P. Geach, Indianapolis, Library of Liberal Arts.

Donagan, A. (1977), *The Theory of Morality,* Chicago, University of Chicago Press.

Dostoyevski, F. (1976), *The Brothers Karamazov,* tr. by C. Garnett, revised by R. Matlaw, New York, W.W. Norton.

Dufrenne, M. (1974), *Art et politique,* Paris, Union Générale d'Editions.

Edie, J. (1973), 'Foreword', in M. Merleau-Ponty, *Consciousness and the Acquisition of Language,* tr. by H. Silverman, Evanston, Northwestern University Press.

Edie, J. (1981), 'The meaning and development of Merleau-Ponty's concept of structure', in J. Sallis, *Merleau-Ponty: Perception, Structure, Language,* Atlantic Highlands, Humanities Press.

Edmaier, A. (1968), *Horizonte der Hoffnung,* Regensberg, Verlag Friedrick Pustet.

Falk, W., (1953), 'Goading and guiding,' *Mind,* vol. 62, no. 246.

Flynn, T. (1983), 'From "Socialisme et Liberté" to "Pouvoir et Liberté": the case of Jean-Paul Sartre', in W. McBride and C. Schrag (eds), *Phenomenology in a Pluralistic Context,* Albany, State University of New York Press.

Flynn, T. (1984), *Sartre and Marxist Existentialism,* Chicago, University of Chicago Press.

Foucault, M. (1978), 'Politics and the study of discourse', *Ideology and Consciousness,* no. 3, pp. 8–26.

Frankena, W. (1973), *Ethics,* 2nd edn, Englewood Cliffs, Prentice-Hall.

Fuller, L. (1964), *The Morality of Law,* New Haven, Yale University Press.

Gadamer, H.-G. (1975), *Truth and Method,* tr. by G. Barden and J. Cumming, New York, Seabury Press.

Gadamer, H.-G. (1976) *Philosophical Hermeneutics,* tr. D. Linge, Berkeley, University of California Press.

Gadamer, H.-G (1981), *Reason in the Age of Science,* tr. by F. Lawrence, Cambridge, Mass., MIT Press.

Gewirth, A. (1980), 'Introduction', in Marsilius of Padua, *Defensor Pacis,* tr. by A. Gewirth, Toronto, University of Toronto Press.

Giddens, A. (1979), *Central Problems in Social Theory,* Berkeley, University of California Press.

Gierke, O (1900), *Political Theories of the Middle Ages,* tr. by F. Maitland, Cambridge, Cambridge University Press.

Goldmann, L. (1977), *Lukács and Heidegger,* tr. by William Boelhower, London, Routledge & Kegan Paul.

Gould, C. (1978), *Marx's Social Ontology,* Cambridge, Mass., MIT Press.

Habermass, J. (1973), *Theory and Practice,* tr. by J. Viertel, Boston, Beacon Press.

Habermas, J. (1975), *Legitimation Crisis,* tr. by Thomas McCarthy, Boston, Beacon Press.

Habermas, J. (1976), *Communications and the Evolution of Society,* tr. by Thomas McCarthy, Boston, Beacon Press.

Habermas, J. (1982), 'A reply to my critics', in J. Thomson and D. Held (eds), *Habermas: Critical Debates,* Cambridge, Mass., MIT Press.

251

Bibliography

Halda, B. (1966), *Merleau-Ponty ou la philosophie de l'ambiguité*, Paris, Les Lettres Modernes.

Hamrick, W. (1963), 'Interests, justice, and respect for law in Merleau-Ponty's phenomenology', in W. McBride and C. Schrag (eds), *Phenomenology in a Pluralistic Context*, Albany, SUNY Press.

Harent, S. (1939), 'Espérance', in A. Vacant and E. Manegot (eds), *Dictionnaire de Théologie Catholique*, Paris, Librairie Letouzey.

Harré, R. (1979), *Social Being*, Totowa, Rowman & Littlefield.

Hart, H. (1967), 'Problems of philosophy of law', in P. Edwards (ed.), *Encyclopedia of Philosophy*, New York, Macmillan.

Hegel, G. (1942), *Philosophy of Right*, tr. by T.M. Knox, Oxford, Clarendon.

Hegel, G. (1977), *Phenomenology of Spirit*, tr. by A. Miller, Oxford, Clarendon Press.

Heidegger, M. (1949), 'On the essence of truth', in W. Brock, *Existence and Being*, Chicago, Regnery.

Heidegger, M. (1962), *Being and Time*, tr. by J. Macquirrie and E. Robinson, New York, Harper & Row.

Heidegger, M. (1967), 'Wer ist Nietzsches Zarathursta?', in *Vorträge und Aufsätze*, Pfullingen, Neske.

Heidegger, M. (1971), *Poetry, Language, Thought*, tr. by A. Hofstadter, New York, Harper & Row.

Heidegger, M. (1982), *The Basic Problems of Phenomenology*, tr. by A. Hofstadter, Bloomington, Indiana University Press.

Held, D. (1982), 'Crisis tendencies, legitimation and the state', in J. Thomson and D. Held (eds), *Habermas: Critical Debates*, Cambridge, Mass., MIT Press.

Heller, A. (1982), 'Habermas and Marxism', in J. Thomson and D. Held (eds), *Habermas: Critical Debates*, Cambridge, Mass., MIT Press.

Hobbes, T. (1949), *De Cive or The Citizen*, ed. by S. Lamprecht, New York, Appleton-Century-Crofts.

Hobbes, T. (1973), *Leviathan*, London, J.M. Dent.

Husserl, E. (1970), *The Crisis of European Sciences and Transcendental Phenomenology,* tr. and with an introduction by D. Carr, Evanston, Northwestern University Press.

Hyppolite, J. (1969), *Studies on Marx and Hegel*, tr. by J. O'Neill, New York, Basic Books.

Ingarden, R. (1983), *Man and Value*, tr. by A. Szylewicz, Washington, Catholic University of America Press.

Jonas, H. (1984), *The Imperative of Responsibility*, Chicago, University of Chicago Press.

Jouvenel, B. de (1949), *On Power*, tr. by J. Huntington, New York, Viking Press.

Jouvenel, B. de (1957), *Sovereignty*, tr. by J. Huntington, Chicago, University of Chicago Press.

B. Jouvenel, de (1958), 'Authority: the efficient imperative', in C. Friedrich (ed.), *Authority, Nomos I*, Cambridge, Mass., Harvard University Press.

Jouvenel, B. de (1963), *The Pure Theory of Politics*, Cambridge, Cambridge University Press.

Kant, I. (1952a), *Critique of Practical Reason*, tr. by T. Abbott, Chicago, Great Books of the Western World.

Kant, I. (1952b), *Fundamental Principles of the Metaphysics of Morals*, tr. by T. Abbott, Chicago, Great Books of the Western World.

Kant, I. (1965), *The Metaphysical Elements of Justice* (Rechtslehre), tr. by J. Ladd, Indianapolis, Library of Liberal Arts.

Kenny, A. (1976), *Will, Freedom and Power*, New York, Harper & Row.

Kierkegaard, S. (1974), *Fear and Trembling* and *Sickness Unto Death*, tr. by W. Lowrie, Princeton, Princeton University Press.

Kojève, A. (1963), 'Tyranny and wisdom', in L. Strauss, *On Tyranny*, New York, Free Press.

Kruks, S. (1981), *The Political Philosophy of Merleau-Ponty*, Atlantic Highlands, Humanities Press.

Langan, T. (1982), 'A strategy for the pursuit of truth', *The Review of Metaphysics*, vol. XXXVI, pp. 287–301.

Leibniz, G. (1972), 'Portrait of the prince', in P. Riley (tr. and ed.), *The Political Writings of Leibniz*, Cambridge, Cambridge University Press.

Locke, J. (1952), *Second Treatise of Government*, Indianapolis, Bobbs-Merrill.

Lucas, J.R. (1980), *On Justice*, Oxford, Clarendon Press.

Lukes, S. (1982), 'Of gods and demons: Habermas and practical reason', in J. Thompson and D. Held (eds), *Habermas: Critical Debates*, Cambridge, Mass., MIT Press.

McCarthy, T. (1978), *The Critical Theory of Jürgen Habermas*, Cambridge, MIT Press.

McCumber, J. (1984), 'Reflection and emancipation in Habermas', *The Southern Journal of Philosophy*, vol. XXII, pp. 71–81.

Machiavelli, N. (1984), *The Prince*, tr. by M. Musa, New York, Oxford University Press.

MacIntyre, A. (1981), *After Virtue*, Notre Dame, Notre Dame University Press.

Maitland, F. (1920), *Equity, also the Forms of Action at Common Law*, Cambridge, Cambridge University Press.

Marcel, G. (1951), *Homo Viator*, tr. by E. Craufurd, London, Victor Gollancz.

Marcel, G. (1962), *Man Against Mass Society*, tr. by G. Fraser, Chicago, Gateway Books.

Marcel, G. (1964), *The Mystery of Being*, tr. by G. Fraser, Chicago, Gateway Books.

Marx, K. and Engels, F. (1974), *The Communist Manifesto*, tr. by S. Moore, New York, Washington Square Press.

Maxwell, N. (1980), 'Science, reason, knowledge, and wisdom: a critique of specialism', *Inquiry*, vol. 23, pp. 19–81.

Meisenhelder, T. (1982), 'Hope: a phenomenological prelude to critical society theory', *Human Studies*, vol. 5, pp. 209–10.

Merleau-Ponty, M. (1945), 'Pour la vérité', Paris *Les Temps Modernes*.

Bibliography

Merleau-Ponty, M. (1962), *Phenomenology of Perception*, tr. by C. Smith, London, Routledge & Kegan Paul.

Merleau-Ponty, M. (1963), *In Praise of Philosophy*, tr. by J. Wild and J. Edie, Evanston, Northwestern University Press.

Merleau-Ponty, M. (1964a), *The Primacy of Perception*, ed. and tr. by J. Edie, Evanston, Northwestern University Press.

Merleau-Ponty, M. (1964b), *Sense and Non-Sense*, tr. by H. Dreyfus and P. Dreyfus, Evanston, Northwestern University Press.

Merleau-Ponty, M. (1964c), *Signs*, tr. by R. McClearly, Evanston, Northwestern University Press.

Merleau-Ponty, M. (1965), *The Structure of Behavior*, tr. by A. Fisher, London, Methuen.

Merleau-Ponty, M. (1968), *The Visible and the Invisible*, tr. by A. Lingis, Evanston, Nothwestern University Press.

Merleau-Ponty, M. (1969), *Humanism and Terror*, tr. by J. O'Neill, Boston, Beacon Press.

Merleau-Ponty, M. (1970), *Themes from the Lectures at Collège de France 1952–1960*, tr. by J. O'Neill, Evanston, Northwestern University Press.

Merleau-Ponty, M. (1973a), *Adventures of the Dialectic*, tr. by J. Bien, Evanston, Northwestern University Press.

Merleau-Ponty, M. (1973b), *The Prose of the World*, tr. by J. O'Neill, Evanston, Northwestern University Press.

Metz, J. (1970), 'Religion and society in light of a political theology', in W. Capps (ed.), *The Future of Hope*, Philadelphia, Fortress Press

Mill, J. (1957), *Utilitarianism*, New York, Liberal Arts Press.

Miller, J. (1979), *History and Human Existence*, Berkeley, University of California Press.

Misgeld, D. (1976), 'Critical theory and hermeneutics: the debate between Habermas and Gadamer', in J.O'Neill (ed.), *On Critical Theory*, New York, Seabury Press.

Montesquieu, C. de (1975), *The Spirit of the Laws*, tr. by T. Nugent, New York, Hafner.

Nozick, R. (1974), *Anarchy, State and Utopia*, New York, Basic Books.

Oakeshott, M. (1962), *Rationalism in Politics and Other Essays*, New York, Basic Books.

Oakeshott, M. (1975), *On Human Conduct*, Oxford, Clarendon Press.

Parekh, B. (1981), *Hannah Arendt and the Search for a New Political Philosophy*, Atlantic Highlands, Humanities Press.

Partridge, P. (1967), 'Freedom', in P. Edwards (ed.), *Encyclopedia of Philosophy*, New York, Macmillan and Free Press.

Pascal, B. (1976), *Pensées*, ed. by P. Selbier, Paris, Mercure de France.

Paton, H. (1965), *The Categorical Imperative*, New York, Harper Torchbooks.

Pfaff, W. (1980), 'Reflections: Finlandization', *The New Yorker*, 1 September, pp. 30–4.

Pfander, A. (1967), *Phenomenology of Willing and Motivation*, tr. by H. Spiegelberg, Evanston, Northwestern University Press.

Plamenatz, J. (1963), *Man and Society*, New York, McGraw-Hill.

Plato (1961), *The Collected Dialogues*, ed. by E. Hamilton and H. Cairns, tr. by Lane Cooper *et al.*, New York, Pantheon.

Quinton, A. (ed.) (1967), *Political Philosophy*, Oxford, Oxford University Press.

Rabil, A. (1967), *Merleau-Ponty: Existentialist of the Social World*, New York and London, Columbia University Press.

Rawls, J. (1971), *A Theory of Justice*, Cambridge, Mass., Belknap Press.

Richardson, W. (1978), 'The mirror inside: the problem of the self', *Review of Existential Psychology and Psychiatry*, vol. XVI, pp. 95–112.

Ricoeur, P. (1950), *Philosophie de la volonté: le volontaire et l'involontaire*, Paris, Aubier.

Ricoeur, P. (1965), *History and Truth*, tr. by C. Kelbley, Evanston, Northwestern University Press.

Ricoeur, P. (1966), *Freedom and Necessity*, tr. by E. Kohak, Evanston, Northwestern University Press.

Ricoeur, P. (1973a), 'Ethics and culture: Habermas and Gadamer in dialogue', *Philosophy Today*, vol. 17, pp. 163–4.

Ricoeur, P. (1973b), 'The task of the political educator', tr. by D. Stewart, *Philosophy Today*, vol. 17, pp. 142–52.

Ricoeur, P. (1976), *Interpretation Theory: Discourse and the Surplus of Meaning*, Fort Worth, Texas Christian University Press.

Ricoeur, P. (1977), *The Rule of Metaphor*, tr. by R. Czerny, Toronto, University of Toronto Press.

Riley, P. (1982), *Will and Political Legitimacy*, Cambridge, Mass., Harvard University Press.

Rockmore, T., Gavin, W., Colbert, J. and Blakeley, T. (1981), *Marxism and Alternatives*, Dordrecht, D. Reidel.

Rousseau, J.-J. (1964), *The First and Second Discourses*, tr. by R. Masters and J. Masters, New York, St Martin's Press.

Ryle, G. (1964), *Dilemmas*, Cambridge, Cambridge University Press.

Sandel, M.J. (1982), *Liberalism and the Limits of Justice*, Cambridge, Cambridge University Press.

Sartre, J.-P (1968a), *Being and Nothingness*, tr. by H. Barnes, New York, Washington Square Press.

Sartre, J.-P. (1968b), *The Communists and Peace, with a Reply to Claude Lefort*, tr. by M. Fletcher and P. Berk, New York, G. Brazillier.

Sartre, J.-P. (1968c), *Search for a Method*, tr. by H. Barnes, New York, Vintage Books.

Sartre, J.-P. (1976a), *Critique of Dialectical Reason*, tr. by A. Sheridan-Smith, London, New Left Books.

Sartre, J.-P (1976b), *No Exit and Three Other Plays*, New York, Vintage Books.

Saussure, F. de (1966), *Course in General Linguistics*, tr. by Wade Baskin, New York, McGraw-Hill.

Schmitz, K. (1983), 'Community, the elusive unity', *The Review of Metaphysics*, vol. XXXVII, pp. 243–64.

Schoenborn, A. von, 'Political authority: some preliminary remarks', unpublished manuscript.

Bibliography

Schürmann, R. (1981), 'Principles precarious: on the origin of the political in Heidegger', in T. Sheehan (ed.), *Heidegger: The Man and the Thinker*, Chicago, Precedent.

Sherover, C. (1984), 'The temporality of the common good: futurity and freedom', *The Review of Metaphysics*, vol. XXXVII, pp. 475–97.

Simon, H. (1947), *Administrative Behavior*, New York, Macmillan.

Simon, H. (1957), *Models of Man: Social and Rational*, New York, Wiley.

Simon, H. (1982), *Models of Bounded Rationality*, Cambridge, Mass., MIT Press.

Skinner, B. (1971), *Beyond Freedom and Dignity*, New York, Knopf.

Skinner, Q. (1978), *The Foundations of Modern Political Thought*, Cambridge, Cambridge University Press.

Sokolowski, R. (1977) 'Picturing', *The Review of Metaphysics*, vol. XXXI, pp. 3–28.

Sokolowski, R. (1978), *Presence and Absence*, Bloomington, Indiana University Press.

Spiegelberg, H. (1974), 'Ethics for fellows in the fate of existence', in P. Bertocci (ed.), *Mid-Twentieth Century Philosophy*, New York, Humanities Press.

Spiegelberg, H. (1981), 'Sartre's last words on ethics', *Research in Phenomenology*, vol. XI, pp. 90–107.

Taminiaux, J. (1977), *Le Regard et l'excédent*, The Hague, Martinus Nijhoff.

Taylor, C. (1982), *Hegel and Modern Society*, Cambridge, Cambridge University Press.

Tolbert, M. (1983), 'Defining the problem: the Bible and feminist hermeneutics', *Semeia*, vol. 28, pp. 113–26.

Turnbull, C. (1972), *The Mountain People*, New York, Simon & Schuster.

Schürmann, R. (1981), 'Principles precarious: on the origin of the political

Waelhens, A. de (1970), *Une Philosophie de l'ambiguité: L'Existentialisme de Maurice Merleau-Ponty*, Louvain, Nauwelaerts.

Walsh, J. (1976), 'Revolutionary violence in Merleau-Ponty, Marx and Engels', unpublished dissertation, Brandeis University, Massachusetts.

Walzer, M. (1983), *Spheres of Justice*, New York, Basic Books.

Watt, E. (1982), *Authority*, New York, St Martin's Press.

Weber, M. (1947), *Theory of Economic and Social Organization*, ed. by T. Parsons, tr. by A. Henderson and T. Parsons, New York, Oxford University Press.

Wolin, S. (1960), *Politics and Vision*, Boston, Little Brown.

Wolin, S. (1980), 'The idea of the state in America', *Humanities in Society*, vol.3, pp. 151–68.

Wrong, D. (1979), *Power*, New York, Harper & Row.

Index

Index